SOMEONE LIKE ME

For the last twenty years Miles Kington has written a humorous column in which everything has been made up and nothing can be trusted. Now he has written an autobiography by those same exacting standards. Was his father a German spy? Did his mother insist on permission from the Vatican before dancing on Sundays? Was baby Miles the victim of pram napping and can he really claim credit as co-creator of the anti-squirrel device? Who cares when a book is as brilliantly entertaining as this one.

Action, adventure, sex education, intrigue, tears, laughter, a homicidal brother with a penchant for amateur dramatics—*Someone Like Me* has got it all and then some. Filled with fabulous tales of Dadaist dog training, decadent ears, borrowed lawnmowers and visions of the Virgin Mary, this is one of the funniest and most original books you'll have read in decades.

SOMEONE LIKE ME

ME

Tales from a Borrowed Childhood

Miles Kington

WINDSOR
PARAGON

First published 2005
by
Headline Book Publishing
This Large Print edition published 2006
by
BBC Audiobooks Ltd by arrangement with
Headline Book Publishing

Hardcover ISBN 10: 1 4056 1402 1
ISBN 13: 978 1 405 61402 3
Softcover ISBN 10: 1 4056 1403 X
ISBN 13: 978 1 405 61403 0

Printed and bound in Great Britain by
Antony Rowe Ltd., Chippenham, Wiltshire

Contents

Prelude:

My Father's War

It was 1941, coming up to 1942. The war was still very much in the balance.

Although the Americans had come in on the Allies' side, the German war machine was barely dented and the tide had not yet turned against it. We know now who won the war, but back then the result was still uncertain, and bookmakers were still taking a lot of money on both sides. There were some in the Foreign Office who wrote very guarded memos when asked their honest opinion about the end result of the war. There was one famous occasion on which a source close to the Foreign Secretary was asked when hc thought we would win the war by. After thinking hard and long, he said, 'I'm not sure you're asking me the right question. I think the question you should be asking me is "Do you think we will actually win the war or not?"'

'All right,' said his interlocutor. 'Do you think we will actually win the war?'

The important man thought hard and long again and then said, 'I really don't think that that is a question you ought to be asking me.'

Truly has it been said that a politician is the best person to drop behind enemy lines, because if a politician fell into the hands of the enemy and they tortured him to get the truth, he would resist all attempts to get it out of him. If a politician will not tell his friends the truth, why should he tell his

1

enemies?

Yes, it was 1941, nearly 1942.

The war was desperate, as it always is when both sides still think they can win.

And in a small Shropshire town one man prepared to go forth and do battle with the enemy.

In Shropshire.

That man was my father.

He had volunteered for the Army in 1939.

He had volunteered again in 1940.

He had volunteered once more in 1941.

Each time he had been turned down for reasons of height.

Each time he hoped against hope he had grown meanwhile.

Nothing doing.

In 1940, in fact, he had even shrunk a little, though this turned out to be entirely due to the thinness of the poor-quality wartime socks he was wearing.

Every time he was interviewed, he stressed his qualifications for taking part in a world war, such as his ability with languages. '*Können Sie Deutsch sprechen?*' said the interviewing officer in 1941.

'*Ja, ziemlich gut,*' said my father, '*aber nicht so gut wie Ich es schreiben kann.*'

The officer stared at him blankly.

As an officer he had been trained to ask the right questions and to recognise '*Ja*' and '*Nein*' as answers, but this was beyond him.

'What does that mean?'

'It means I speak German pretty well, but not as well as I write it.'

'Does it indeed?' said the officer heavily. 'Very impressive, I'm sure. And what use would this be

2

to us?'

'Well,' said my father, 'you could drop me behind enemy lines.'

'And then what?'

'And then, using my German and my ability to live off the land, I would gradually travel back towards the British lines and eventually rejoin our forces.'

'Having achieved what?'

My father thought about it and could think of nothing he would have achieved.

'You see,' said the officer, 'you must leave these things to us. We will send for you if we need you. Meanwhile, back to civvy street.'

But he was so desperate to get to the fighting in 1941 that he had gone straight from the Army to volunteer to join the Navy.

'You're too small,' they told him.

'Put me in midget submarines!' he implored them.

'We've already got all the midget submariners we can handle,' they told him. 'Did you know that there hasn't been a pantomime production of *Snow White* anywhere in Britain since 1937?'

'You mean . . . ?'

'Yes. You can't get seven dwarves anywhere, for love nor money. They're all in midget submarines.'

And then an amazing thing happened. After all that rejection, the Army did send for him. A Captain Webb summoned him to a small Army office in Ellesmere and said that after reviewing his qualifications—especially the fact that he spoke several languages, including German, combined with his persistence in trying to get into the Army and the fact that he had done a lot of

3

amateur acting—they thought he was just right for a new secret project which had just been dreamt up by someone at the highest level.

'What I am about to tell you is in the highest confidentiality and you must not pass it on to a single soul.'

My father agreed.

Captain Webb then discreetly unfolded the current difficulty in which the government found itself. The trouble was that there was a general apprehension in the country as a whole that the Germans were going to invade Britain. The creation of the Home Guard had not only allayed fears, it had increased them . . .

'How can it do both?' asked my father.

'Well, the presence of the Home Guard reassures people that we are ready to withstand an invasion. But people hadn't really thought there were real fears of an invasion until the government created the Home Guard. Also, most people know someone who is in the Home Guard, and usually that someone is a bit old and past it, so most people privately doubt whether the Home Guard will be up to repelling the Germans. Unless the Germans send in an army of old-age pensioners. Which is unlikely.'

There was a pause. My father said nothing, as he felt they hadn't reached the crux of the matter yet.

'The crux of the matter,' said the officer helpfully, 'is that we know that before the Germans invade they will have to gather a lot of intelligence first, which means planting a lot of agents and spies in Britain. Now, we simply haven't got the manpower to mount a thorough counterintelligence operation, so we are going to have to rely on the common sense and co-operation of the British public to recognise the presence of agents and report their activities. We have appealed to them to do so and they are beginning to respond, but we simply don't know if they are up to it.'

My father said nothing again, as he felt that although the officer had said he had come to the crux of the matter he had not in fact really done so yet.

'What we are going to do is mount a secret operation to test the reactions of the British public. We want people to go out into the towns and countryside and behave suspiciously and discover if anyone takes any notice of them. In other words, we want you to devise various situations in which you might be a German spy and see what happens.'

'In other words, you want me to be shot?' said my father, who thought he knew a crux when he saw one.

'I don't think it will come to that,' said Webb smoothly. 'That's not the British way of doing things. We don't go out and lynch people.'

'Then what do we do?'

'We report them to the police,' said Webb. 'There was a German spy caught in Portsmouth last month. He had been photographing the movement of ships for weeks. Everyone assumed he was a harmless ship-spotter.'

'So how was he rumbled?'

'He left his car in a space reserved for the admiralty and got done for illegal parking. They found enough German stuff in his car to incriminate a dozen spies.'

5

'And what happened to him?'

'Ten years for spying. Three-pound fine for illegal parking.'

'I don't remember reading about that.'

'Oh, we don't put too much stuff about German spies in the papers. It might affect morale if people thought we were being spied on.'

'So what would you want me to do?'

'As I said, go out into the wilds of Shropshire and act suspiciously. See what happens. See if you get challenged as a German spy. We've got people doing this in almost every county now. Helping to make people aware of the Hun threat. We'll give you a petrol allowance and your own parachute.'

'*Parachute*? What would I want a parachute for? I've never done a parachute jump in my life.'

'Oh, you wouldn't have to jump with it. All you would have to do is take it somewhere and unfold it, probably in a tree. It's the classic way in which spies are supposed to arrive, dropping out of the sky in a parachute in some deserted part of the country. If you drove past a wood and saw a man rolling up a parachute, what would you think?'

'How nice it was to see people keeping the countryside tidy?'

'No, you wouldn't,' said Webb briskly. 'You'd think to yourself, "There, if I am not much mistaken, goes a German spy!" Now, get out there and act suspiciously!'

It was 1941, going on 1942, and much to his surprise my father had now been hired by the Army to masquerade as a German spy to test the intelligence of the British public. It was just his sort of thing. He set to work immediately. He drove round the countryside looking at everything

6

through binoculars, writing things down in a little notebook and clicking away with a camera which hadn't got any film in. He went into pubs and shops and ordered things with a foreign accent. He even hung around the barracks in Shrewsbury trying to look suspicious, sometimes reading a German daily newspaper when he was feeling brave, though with its heavy typeface it looked very like the *Daily Telegraph* and was in any case a 1937 edition, as during the war it was next to impossible to get hold of current German papers in Britain.

The trouble was that people in Shropshire are not generally, even now, predisposed to think of other people as potential enemies (except for the Welsh across the border) and there was not a lot of industry in Shropshire to attract potential spies. It is true that the industrial revolution had started in Shropshire, at Ironbridge, so that for a few short years Shropshire had all the heavy industry in the world, but it had quickly moved on elsewhere and now it probably had the least heavy industry of anywhere in the world. To this day Ironbridge still has the oldest metal bridge in the world. The significant thing about that is not that they built it, but that they never replaced it.

One day he drove over to Lake Vyrnwy, which sounds very Welsh and natural but is actually one of the largest artificial reservoirs in the country. Wales is dotted with large lakes whose only purpose is to supply people in Birmingham or Liverpool with drinking water and this has caused enormous resentment among the Welsh in recent years, for two reasons: 1) because the English are taking Welsh water away from the Welsh; 2) because it gives the impression that water is the only thing worth taking out of Wales. However, in World War II Welsh nationalism was at a low ebb, subsumed to the common good, and if anyone was guilty of setting English second homes in Wales on fire during the war, it was not the Welsh; it was the German air force.

Why, wondered my father, had the Germans never targeted places like Lake Vyrnwy? Easy to hit, undefended, full of priceless water. One big bomb on the dam holding back Lake Vyrnwy, and nobody in Birmingham would have a bath for a fortnight. That would send British morale crashing. So reasoned my father (he found himself more and more adopting the philosophy of a German spy, without even trying) and he spent a most enjoyable afternoon over there, wandering around the lake, photographing and taking copious notes. However, he was virtually unobserved and saw nobody except a man walking his dog who sheered off nervously when he saw my father approaching.

It was at this point that my father reflected that, although being a spy was sometimes painted as a dangerous and harassed existence, with the threat of capture and torture always close by, in fact it turned out to be a very lonely existence. It is very easy to pass unnoticed in a crowd. It is very easy, too, to pass unnoticed by Lake Vyrnwy if there is nobody else around excepting a nervous man with a dog.

'I had a very strange mission,' my father pointed out years later. 'I was employed to masquerade as a spy, that is to attract no attention whatsoever. Yet I was also asked to attract attention in order to test the British public's reaction to my "activities".

8

Now, how is it possible to unobtrusively seek attention? That was my objective in the middle of the war.'

Every week he was required to report back to the small Army office in Ellesmere and tell Captain Webb what reactions he had got from the public.

'So, what is your estimate of the gullibility of the British public this week past?' Captain Webb would say. 'Do they show any symptoms of invasion hysteria?'

'Quite the opposite,' my father would say. 'They show a *sangfroid* which is hard to overestimate. They are not afraid of the Germans. They make fun of them. The danger of German spies is not very real to them.'

'They make *fun* of them?'

Captain Webb seemed almost cross at this.

'They make fun of everything,' said my father. 'When I am sitting in a pub with the British, I am struck by their attitude of mockery towards everything. Not just towards the other side. But towards the Frogs too. And the Yanks. And not just towards the Allies, but us as well. They make fun of Churchill's voice and of wartime regulations and the blackout and the black market and everything.'

You would think Captain Webb would have been pleased by this, but he wasn't.

'Then you must try harder!' he told my father. 'Take more risks. Pretend to be more German than heretofore.'

The next week, obeying these instructions, my father went to Shrewsbury railway station, to be observed monitoring the movement of rail traffic up and down the line. He was observed all right, by several young boys who were also on the platform with notebooks and pencils. One of them came over to him and said: 'Seen any Castle class come through here this week?'

'*Nein*,' said my father gruffly.

'Nine!' said the boy, hugely impressed.

To get away from the boys and their train-spotting chatter my father adjourned to the station buffet where there was nobody else present except a man with his dog who came and sat down beside him. My father sipped at his mug of tea. The man ate a large biscuit very slowly.

Then he turned to my father and said very softly, 'Also, *Wie geht es Ihnen?*'

'*Ganz gut*,' said my father without thinking.

Then he froze.

The man had spoken to him in German.

And the man had also expected my father to reply in German.

Which, indeed, he had.

All this time my father had been bracing himself for the moment when he was going to be arrested for being a spy, or lynched for being a spy, or at the very least just jostled for being a spy, at which point he would attempt to claim convincingly to be Dutch, a language that he could also speak.

What he had never expected was to be greeted warmly and clandestinely by someone who was also German.

'*Ich habe Sie letzte Woche in der Nahe von Lake Vyrnwy gesehen*,' said the man, even more softly.

I saw you last week near Lake Vyrnwy.

Good God!

He recognised him now.

This was the man with the dog who had avoided him up at Lake Vyrnwy.

What should he do now?

He, my father, was a pretend German spy whose intention was to raise the consciousness of the British public and make them more aware of real German spies.

Aware of German spies such as, to take an example, the man with the dog now sitting beside him in Shrewsbury railway station.

Should he now, then, raise the hue and cry and denounce the man as a German spy?

Not really.

For one thing, he already knew from experience that people were not likely to be interested or convinced.

For another thing, he would have a hard job explaining how he *knew* that the man was a German spy.

For a third thing, there was no-one else in the station buffet except an elderly lady behind the tea-urn.

So he decided, quite sensibly, to continue chatting to the spy.

'A good target, Lake Vyrnwy,' he said casually.

'Yes,' said the other man. 'We ought to report back that it is worth . . . attending to.'

'Yes,' said my father. Then, 'Have you been over here long?'

'Several years. I came in 1938.'

'Before the war?'

'*Natürlich*. It is always easier to get settled in before a war. Dropping in by parachute is such a messy business.'

'Of course. Did you . . . bring the dog with you?'

'No,' said the spy, looking down with fondness. 'I bought Otto here. He is the perfect alibi. You can go anywhere in England if you're walking with a dog. No-one ever suspects you.'

'And what do you do when you are not . . . ?'

'I teach German at a large public school.'

'So they still teach German . . . ?'

'Oh, yes. The English educational system is very fair like that. They do not ban things they are fighting against, as we have banned Mendelssohn.'

Still nobody had come into the buffet, so my father asked the man for his telephone number and promised to get in touch with him, then left. He drove straight to Ellesmere, where he reported to Captain Webb that an unbelievable stroke of good luck had befallen him. He had fooled a German spy into giving away his identity to him! Accidentally, of course, but . . .

Captain Webb looked a bit taken aback, but he promised my father that he would look into it and took the phone number from him.

Two days later, having heard nothing, my father went back to Ellesemere and was thunderstruck to find that there was no sign of the little Army office any more. Where it had been was now occupied by a coal delivery business.

'What happened to the Army office?' he asked the coal official inside.

'Left in a hurry,' said the man. 'Scarpered. We desperately needed the premises, so we moved in. They took everything with them. Except this envelope. Left it for someone called . . .' He looked at it. It was for my father.

My father took it and opened it. It contained his petrol money and most recent pay packet. There

12

was a note saying, 'Mission now completed. Thank you for all. Webb.'

There was something not quite right about all this and my father had the good sense to go back to the original Army officer who had interviewed him for the Army in 1939, 1940 and 1941.

'You remember,' said my father, 'that after I had failed to get into the Army in 1941, the Army got in touch with me again to put me on the German spy scheme?'

'Pardon?' said the man.

'Well, presumably you must have known about it, otherwise Captain Webb would never have been able to get in touch with me.'

'Captain who?'

My father sighed and went through the whole story. He had even kept a copy of the telephone number the spy had given him.

'Wait here a moment, would you?' said the officer. 'I have some phone calls to make.'

My father was kept there waiting for three days, under close arrest, before the officer came and explained things to him.

'Your Captain Webb, as you must have guessed by now, was not a bona fide English Army officer. As a matter of interest, we have never had an Army office in Ellesmere. No—Captain Webb was in fact a German agent who had set up a fake agency to send people out into the English countryside masquerading as German spies in order to weaken the morale of the British public. He must have had some sort of source inside the Army to get names of possible recruits like you. That phone number, incidentally, was the German Embassy in London.'

The world swam round my father for a moment. He remembered suddenly that Captain Webb, although he spoke English perfectly, had one or two oddly Teutonic turns of phrase. *Thank you for all . . . What is your estimate of the gullibility of the British public this week pas . . . ?*

'You mean . . . ?'

'Yes. You have been working as a German spy—for the Germans.'

'Hold on a minute!' said my father. 'I wasn't working as a spy! I was *acting* as a spy! I never found out anything and I never gave away any secrets!'

'Oh no?' said the officer. 'How about your suggestion that Lake Vyrnwy would be a good target for German bombers?'

The world swam round my father again.

'How on earth did you know that? The only person I ever told that to was . . .'

He tried to think who it was.

'A man with a dog at Shrewsbury station,' said the officer.

'How on earth do you know that . . .'

'He wasn't a German spy as you thought he was,' said the officer. 'He was one of ours.'

My father started to get the feeling that the world wasn't going to stop swimming round him for a while yet.

'So you're going to have me up for treason, are you?' he said dully.

'Good Lord, no,' said the officer. 'We quite like the way you've been operating. And after all, you didn't think you were working for the Germans. So it wasn't treason, not really. And we've got a proposition for you now. We'd like you to do a job for us.'

'I'm not tall enough, remember?' said my father.

'Ah, but this isn't an Army job! This is a spying job! And there are no height requirements for spies!'

'I see. What does it consist of?'

'Well,' said the officer, 'we want to test the reactions of the British public to the presence of possible German agents among them. We want you to go out and devise situations in which you *could* be mistaken for a German spy . . .'

'That's exactly what I did for the Germans!'

'Two things you have to get used to in this spying job,' said the officer. 'One, it doesn't matter how tall or small you are. Two, it doesn't matter which side you're working for, as long as you remember which side it is.'

And so it happened that my father ended up doing for British Intelligence exactly what he had already done for German Intelligence. He once told me that he wished he had gone on to do the same job for American Intelligence.

'Why? To complete your set of three?'

'Well, partly that, of course. But mostly because they get paid so much better.'

I Am Born

I was born on 13 May 1941.

Of course, I only have my mother's word for that.

'You never forget things like that,' my mother told me when, as she lay on her deathbed, I asked her about my birth. 'I remember the day of your birth quite clearly, even if you don't. And now, if I pass away, you will have a clear memory of my last days on earth. So it all evens out in the end.'

A couple of days later she was up and about again, as right as rain, as she usually was after one of her deathbed scenes, so she was wrong about her dying moments, but she was right about my birth. I couldn't remember anything about it at all. Since then I have been privileged to be present at a couple of births (once at the birth of my own child, once when I took a wrong turn in a hospital in Ireland) and on both occasions I have come to realise why a baby can never remember his or her own birth. There is simply too much to take in, and too many people milling around.

One of the worst things in the world is finding yourself at a party where you don't know anyone and don't recognise any of the drinks either. Being born is even worse than that. A moment before, you thought the world was a small, dark, squishy place, then you come out into a place like the Millennium Dome full of people saying things like, 'Isn't he lovely?' and 'If you're not the father then you've no right to be here at all' (though I have only heard that once, in that hospital in Ireland). It must be such a confusing experience for the baby that the memory refuses to accept it.

The American writer Gore Vidal claims that he retained a clear image of being born to his mother, and even gives the impression that he disliked her immediately, although they hadn't yet exchanged a word, but I cannot match that. In a funny sort of way, though, I can beat it, because I do have a strange memory of a moment *before* I was born.

It's more like a dream than a memory, actually.

I am sitting in a room with an unseen figure who is asking me what I want to be.

'Who do you want to be?'

'How do you mean?' I say.

'Just that. What sort of person do you want to be?'

'How do you mean, person?'

'Look, we haven't got much time,' says the figure. 'You're going to be born pretty soon. Just tell me what you want to be. Population figures are going up all the time, so the choice is quite wide.'

'Choice?'

'Oh, for heaven's sake,' says the voice. 'Boy or girl?'

'Boy,' I say.

'Money or no money?'

'Money.'

'Brother or sister or only child?'

'Brother.'

'Now, class. What class?'

'Class?'

'Middle, upper or lower?'

'Middle.'

Looking back, I realise that I didn't make a rational choice at all. I just went for the first option in each case. That's how I still make a lot of choices. For instance, if I am faced with a wine list in a restaurant on which I don't recognise a single wine, I always find myself choosing the third one down from the top of the list. It's near the cheap end, but not so cheap that it looks cheap. Just . . . reasonable. Whenever I back horses, which isn't often, I use the same approach. Not the favourite, but nearly the favourite. I often wonder if other

17

people use the same system. If so, a lot of restaurants must find that their third wine down the list sells as well as all the others put together and they have to reorder that particular wine all the time.

Of course, if and when they run out of that particular wine they must strike it off the wine list and then another wine moves up and becomes the third wine down. Or swap the order of the list about a bit to get the other wines selling.

I must remember to ask a restaurateur, the next time I meet one.

Going back to the questionnaire, if I really was remembering a moment before my birth, then I clearly didn't take the process very seriously. These were all life-altering decisions, and in each case I was just taking the first option offered.

It's fairly clear that Gore Vidal would have taken his pre-birth interview much more seriously . . .

'What sort of person do you want to be?'

'I want to be a Roman emperor.'

'I'm afraid that's not possible.'

'Why not?'

'Wrong period, I'm afraid. You will be born at least 1,500 years after the collapse of Rome.'

'Oh. Then I want to be in the White House.'

'Mmmm . . . Well, we can get you born in and around the White House, though we can't give you any power.'

'Why not?'

'Well, in a democracy you have to be elected to get power.'

'No, you don't. All you need is the backing of the military-industrial complex.'

'Look! I'm not going to get drawn into a political discussion with an unborn child . . . What do you want to be called?'

'Something very interesting and unusual.'

Something very unusual and interesting, indeed. Gore Vidal was lucky not to be called Truman Capote, and vice versa. But most people never get to choose their own names. If they did, the world would be full of interesting names. As it is, we are given a name at birth and have to make the best of it, whether we like it or not, and I think it is fair to say that most people do not like the names they have been given.

I used to think that, given the chance of a name change, most people would go for something exotic or memorable and I would always point to the fragrant aliases chosen by film stars when they adopted a stage name. 'Look at Rock Hudson and Victor Mature!' I would say. What I did not realise was that these were rare exceptions. Many performers have been lumbered with odd or outlandish names in the first place and almost always opt for the quiet life when changing name. So Frederick Austerlitz becomes Fred Astaire, and Marion Morrison settles gratefully for John Wayne, and Lucille le Sueur turns into Joan Crawford, and Michael Dumble-Smith turns into Michael Crawford. When I read somewhere that Walter Matthau had started life as Walter Matuschanskayasky, I thought I had discovered the ultimate name change. That was before I learnt that Tom Cruise had started life as Thomas Mapother IV.

Anyway, I was born, as I say, on 13 May 1941, though I have no idea what time of day it was. I was once asked this by a girl called Sarah who was mad keen on astrology and wanted to know exactly what time of day I was born so that she could work out an accurate horoscope for me. I thought at the time that this interest meant that she was mad keen on me, but I was only a case study; it was astrology she was mad keen on, not me.

'I really don't know,' I said. 'My mother never told me.'

'Well, let's ask her!' said Sarah.

'She's dead,' I said.

Things like that don't deter horoscope-loving girls like Sarah.

'I'm going to a spiritualist séance next week,' she said. 'Come along with me and let's try and get in touch with your mother and ask her when you were born!'

'I don't really believe in things like . . .'

'Oh, you will, you will!' said Sarah who was terribly bright and breezy and made people round her feel unaccountably tired. 'I didn't think I would be impressed by mediums either, but the first time I went I got straight in touch with my late Uncle Fred who told me where the missing family photographs were! It was incredible!'

'And where were they?'

'Down the back of the old family desk. Well, that's what he said. In fact when we went to look down the back of the desk there was nothing there at all, so they must have been moved since Uncle Fred died. But it was incredible to think that he knew!'

If I hadn't been physically attracted to Sarah I would never have got drawn into a spiritualist séance, but I let myself be taken along and just when I was getting a little bored with the whole thing—I thought I could see how the medium was telling people what they wanted to hear—someone said, 'Has anyone here got a mother called Jean?'

'Yes,' I said, startled.

'Do you have a message for her?'

'What time of day was I born?' hissed Sarah.

'Uh . . . I would like to know if she can remember what time of day I was born.'

'That is a fairly unusual request. Normally we like to pass on messages of fondness . . .'

'No, I would like to ask her that.'

The question was duly asked, but no answer seemed to be forthcoming. Instead, the medium made moaning noises and said something vaguely like, 'Oh no, oh no,' and then shortly afterwards woke up.

The person in charge of the séance said, somewhat strictly, that asking my mother about my birth had brought on memories of those difficult times and what we had heard was almost certainly my mother reliving the pangs of birth.

I disagreed, though I said nothing. I knew that what we had heard was the very familiar sound of my mother doing one of her deathbed scenes. But this raised two difficult questions. One was the question of whether what I had heard was really genuine. The other, rather simpler, was why—if it was genuine—my mother should feel it necessary to stage a deathbed scene *after* she had died.

Perhaps old habits die hard.

Kidnapped!

My earliest memories are of my pram, in which I lived for what seemed like years. I have little memory of the first house we occupied, but very clear memories of the pram I was put in. Is that because a house is, all through your childhood, a place you have to share with other people, but a pram is somewhere you get all to yourself? Whatever the reason, I still remember the stiff framework, the way it bounced up and down and excitingly side to side if you shook it, the darkness of the interior and the contrasting shocking brightness of the outside world, viewed through that primitive proscenium arch. Not just the pram itself, but the infinitely fascinating foliage under which you were often left, blown by the wind in patterns which never repeated themselves. The ever-changing sky if there was no tree to study. The pram was where I was and the world was where everyone else was, and in my mind they both seemed the same size and had the same importance.

I am afraid that most modern children do not get the pram experience. Only the buggy experience. Even when *I* was a baby the big Victorian pram had more or less receded into history, along with the huge lawn mowers and rollers of earlier times, but my pram was still recognisably a pram in which you could lie flat, a four-wheeled thing, a distant descendant of the stagecoach and hansom cab.

Now we have the buggy.

A sort of shopping basket on wheels.

A kind of limp wheelbarrow for children.

Buggies are very convenient for parents because they can be folded, and put on aeroplanes, and steered through crowds, and everything a pram cannot, but they are disastrous for a child. Being put in a buggy instead of a pram is like being given a moped when you expected a car, or a skateboard when you expected a moped. A pram could be your home and your kingdom. A buggy can only be a way of getting from A to B. Is it possible that a whole generation of children has been warped by never knowing the pram experience? Children who have started life in prams have known security and peace, whereas life in a buggy is a rootless, asylum-seeking existence.

I have noticed that transport for small children has become more and more 'practical', until we have ended up with parents carrying children on their backs in rucksacks, or on their fronts in slings, not unlike some of the bigger animals in David Attenborough programmes. It is all very well getting back to nature, but there are risks involved. I have noticed, for instance, that when a child is in a sling on a mother's chest, the child is almost always facing the mother with its head crushed up against the mother's breast or, rather, bra.

Has anyone ever thought through the implications of this?

With its head jammed against the mother (or father, come to that) it cannot see anything except the parent spaceship and it must be conscious the whole time of the parent's heartbeat, inches away from its ear. Thud thud thud thud thud—a regular tribal drumbeat, linking the child and parent in a primeval bond. Then, suddenly, one day the child gets too heavy to carry, is forced to walk and is never again so close to the parent's heart. It is deprived for all time of the aural equivalent of mother's milk. Wildly, it looks for a substitute and finds it in the pulse of modern music. That is why so many teenagers have a bass beat thudding in their ears from an enclosed personal stereo. It's mummy's heartbeat all over again!

(Recently, in the first years of the twenty-first century, it has become fashionable to sell water in plastic bottles which have a kind of nipple on, allowing you to suckle it. No comment.)

Having been brought up in a pram, I now have no need of a personal stereo. But prams bring their own risks. My first memory of anything really exciting is of my first kidnapping. When I was ten months old and lying in my pram in the garden, it was removed at high speed down the suburban streets of the small Shropshire town we were living in. (Actually, all towns in Shropshire are pretty small, even Shrewsbury. Especially Shrewsbury, because it thinks itself big.)

I don't really remember the event itself, of course. Nobody genuinely remembers anything from that age. But I do recall being told about it and I came to remember all the different accounts of my kidnapping as if I had really been there. Which I had. The normal custom in autobiography, or memory, is to amalgamate all the accounts into one colourful, if unreliable, reminiscence, but I have always managed to keep these accounts separate in my mind and I bring them to you now.

24

My mother's story
'I was in the kitchen. It was a nice summer day and I had left you out in the garden in your pram, under an old apple tree.'

Author's Note: I remember that apple tree, come to think of it. Bits of twig used to fall off it into my mouth. So did the occasional insect. But never an apple.

'I was making some biscuits, I think, when all at once I didn't hear a cry. By that I mean that out in the garden you had been making a kind of babyish moaning noise which sounds like moaning but is really quite happy, so you would probably describe it as gurgling. Suddenly, I became aware that the noise had stopped. Presumably you had gone to sleep. I glanced out into the garden and saw to my horror that the pram had vanished!

'Well, I rushed outside and looked around and there was no sign of you anywhere. It was just possible that you had been taken for an impromptu walk by your father, so I came back into the house screaming for your father. Unfortunately, he was there.'

My father's account
'By that she means that, if I hadn't been there, there would have been a chance that I had taken you for a walk. Because I was there it meant that you had been taken by someone else. So we rushed out into the street and looked up and down and saw two people with a pram at the very end, where it joined the main road, and we ran after them, but by the time we got to the main road they had vanished. Luckily, a woman coming the other way

had passed them and she gave us a good description of them and that's how we found out that it was two men who had taken you. But they must have been moving fast, because they had vanished from sight in a mere fifteen seconds. I don't know how fast a pram can travel, but I suppose it's pretty fast.'

Extract from *A History Of Perambulators* **by Ronald Osgood (Tavistock Press, 1947)**
PRAMS AND SPEED: Pram design has always put space and comfort ahead of speed and road-holding. Some designers have attempted to add a small engine to a pram for charity pram races, but it is hard to see the point of this for if it goes any faster than a human being then the 'driver' or pram-pusher will not be able to keep up with it and control it. Unless, of course, he gets into the pram, but then by definition it ceases to be a pram and becomes a small sports car.

My father's account (continued)
'I was surprised to hear that it was a male kidnapper, or kidnappers, who had taken the pram, because almost always babies are stolen by women who are desperate to have a baby. But two men? This was back in the 1940s, mind, long before gay pairs set out to adopt children, and that kind of thing just hadn't been heard of. In any case, none of this ran through my mind at the time. What struck me was the advantage of knowing that the pram had been taken by two men, because this made the pram easily identifiable—if we rang up the police and asked them to look for two men with a stolen pram, they should be able to spot it

26

pretty soon.

'And I did ring the police up and they did go out looking for it, and they found it almost immediately.'

From the police report
A report was received at 2.39 p.m. of a missing pram with a baby in it being pushed by two men. At 2.46 Constable Pritchard encountered two men and a pram answering to the description and challenged them to stop. They left the pram behind and ran off, pursued by the Constable who shouted to a passing woman to mind the baby. After Constable Pritchard had effected an arrest he returned to find that the lady was still in charge of the pram, but she said that there was no baby in the pram and had not been at the time of the handover to her from Constable Pritchard. A thorough search of the pram revealed no trace of a baby.

Upon the two arrested men being asked what they had done with the baby, they disclaimed all knowledge of an occupant and said it was only the pram they were after.

My mother's story (continued)
'I had been left behind in the chase after the two men and the pram, so I came back to the house to continue making biscuits, and as I came in through the gate I heard a familiar gurgling sound. It was you, my dear baby boy, rolling in some leaves under a bush in our garden still in your pram clothes. They had obviously dropped you out of the pram when they took it, so I just picked you up and hugged you, I was so glad to see you, then

looked round for a pram to put you into, but of course we didn't have one so I took you indoors and put you in the high-chair and phoned the police to say you had been found.'

My father's account (continued again)
'I was at the police station when the news came through, and I was delighted, of course, but puzzled too by the fact that what had seemed like a kidnapping wasn't a kidnapping at all. The police weren't at all surprised, though. They said that very often it was the pram that thieves were after, not the baby, as prams had a commercial value and babies didn't.

'"In your case," the policeman told me, "I am not surprised they took the pram because you've got a very nice model there. Those old heavy ones are much in demand by photo-thieves."

'"Photo-thieves?" I said. It was an expression I had never heard before.

'The police explained to me that sometimes thieves stole to order and that they would go round places with a lot of valuables in them, photographing the objects wherever necessary or possible. If, say, there was a garden with a lot of statuary in it, they would go round snapping the different statues, masquerading as tourists. Later on, they would put all their photos into an album and use it as a sort of shopping catalogue. They would show it to prospective buyers and when the buyer said, "Oh, I'd like that!" pointing to a photo, the thief would fix a price and then go off and nick it at the first opportunity.'

Headline from a small-town Shropshire newspaper, 1942
Pram Recovered After High-speed Chase

Well, there it is. The day I was kidnapped by a gang of pram thieves. And yet I wasn't kidnapped because they didn't take me, and it couldn't have had a drastic effect on me because I didn't know it had happened, and I didn't feel cruelly rejected at being left behind in favour of a much more attractive pram because I didn't know I had been rejected. In fact I would never have known it had happened if my parents hadn't talked about it, which they did at the drop of a hat, much to my embarrassment.

'Have we ever told you about the time he was kidnapped?' they would say to new friends and acquaintances. 'Well, more precisely, the pram was taken and he was left behind, which shows that they had discrimination, doesn't it! Anyway, the way it happened was this . . .'

When you are trying to become a troublesome teenager, leaving short trousers and a treble voice behind, it doesn't help if your parents constantly remind the world of the days when you were a chubby little baby, lying on your back and dribbling, and I always left the room when this performance was being gone through.

But at the time it all happened, I resumed life in my pram unaware that anything had occurred and the only difference, I suppose, was that my father, who had an inventive bent, was now determined to create a security device which would make it

29

impossible to steal prams. At first he was in favour of padlocking the pram to the nearest fence with a big chain, which would probably have done the trick but was unwieldy, and he also tried to talk my mother into letting him handcuff me to the side of the pram, but I am glad to say she stood firm on that one and wouldn't hear of it. As she said, if that had been in operation when the two men had taken the pram, I would have been stolen as well. And probably had my chubby little arm cut off at the wrist.

'If I was working on a pram anti-theft device nowadays,' he once said to me much later when we were reminiscing about old times, 'it would be so much simpler. You could just fix on a small tagging device of some kind so that you could locate the pram as soon as it was stolen.'

'That's not an anti-theft device,' I said. 'It's a pro-recovery device. It doesn't stop it being stolen.'

'I considered affixing a small explosive charge to the pram as well,' he said, ignoring me.

'What good would that do?'

'It would be timed to go off in 24 hours. At home you'd have to deactivate it and reset it every day. But a thief wouldn't know that. The day after he stole it—BOOM!'

'Dad, be sensible!'

'Your mother's very words,' he said. 'So then I devised a kind of booby brake which would also come on if not deactivated regularly and which would prevent the pram from being removed.'

'And did it work?'

'I don't know,' said my father. 'Nobody ever tried to take it again, so I never found out. It was a bit like the people I always feel so sorry for, those magnificent medieval castle builders who put up huge fortresses designed to withstand any attack and did it so well that nobody ever attacked them.'

'I wonder if the people who built the great churches come into the same category,' I said.

My father looked at me queerly.

'I don't think many churches have been built for defensive purposes,' he said.

'No,' I said, 'but they were built to make people better and holier. Now that these churches are almost as unused as the great castles are unattacked, can we assume that they have achieved their purpose of improving humanity?'

'Whenever you make a remark that is too clever by half,' said my father, 'I feel quite justified in ignoring it.'

Aunt Flo and the Photos

Being in a pram is like sunbathing next to a main road. Anyone can stare in, and they usually do. After a while I began to get used to being stared at by people and told what a pretty baby I was. So I was justifiably startled one day when I suddenly realised I was being stared at by a giant frog who didn't seem to approve of me at all.

I was lying in my pram at the time, looking malevolently up at the five plastic balls on elastic which someone had thoughtfully strung across my pram for me to play with. I had already played with them weeks before and was now trying to destroy them, but to a grown-up both activities must look

31

identical. Of course, a grown-up has never lain on his back beneath five giant balls on a length of rope above his head, but if he had he would know that it is a fairly threatening and oppressive experience. The next time you pass a pram with a baby lying on its back, apparently trying to make contact with the five plastic balls above it, remember that it is desperately trying to get them out of its line of sight. Do it a favour. Lean over while the mother is not looking, unhook the balls-on-a-string and throw them away.

So there I was, lying on my back in my pram, grimly planning the destruction of the five black balls above me (no matter what colour they are, they always look black against the sun or sky) when suddenly a giant frog pushed its face round the pram and stared at me.

This was Aunt Flo and the reason why she looked like a frog is that she was squinting at me through a pair of opera glasses. She was terrifically short-sighted and claimed she could see nothing without artificial aids. I knew nothing of this, of course. All I could see was a human face with what seemed to be a glass mask staring at me and I went into a terrible shrieking fit of fear and panic. My mother told me later that she had come rushing out into the garden thinking I had been attacked by bees or was being abducted by kidnappers again and found only Aunt Flo staring fixedly at me through her wretched opera glasses.

'They weren't even a very good pair,' said my mother. 'She had stolen them from the Opera House in Buxton, I think, which isn't a very big place, so the audience don't need very strong magnification, even when they are sitting at the back. She was always stealing opera glasses.'

'Actually, that's not quite fair to old Aunt Flo,' said my father, who had been listening. 'She never made a habit of stealing. She only stole one pair of opera glasses, the first one. After that, if she found a pair she liked better she would take it but leave the old one behind in the theatre in exchange, so in a sense she always swapped opera glasses.'

'It's an expensive way to acquire opera glasses,' I said, 'if you have to buy a ticket to the opera every time you want to upgrade your viewing.'

'Not if you like opera,' said my father. 'Then you get an evening of opera *and* a new pair of glasses for the price of your ticket.'

'Why do people in opera houses have to have binoculars?' I said. 'People in theatres never need them. And yet some theatres are just as big as opera houses. So it must be just as hard to see the actors.'

'It's a good point,' said my father. 'I would imagine the answer is that as opera singers spend most of the time standing still it is possible to focus on them, whereas actors are always moving and by the time you get a close-up of one he will have gone somewhere else.'

'And theatre isn't boring in the way that opera usually is,' said my mother. 'So you don't need to distract yourself so much, or try to keep yourself awake.'

Apparently, my mother pulled Auntie Flo off the pram as I lay there screaming and all she said was, 'He needs feeding up.'

'He needs not to be scared to death by people staring at him through opera glasses,' said my mother.

'If he was fed properly, he wouldn't get scared by people just looking at him,' said Aunt Flo.

Aunt Flo took these opera glasses with her wherever she went and would have attracted permanent mockery to her for that reason had she not once found them unexpectedly useful. She was standing outside a bank when two bank robbers came running out of the building, jumped into the getaway car and shot off at lightning speed. The car was forty yards away before anyone thought to take the number and of course it was too far away to read by then. Unless you had opera glasses. When the police arrived they found that Aunt Flo was their prime witness.

'She had written the number down already,' said my father. 'Quick thinking.'

'I thought getaway cars always had false number plates,' I said.

'Yes, this one did too,' said my father. 'But she had also managed to read the name on the briefcase which one of the robbers was carrying the notes in.'

'How on earth did she manage to read a name on a briefcase inside a moving car forty yards away?' I asked.

'She didn't. She read the name on the briefcase before the robber got in the car. The judge commended her highly in court and said she was a very resourceful young woman. She loved being called resourceful.'

'She loved being called young,' said my mother.

'And ever afterwards she felt justified in having these wretched opera glasses round her neck. Occasionally, it fitted in. At the opera, of course. And at point-to-points. And when she was out walking and an interesting bird came past. But most of the time it just looked silly.'

'What does Aunt Flo look like?' I asked.

I didn't remember ever having met her. Some aunts and uncles seem to come round quite often on the luggage carousel of life, whereas others are never seen and gain mythical reputations in their absence.

'Well, she's . . .'

My mother thought about it for a moment, then said, 'I'll get the family photos out and show you. There's a photograph of her with a family group standing on a lawn somewhere, I think.'

My father groaned. Getting the family photographs out was quite a performance. My mother, for some reason, had taken it on herself to organise the family photos. Not that she took any photographs herself, but she saw herself as the family archivist. She had become exasperated by her own family's failure to sort out their family photos and had decided that ours would be properly organised.

'When I was a young girl, whenever we looked through our great heap of family photos,' she told me once, 'we found that we didn't know who half the people were. A few photograph albums had names written in, of course, but people are always very bad about captioning people in photographs. At the time, I suppose, it doesn't make much sense to do so. You take a photo of Aunt Maisie. You stick it in a book. You don't write "Aunt Maisie" underneath because, for heaven's sake, everyone knows who Aunt Maisie is. But gradually, over the years, everyone who knew who Aunt Maisie was dies off and eventually you're left with the yellowing picture of a stout matron standing on a lawn under a cedar tree wearing sort of 1930ish clothes and you think, "Who on earth is this old frump?" '

It was for this reason that my mother decided to do something that, as far as I know, has not been done by anyone else in the history of the world. She decided it would be safer to get the captions *inside* the photograph. That is to say, whenever we had photographs taken at home or at family gatherings, she always had cards written out for people to hold up to the camera on which would be written 'Uncle Tom', or 'Great-Aunt Edith' and so on. And there would usually be another placard standing casually in the corner of the scene with the place and date written on it: 'Elmwood House, June 1937', or 'The Beach at Paignton, 1958'— something like that.

The net result of this was that all our family photos had a certain resemblance. In each one, everyone stood somewhat self-consciously holding a placard with their name on. This did not allow for much spontaneity, so you never got the impression that anyone in the photos was having a good time. Indeed, you got the impression that all our family were a solemn and embarrassed lot.

'I don't care,' said my mother when people pointed this out to her. 'I suffered a lot from growing up with a collection of relatives in photographs who were all unidentifiable and I would prefer to have a family who will be instantly recognisable to posterity, even if they look mannered, which I admit they do.'

'Oh, but will they?' said my father. 'Do you really think that a photo of a lady holding a card saying "Richard's fiancée, Gladys" is going to mean anything to someone in fifty years' time? Especially if they don't know who Richard is?'

'Then draw a family tree,' said my mother. 'Number the photos. Indicate on the family tree which person goes with which number.'

'If we did that,' said my father, 'we wouldn't need to have this ridiculous charade of getting everyone to hold up cards.'

Still, at least it meant that when I innocently asked what Aunt Flo looked like, my mother knew she would be able to dig up the evidence from her family picture album.

The reason that I had no idea what Aunt Flo looked like, by the way, was that she had gone out to New Zealand when I was eight and never come back. She had fallen in love with a cricketer and followed him out there. Uncle Sidney (that was his name) was not a New Zealander, as you might assume; he was an English cricketer who had gone out to play on a tour of New Zealand and liked it so much that he had stayed there.

And when I say that Aunt Flo followed him out there, that is the exact truth; she was waiting for him to come back and when he didn't she went after him.

'When he was in England, she used to follow him from county ground to county ground,' my mother told me. 'We all thought she was a bit cracked. Spending days on end in half-empty cricket stands just to be near her loved one? With Uncle Sidney hardly visible to her?'

'That's not fair,' said my father. 'After all, she did have her opera glasses. I think it was when she fell in love with a county cricketer that her opera glasses finally started to pay their way. She took me to a game once, just to see Sidney play, and I marvelled at the way that woman handled those glasses. I find binoculars really hard to manoeuvre. I can never quite get them focussed, and even when they are focussed it's only for one eye, so I spend ages trying to get the other eye to act in conjunction with its mate, and then when everything is beautifully co-ordinated I can never find the thing in the lenses which I can see with my naked eye. Have you ever noticed that? Look at that bird, someone says, and you look through their binnies, as they always call them, and all you can see is sky and branches . . . Where was I?'

'Cricket. Flo. Sidney,' said my mother.

'Oh, yes. It's an odd thing, but on the few occasions when I have been to a big cricket match I have found it extremely hard to see the ball. Especially if you're sitting sideways on. The bowler runs up and swings his arm; a second later the batsman swings his bat; a second later a fielder starts running and then *he* swings his arm from the outfield, and all this time I haven't seen any sign of the ball. It is as if they are all miming it. And I have sometimes wondered whether, if they *did* start playing Test cricket without a ball and just mimed the actions, anyone would notice . . . Where was I?'

'Where you were before,' said my mother. 'Cricket. Flo. Sidney.'

'Seems odd for two people named after great cities to marry each other,' said my father reflectively. 'Sidney . . . Florence. Anyway, she followed him out to New Zealand, determined not to let him fall into the hands of those Kiwi sirens,

38

and they lived happily ever after.'

'Here she is,' said my mother, stopping at a page in the photograph album. 'Oh, no! Oh, how terrible! Oh, that's awful!'

It's not often that you get that sort of reaction from an old family picture album, so we crowded round to see what had gone amiss.

'Look!' she said, pointing at some sort of tea party on some sort of lawn in some sort of decade or other. The 1930s, probably, on the grounds that everyone looked bravely dowdy. At the right-hand edge of the group stood two young women. One held a card saying 'AUNT FLO' and the other one held a card saying 'MISS SATTERTHWAITE, AUNT FLO'S FRIEND WHO CAME DOWN FROM LONDON FOR THE DAY'. You couldn't see much of Miss Satterthwaite, due to the fact that her card had to be large enough to accommodate all that description.

'What's so terrible?' I asked.

'That's not Aggie Satterthwaite at all!' said my mother, jabbing with her finger. 'That's Aunt Flo! She and her friend have swapped places! Or do I mean that they've swapped cards by accident?'

You could tell from the two young women's expressions that it wasn't an accident. Alone of the people in the group they were laughing and grinning broadly, fully conscious of the fact that they had thwarted Mother's plans. Miss Satterthwaite, holding Aunt Flo's card, was tall and plump and jolly. Aunt Flo, holding the Satterthwaite caption, was, as far as you could tell, smaller and prettier. They had waited a good few years for their joke to become effective, but they were still laughing.

'That's the flaw in the whole scheme,' said my father. 'If the people in the photograph are holding the wrong cards, there's not a damned thing you can do about it. If the caption was written underneath, you could correct it. But you can't change a caption inside a photograph.'

'Stalin could,' said my mother, defensively. 'He was always altering photos to get rid of people who had fallen from favour.'

'Well,' said my father, 'I sense that Aunt Flo has fallen from favour in the last few minutes, but I think it's going a bit far to try to airbrush her out of history.'

'Hold on a minute,' I said. 'If one photo can be wrong, how do you know there aren't others in the family archives? Shouldn't you go through all the photos again, checking for people who might have got their cards wrong?'

'Certainly not,' said my mother, grimly.

'What worries me,' said my father, 'is if some future historian comes looking for pictorial evidence of Aunt Flo *and uses the picture of Miss Satterthwaite instead*!'

'What nonsense,' said my mother. 'Who would want to write a life of Aunt Flo?'

'All right then,' said my father. 'What happens if someone comes here doing research into Miss Satterthwaite and prints Aunt Flo's picture instead?'

'Nonsense,' said my mother, not quite so firmly. 'Who would want to write anything about Aggie Satterthwaite?'

'Who knows?' said my father. 'That all depends what happened to Miss Satterthwaite. Maybe she married rich and has a title. Maybe she changed

40

her name and became a famous actress. Maybe, under an assumed name, she has become a celebrated murderess whose new name we would all recognise. And maybe we shall never hear of her again.'

But we did, albeit briefly, as you will find out in due course.

Murder Most Feeble

It is somewhat daunting, when you are not yet two years old, to realise that someone is trying to murder you.

I know now that all elder children resent the arrival of a younger sibling, but it came as a shock at the time to realise that, when my older brother Ralph looked at me over the edge of the pram, it was with a murderous look in his eye.

You think I am making it up?

But a baby knows. Babies are used to people looking into their prams and saying, 'Isn't he sweet!' or 'Hoochy coochy coochy coochy' or 'Hello, darling!'. They may not understand the words, but they recognise the tone of total adoration in which the words are wrapped. So when someone looks at you in your pram and says, 'I'm going to kill you, you little . . .', or words to that effect, you don't need a command of vocabulary to sense the difference.

Ralph wasn't very good at looking in over the edge of the pram because he wasn't quite tall enough to do it, so he had to stand on a stool to get a good view of me and I quite clearly remember him, just after he had issued his death threat, suddenly disappearing from view as he fell sideways off it, twisting his ankle and bursting into tears. I can remember him briefly reappearing over the edge of the pram, saying, 'I'm going to get you for that,' and vanishing again before my mother came along to see what the noise was all about. Both of us were crying by that time, Ralph because he had hurt his foot and me because I was about to die.

Having dealt with Ralph, she looked into my pram and said, 'Gosh, he is in a paddy, isn't he?', as I lay there wailing, with my chubby little arms flailing about.

She thought I was crying.

But I wasn't.

I was saying, 'That man is going to try to kill me! The one over there! Yes, that one! As soon as he can put weight on his foot, he is going to kill me!'

(I can distinctly remember that I thought of four-year-old Ralph as a 'man'. I think all babies think of anyone bigger than them as a grown-up, just as later on we think of all teachers as being immeasurably older than us, even though some of them are only four or five years older.)

My mother, of course, had no idea that I was letting her in on a murder plot, so she said, 'Good boy!', asked Ralph to keep an eye on me and went back to the kitchen. Leaving me alone with a murderer. Whom she trusted.

The trouble was that I had no means of defence against Ralph. The one weapon I had used in my short life so far to get what I wanted—angelic innocence—was not going to work against him. Indeed, it was probably my angelic innocence as

42

much as anything else which had brought on his murderous fit. No wonder that, out of sheer terror, I proceeded to fill my nappy, so that when Ralph next looked over the side of the pram he recoiled from the rich, dung-laden odour.

'Mother!' he called. 'I think the baby's nappy needs changing.'

This taught me a lesson. It taught me that no-one likes to murder a soiled victim. Killers like victims to be clean, like a sacrificial victim in some ancient Greek or Inca ritual, going calmly and palely to join the gods. So it stood to reason that Ralph would not try to do away with me when I was needing changing. If only I could always fill my nappy at his approach . . .

Well, I did once or twice, but a baby really can't keep up that sort of thing and some time during the next day, when I had been left alone in the pram (even though I had again told my mother that Ralph was trying to kill me and she had smiled and said, 'Baby baby bunting'), I sensed that I was not alone in the room and that Ralph was creeping up on me.

Physical resistance was useless.

Protest was useless.

I had had a nappy change less than ten minutes previously.

There was only one thing for it.

I feigned dead.

I closed my eyes and stopped breathing.

I let all my limbs go limp.

It must have looked as if I were sleeping at first, but of course when people are sleeping they make little breathing noises and I wasn't making any noises at all.

I looked dead.

Moments later, I could hear Ralph running down the passage crying out, 'Mother! I think the baby's dead! Come quick!'

She came very quick. By that time I was gurgling and waving my thumbs and smiling.

'Honest,' Ralph was saying, 'he was lying very still and quiet and I thought he was . . .'

Mother went back to the kitchen. Stillness resumed. I feigned dead again. This time, I could hear Ralph creeping across the floor to the pram. He was breathing audibly. His footsteps made a noise. Through nearly closed eyelids I could see him appear over the edge of the pram. He looked very determined.

I only had one line of defence left, now.

I used it.

I suddenly opened my eyes wide and shouted, 'Boo!'

It may not have been 'Boo!'

It may have been some more barbarous sound.

But it worked.

Ralph got the shock of his life and fell off the stool again. I immediately went limp and closed my eyes. It had worked once. It might work once more.

I could hear Ralph picking himself up.

I could hear him hoisting himself up alongside the pram.

Then I heard him say, not a foot away from me, 'What did you say?'

I opened my eyes again and said what I fondly imagined was 'Boo!'

He stared for a moment and then burst into laughter. He laughed so loud that mother came running to see what the matter was.

'He's a funny baby,' said Ralph.

From that moment on, Ralph changed his attitude to me entirely and started looking after me. I had made him laugh. I was a possible playmate, or at least a possible plaything. I was no longer a potential murder victim.

'Do you remember,' I said to him years later, 'when you tried to kill me as I lay defenceless in my pram?'

He claimed he had no memory of any such thing.

'Yes, you did,' I said. 'I had a very strong feeling that you resented my coming and were trying to kill me. It was a sort of Oedipus triangle at another level. Deep down, you wanted to sleep with your mother and murder your little brother.'

'That's absolutely not true,' said Ralph. 'As I remember it, I didn't resent you at all—I only resented Mother for having you. I remember wondering how she could possibly let her body be used to give birth to a blob like you when she had already had someone as wonderful as me. It wasn't you I had it in for. It was her and her treachery.'

'But you were always appearing over the edge of my pram and trying to kill me!'

'Kill you? Nonsense! All I was doing was checking to see if you were all right. I always loved it when there was something wrong with you because then I could call our mother and worry her. I only wanted to get at her through you. I never harmed you once. God forbid . . .'

As you can imagine, this came as a great shock to me. I had so often told people the story of how my brother tried to kill me that I had come to

45

believe it. Now, it seems, the opposite was true and therefore I could never tell the story again. I hope and pray that anyone reading this will not repeat my great error and will avoid checking up on the truth of any episode of family history.

First Day at School

When I was delivered to school for my first day there, I was conscious only of there being a lot of nice people around and a lot of nice things to play with, which seemed like a lot of fun, so I got stuck in straightaway. Or I was about to, when I suddenly became aware of my mother hovering on the doorstep. I thought she had gone. I thought she had just left me to have fun. But, no, she was hovering, looking rather anxious but pretending to be cheerful.

All at once it was borne in on me that for her this was a momentous day. This was the first day of her life on which I would be taken away from her and she would have to spend the rest of the day alone. One day far in the future I would leave home and not come back and then she would be alone all the time and this was a foreshadowing of that awful day. No wonder she looked sad. And how selfish I had been! I was happily going to join the party and forget all about her! Thank goodness that, just in time, I had become conscious of her needs.

So I crossed the schoolroom floor back to my mother, took her hand and said, 'Don't worry, Mother. I'll see you again at tea-time.'

46

'Lunch-time, darling,' she said.

'I'm quite happy to see you again at tea-time,' I said.

'No, it's only till lunch-time,' she said.

A shadow must have passed over my face, and then it occurred to me that I was being selfish again.

'I will see you at lunch-time, then,' I said.

At that moment a teacher spotted that my mother was finding it difficult to tear herself away and came over to distract her attention while I made my getaway. She was called Mrs Panton and I came to like her best of all the teachers there, as she had a mind and could think for herself. All the others were just very good at group games. Take the coloured pencils and dried pasta and tubes of glue away from them and they would have been helpless. But Mrs Panton was different.

I remember that, halfway through that very morning, she came across me sitting in a corner staring into space and said, 'A penny for your thoughts!'

(I had already learnt that this was one of those untrustworthy grown-up statements. I had often told people my thoughts and never once been paid for it. But I went along with Mrs Panton because I knew that grown-ups got unhappy if you didn't and it was up to us children to keep grown-ups happy.)

'I was just wondering,' I said.

'Wondering what?' she said.

'I was wondering who I would be if I wasn't me,' I said.

'Good heavens!' said Mrs Panton. 'What on earth do you mean by that?'

I was surprised. It seemed pretty obvious to me.

'Well,' I said, 'everyone is different. I am not the same person as Johnny, and he is not the same as Molly-who-cries-all-the-time, and Molly is not the same as Sally, even though she cries all the time too.'

I stopped there for a moment. Those were all the names of the children I had got to know at school that morning.

'Well, anyway,' I said, 'if the things that make me different were changed and I was somebody else, who would I be? I couldn't be Johnny, because Johnny is already Johnny, and so I would have to be someone else. But who? I would have to be someone who does not exist yet. But how can I be someone who does not exist?'

You may not believe that I thought these things, but I did. I often sat and thought about things. I remember once at about that age looking up at the night sky and thinking how much bigger the sky was at night than by day. By day it was filled with clouds, which were all just above your head. At night it was filled with stars, and they were millions of miles away. But the question I wanted to know the answer to was: what happens when you run out of stars? When you come to the end star—and there must be an end star—what lies beyond?

I asked my mother once and she hadn't got the faintest idea.

I asked my father once and he said, 'If there is something beyond what you think is the end star, then what you thought was the end star wasn't the end star after all,' which was true but not very helpful.

I asked Ralph once and he said that he couldn't imagine any form of life without stars, though I suppose he was thinking of people like Marilyn Monroe and Laurence Olivier.

It so happened that Mrs Panton had been to university and had studied philosophy, before she got married and found herself reduced to kindergarten work, and so she must have been staggered to hear a child at kindergarten ask a question like the one that I had just asked.

And I don't suppose I would have asked it in the first place if it had been explained to me what school was all about.

It's a funny thing, but when children go to school nobody ever tells them what the whole idea of school is.

They just tell them they are going to have fun.

Nobody ever gives them the real low-down, as follows: 'In fifteen years' time, children, you are going to go to university to study something like philosophy, which is all about the way we think and reason. But before that happens, you have to go to a big school and learn languages and maths and history and things, to give you some knowledge of the world we think about. But before that happens, you have to go to a small school and learn about spelling and geography and numbers and shapes and sports and things, so that you have the tools with which to deal with knowledge. But before you can do that, you have to come to this very small school and learn how to be friends with other children and put your coat on the right hook and how to stick dried pasta on to a big bit of paper to make shapes and pictures, which will give you an early inkling of routine and discipline. If you don't do all that, you'll never get anywhere near philosophy.'

I think that pretty much sums it up.

What had amazed Mrs Panton was that she had come across a child who seemed to have bypassed the whole damned system.

Me.

On my first day of pre-pre-pre-school, or whatever it was technically, I had started asking questions which would not be out of place in the first year of university.

Without the benefit of years of dried pasta training, I had moved smoothly into the shallow waters of philosophy.

Well, it was hardly surprising, after living in the same house as Father all those years and being exposed to his perpetual questioning of life, his joy in creeping up on logic from behind and seeing if he could frighten it into doing something unaccustomed.

No wonder that, from time to time during the morning, Mrs Panton came back to look at me in awe and exchange a few words with me.

Unfortunately, I didn't have much time by then to exchange words with her.

I had just discovered the joys of sticking dried pasta on large pieces of paper, of sticking different coloured and different shaped bits of sticky paper on to more paper, and of fighting with other children who were trying to take my bits away from me.

This was something I had never done at home.

It was great!

So much so that by the time my mother came to get me at lunch-time, I was making a rainbow out of curved pasta (though there are never enough blue pasta shapes—are you listening, Italy?) and instead of being glad that she would not be alone for the rest of the day, I was furious that I would have to go home with her and give up my rainbow and burst into tears.

'Oh dear, oh dear, has he been very unhappy on his first day?' said Mother, seeing my misery.

'No, he's been full of beans,' said Mrs Panton. 'And very philosophical,' she found herself adding. 'Darling, ask your mummy the question you asked me earlier . . .'

Of course, she meant the one about who I would be if I wasn't me. But I'd forgotten all about that. So I asked the question which was really bothering me by then.

'Why does Tommy Parker always get all the red pencils?'

Mrs Panton gave me a sad look. I had let her down. I had gone back to being an ordinary child who would have to go through another thirteen years of education after all before he could get back to where he had been at the moment of arriving at his first day at school.

Playing Doctor and Nurses

When I was a little child, one of the most daring games you could play was Doctors and Nurses. I expect most people have played this. If you haven't, what this involves, basically, is boys and girls taking off their clothes and looking at each other. Mostly at the bits you don't normally see. If you were five or six years old this was not only pretty harmless, it was also quite educational. This was especially true if your only sibling was a brother, as in my case, and you had never seen a girl without her clothes on. This meant, of course, that you didn't know what they had between their legs. You knew that they didn't have a willy; what you didn't know was what they *did* have.

The answer, as I finally found out when I was about seven, was that they seemed to have nothing between their legs. We boys had little dangly bits and they had nothing. Well, a sort of curved nothingness, but still nothing. I wasn't disappointed. In fact, I was obscurely impressed. I think, looking back, that this was because I had already entered my train-spotting days. A steam engine was a bumpy thing with valves and pipes all over it, but some of the fastest steam engines had everything hidden away under sleek streamlining, making them look like dynamically shaped rockets whizzing along the rails, or perhaps like smooth licked ice creams. Girls looked streamlined. We boys looked bumpy and old-fashioned. It was only later that I learnt from a train expert that streamlining on steam engines was a nightmare because you couldn't get at the works without taking everything to bits.

'If you ever construct a steam loco, lad, put stuff on the outside where you can get at it easy.'

The very same bit of advice that was heeded by the man who built the Pompidou Centre, and by God when he designed the male form.

Doctors and Nurses, as an educational game, doesn't have a long lifespan. People play Scrabble all their lives, but Doctors and Nurses, which seems so very interesting at the age of six, has already begun to lose its allure two years later. At eight, you are starting to gain inhibitions and to cultivate embarrassment. Six-year-olds can goggle at each other's bodies, but eight-year-olds, I think, are beginning to blush.

One thing I can boast of, though, is that I did once shock my fellow players in a game of Doctors and Nurses. And it happened the very first time I was involved.

It was one afternoon in the holidays, when a boy and a girl had come over to play with me and the boy, who was called Eric, had bravely suggested that we play Doctors and Nurses.

The girl, who was called Jane, agreed.

They looked at me.

I looked puzled.

'Haven't you ever played Doctors and Nurses before?' Eric said.

'Oh, yes,' I said. 'But only with my mother.'

Sensation!

And yet it was true.

Whenever I was ill in bed, my mother would try to find ways of getting me to take my medicine, and the one that seemed to work best was this game she had invented.

'Let's play Doctors and Nurses,' she said, the first time I was laid up in bed.

'What's a nurse?' I said.

I asked that because I already knew what a doctor was. He was a man who smelled of tobacco and had a rough jacket and breathed on you when you were in bed and asked you questions, and then, when you tried to avoid his breath, punished you by giving you nasty stuff to drink.

'Nurses are really nice ladies who look after you in hospital,' she said.

'Do they have nasty breath?' I said, thinking of Dr Glynn.

'Oh, no,' she said. 'They're very kind and sweet and nice. The doctor knows what's wrong with you, and he knows what medicine to give you, but he is too busy to come and give you all the medicines, so the nurses do that.'

'Do the nurses know what is wrong with you?'

'Oh, yes.'

'So why do we need doctors? Why can't the nurses do it all?'

How far ahead of my time I was.

'Because the nurses wouldn't know what was wrong with you if the doctors hadn't told them. Now, I'm going to be your nurse and you're going to take the medicine that Dr Glynn told me to give you. Come on, little man!'

So I took the medicine and it was horrible.

'You've played Doctors and Nurses with your . . . mother?' said Eric.

'Yes,' I said.

'And you both took all your clothes off?' gasped Jane.

'No,' I said. 'Why should we do that?'

'Because that's what you do in Doctors and Nurses.'

'No, you don't,' I said. 'You give each other medicine to make each other better. That's what doctors and nurses do.'

Eric and Jane looked at each other.

'And you didn't take all your clothes off?' said Eric.

'No,' I said.

'Well, we're going to,' said Jane.

'Why?' I asked.

54

It all got a bit embarrassing after that and I can't remember a great deal about it, but I do remember the next time I was ill in bed my mother came in and said, 'I've got some more medicine for you, so it's time we played Doctors and Nurses again!'

And it so happened she was taking off her jersey as she said this, so I shouted, 'No! No, don't! Just leave the medicine there and I'll drink it! Please don't get undressed!'

And she gave me a very odd look, but she left the medicine behind and I drank it and we never played Doctors and Nurses again.

Life in Hospital

Because there was no surplus food during the war, nobody had a chance to overeat and so nobody got fat. It is said, in fact, that our health as a nation was at its finest during the lean war years. I can still remember many happy days spent with my mother harvesting rosehips in the hedgerows, prior to the operation of turning them into roschip syrup, rich in vitamin C.

'Before the war we could get all the vitamin C we needed,' said my mother, 'because we had a plentiful imported supply of . . .'

She paused. The days of plentiful imports were so long ago that she had forgotten what vitamin C came in.

'Bananas? Figs?' she mused. 'No, that's what we get syrup of figs from. Very important, syrup of figs. Keeps you regular. Have you been yet today?'

My mother had a fascination with bodily

functions which, in common with most British people of that time, she thought were vital to health, and at the same time she suffered from an equally British inability to mention them by name. So she issued a series of generalised questions: 'Have you been today?' 'Did you do anything?' 'We are going to go out in a moment, so do you want to go before we go?' To an outsider it would have been incomprehensible, and even with me it took a year or two to catch on. Until that moment of enlightenment, I just politely responded with whatever she seemed to want to hear.

It wasn't just syrup of figs and rosehip syrup that kept us the healthiest we had ever been, of course—there was also extract of malt and cod-liver oil and other things you can't even get in the shops nowadays unless you ask for them. The funny thing was that, although we British were the healthiest we had ever been, we were also the sickest we had ever been. Along with our glowing good health went the largest number of fashionable ailments since the heyday of the Black Death. We had TB, consumption, measles, polio, haemophilia, rickets, shingles, pellagra, scarlet fever, mumps, diphtheria, sago, tapioca and many other afflictions which raged through the nation so widely that we took them for granted. (Except, perhaps, for the most feared afflictions, which were TB and junket.) People took all the precautions they could—had their tonsils and appendices removed, went to the lavatory a second time just to be safe and so on—but still the epidemics came.

I myself had TB for a while, which was one of the more fashionable things to have. This was some time after the war. I contracted it round about the time I did my Eleven Plus, and the two will for ever be connected in my mind—indeed, there was a time when I thought that the Eleven Plus examination must have been some sort of questionnaire sent out by the hospital to get my background straight. I never felt very ill because of TB, but the doctor at the local hospital who examined me diagnosed it immediately.

His name was Dr Jayasyringa and he came from Ceylon. I had never seen anyone with such brown skin before. He was small and nimble and if he had been a young man today no doubt he would have been able to command vast fees as a spin bowler, but in those unenlightened days he was forced to work as a top doctor in a large British hospital. He sat on the edge of my hospital bed and very carefully explained all my symptoms to me and what he thought they meant. Then he asked me if I had any questions.

'Yes,' I said. 'Where do you come from?'

'I am from Ceylon,' he said. 'I am Sinhalese.'

This meant nothing to me.

'Is that like British Celanese?' I asked.

His face darkened, if a Sinhalese face can ever be said to darken. The firm called British Celanese had a vast factory somewhere in the North Wales/Shropshire area and he told me that his nationality was constantly being confused with it.

'I shall be a happy man when that damned factory closes down,' he said. 'Either that, or when our island home reverts to its traditional name of Sri Lanka and when I can call myself Sri Lankan and everyone will know what I mean. Until then I shall have to be Sinhalese. A distinguished word in

57

its own right, as it is the only word in English which has an "n" followed immediately by an "h".'

'What about "henhouse"?' I said.

He looked at me closely and thought for a moment.

'You are a clever young man and will go far,' he said. 'Assuming your TB clears up.'

'Is TB the same as consumption?' I asked.

'They are two words for the same thing,' said Dr Jayasyringa. 'Very often in this life this happens. It is the same with Ceylon and Sri Lanka, also with Wales and Cymru.'

I learnt in time that Dr Jayasyringa identified very strongly with the Welsh. This was because he perceived them as being overwhelmed and bullied by the English in the same way as the Sinhalese were historically dominated by the Indians. This simple piece of hero-and-victim casting was slightly complicated by the arrival of the hated English in India, as they were not quite so hated in Ceylon.

'But there is a good reason why England should be hated in Wales and loved in Ceylon. When you have a big country dominating a small country, and then an even stronger country comes along and starts to dominate the big country, then of course the small country will feel friendship for this new, strong country. That is why the Italians welcomed the arrival of the French under Napoleon. He got rid of the Austrians. That is why Portugal is England's oldest ally. The English represent protection against the overbearing presence of Spain. So when the English arrived in India and started ruling them, we in Ceylon did not say, "Oh dear, oh dear, oh deary me." We said, "Ha ha! Very good! That will show the almighty bloody

58

Indians where they get off!" '

I learnt quite a lot about world politics and colonial history and the movement of populations worldwide from Dr Jayasyringa. I did not, however, learn a great deal about tuberculosis from him.

'Am I getting better, doctor?' I asked him one day after I had surrendered the various samples of this and that which I had to submit for testing.

'I think so, I think so,' he said, sitting on my bed again.

He was the only doctor I have ever met who expressed doubt and self-questioning as breezily and easily as certainty.

'The thing is, young man, that we do not know everything about TB yet. We know that it is very infectious, which is why we have to isolate the patients on the top of mountains in special sanatoriums.'

'But I have not been isolated!' I said. 'I am here in the local hospital!'

'Yes, well, you are a special case.'

'What kind of special case?'

'Special in that we cannot afford to send you away. In any case, I think it is clearing up nicely now.'

On another occasion Dr Jayasyringa told me that in fact his name was Jayasinya, but that people had always made a joke of it and called him Jayasyringa, so he had gone along with it and changed his name.

'I would do anything to succeed,' he said. 'You have no idea how hard it is for an Asian doctor to come to Britain and compete with all the other doctors. If it were not for the cricket . . .'

'What cricket?' I asked him.

It turned out that he was indeed a good cricketer, both at batting and bowling, and as hospitals in those days had enough leisure time for the medical staff to field a cricket team, it was a great advantage when applying for a job to mention your cricketing talent because you might quite easily get a hospital appointment on that alone. Apparently Dr Jayasyringa had edged out a very talented TB specialist from Liverpool who had never played cricket, only football.

'There was another man who applied for a job the other day, in the Ear, Nose and Throat department,' said Dr Jayasyringa, 'who would have been a good man in the department, but unfortunately he was also a wicket keeper.'

'What's wrong with that?'

'Nothing. But we already have three wicket keepers in the hospital. We couldn't afford to carry another one.'

The doctor told me on another occasion that it was very odd having a cricket team which was composed entirely of doctors.

'You see, if anyone is injured on the other side they immediately expect to be treated.'

'And aren't they?'

'Oh, no. Doctors hate to be involved when they are off duty. They don't like to have anything to do with health out of hours. That is why they smoke and drink so much. But the other day in a match this poor chap had some sort of fainting fit on the field while he was batting and it was as much as the umpire could do to get any of the fielding side to look at him.'

'Did you look at him?'

'Oh, yes, I went to have a look and so did the orthopaedic surgeon and also an eye specialist.'

'And what was wrong with him?'

'The eye man thought it was a severe migraine. The surgeon said he'd almost certainly broken a leg. I said it had all the primary signs of TB. We might still be arguing if an anaesthetist hadn't strolled over from fine leg and pointed out that the man had swallowed his tongue.'

'Gosh,' I said. 'What happened then?'

'We got it out and got on with the game.'

I cannot have been in hospital for more than a few weeks, but it seemed an eternity at the time. Children get used to things very quickly, of course, so I came to accept this new world almost as automatically as I had accepted life at home. Most people never get sent away to school, but if they ever want to know what it is like, they only have to think back to any period they ever spent in hospital. The same sort of hierarchy, the same discipline, the same institutionalised correctness and cunning infringement of rules. And the same chance to meet people you would never otherwise meet. Some of them nice, but some of them were like Sister Catherall.

She was, I suppose, the ward matron.

She didn't even attempt to be nice, any more than a sergeant-major does.

'Has Dr Jayasyringe been in today?' she said to me one day.

Getting his name wrong must have been a joke once. By now it seemed to have turned into a habit.

'Yes,' I said, but she was already brushing the corner of the bed where he habitually sat to talk to me, as if getting rid of some unseen Sinhalese threat.

'And what did he tell you today?'

I tried to remember.

'He said that it was very dangerous to swallow your tongue while playing cricket.'

'Oh, did he indeed?' she sniffed. 'And how is that going to help you get better?'

'I don't know. I don't think it was meant to. He was just telling me about things.'

'Less talk, more treatment, that's what I'd like.'

She looked at me closely.

'You like Dr Jayasyringa, don't you?'

This time she pronounced his name properly.

'Yes, I do,' he said. 'He's very nice to me.'

'He's very nice, I'm sure,' she said, 'but that doesn't mean he always knows best how to deal with British diseases.'

'British diseases?'

'He comes from a tropical island where they have lots of tropical diseases like malaria and smallpox and yellow fever, I expect. Well, you don't get things like that here. We've got our own diseases here.'

Something I had read about Christopher Columbus in a history lesson stirred in my memory.

'Well, I think our explorers took a lot of our diseases round the world with them. Didn't a lot of people die of flu when we took it to America? Because they weren't used to it?'

She sniffed and passed on. I realise now that she was dismissing me as one of Dr Jayasyringa's allies. I was in the other faction. In hospitals—as in any enclosed organisation—you get lots of factions

62

building up. That's one of the reasons why so many TV soaps are set in hospitals. Ready-made conflict, ready-made drama. If only I had realised all this at the time, I could have started work on the first hospital soap and made a fortune.

'How are you feeling?' said Dr Jayasyringa the next time he sat on my bed.

'Fine,' I said.

I always felt fine when he came round. It must have been very disappointing for him.

'Is there anything you want to ask me?' he said.

'Yes. When can I go home?'

'When I say so. Next question.'

'When a cricketer swallows his tongue and is taken off the field, can someone else come on instead of him?'

'Yes, but only to field. Not to bowl or bat. And when the man is better, he comes back on. Cricket is the only game I know of where a man can come back on again after he has been replaced.'

He was certainly right about football and rugby, though I found out later that it wasn't so true of ice hockey, where every five minutes the whole team is suddenly replaced by dozens of players who went off for a quick fag five minutes previous to that.

'Anything else?'

'Yes. Do they have TB in Ceylon?'

He looked at me sharply.

'You've been talking to Sister Catherall, haven't you?'

'Well, yes, a bit . . .'

'Sister Catherall has something against me, you know. She thinks that because I am from a far-off country I can only cure far-off diseases. A lot of nonsense. We have imported all your diseases over the years and learnt how to deal with them. If Sister Catherall were on a ward in Colombo Hospital, she would recognise most of the illnesses she saw.'

'And have we imported your diseases?'

'Oh, my goodness, yes. They all came back with the Empire. That is why in London you have a hospital specially devoted to tropical diseases. You go out to build an Empire, you make us work for you in the paddy fields and you come back with our diseases. It is a fair swap.'

Very shortly after that, it was discovered that I didn't have TB and I was sent home.

'Not only are you cured, but you were never ill,' said Doctor Jayasyringa to me, as I left. 'That is the power of modern science.'

I only saw him once again. About six months later I was walking through our local town when he hailed me. He was walking hand in hand with Sister Catherall. I couldn't believe my eyes.

'I have succumbed to one of your Western diseases,' said the doctor happily. 'It is called love. It is different from most other diseases, because even if the patient knows he has got it, he does not wish to be cured.'

'Get along with you, Jaya,' said Sister Catherall, and they both laughed and vanished into the crowd.

The Family Motto

My mother, as a staunch Roman Catholic, seldom gave religion a second thought. My father, however, was a convinced agnostic, so he thought and worried about religion a great deal of the time.

'Wouldn't it have been easier to convert to Catholicism when you got married?' I asked him once.

'Easier than what?' he said.

'Well, than being creedless,' I said. 'Being as certain about everything as a Catholic is takes up no time at all, but being unsure is a full-time activity. You would have saved a lot of time and worry by going over to Rome.'

'I might at least have learnt a bit of Latin,' conceded my father. 'That way we would probably have got a better family motto.'

'Have we got a family motto?' I asked, a bit shocked. 'I mean, have we got a family motto apart from "Wait and see" and "Will we be there soon?" and "Don't ask your father questions he can't answer" and "Nobody appreciates me" and "Never you mind" and "The Bogey Man will get you if you don't go to sleep this very moment" and . . .'

'Those aren't mottoes,' he said. 'Those are catchphrases. Very useful, catchphrases. Unlike mottoes, which never seem to be any use at all. But, yes, we have got a family motto. It came about like this . . .'

Apparently, when my father was courting my mother, he sometimes wanted to take her dancing

65

at the weekend, but she would never go out on a Sunday to a dance. This was partly because she had to be up bright and early on a Monday to go to work, but mostly because she said it was sinful to dance on a Sunday and against her religion.

'Show me!' said my father-to-be scornfully. 'Show me where in the Bible it says you shouldn't dance on a Sunday!'

My mother did have a desultory look in the Old Testament, but found so many injunctions not to do various things that she liked doing, such as eating shellfish, that she gave up quickly.

'No, I don't think it's in the Bible,' she said. 'But it must be in a Papal decree somewhere. I am sure the Pope is against dancing on a Sunday.'

'Of course he is!' said my father. 'He's against any kind of dancing! He's a priest! He's not allowed to dance with women! And he would not be seen dancing with men!'

(In this, my father later admitted, he was absolutely wrong, as Catholic priests and even nuns are allowed to dance, and play golf or go to the cinema or whatever. It's just marrying and the sexual act they're not allowed. In fact, when recruitment to the priesthood began to fall off, my father suggested that the Catholics could have a priest recruitment campaign with a slogan that went something like: 'Join the Catholic priesthood and dance and drink and smoke all you like! And here's more good news—you don't have to have sex afterwards!')

So my father decided to write to the Vatican asking for adjudication on this one. Did the Church allow Catholics to dance on Sunday or did they not? That's all he wanted to know. Not having the Latin, he wrote it in English and then got a friend of his who had done classics at school to translate it into Latin.

'It's much more likely to be answered if I send it in Latin,' he said to my mother. 'Of course there's always the risk that they'll answer in Latin and I won't have the faintest idea if they're letting you dance with me or not, but that's a risk we'll have to take.'

He sent the letter off. It came back a month later, unopened.

Someone had written the words 'NON SATIS PECUNIA' on the envelope.

He took it to his friend to translate.

His friend said that it meant something like 'Money Is Not Enough'.

'Are they trying to teach me that material things don't matter?' said my father. 'I wrote to the Pope for advice on dancing, not to get a sermon on the vanity of filthy lucre! Does the Pope really despise moncy?'

'Of course not,' said the friend. 'The Vatican thinks of little else but earthly riches. If anyone has learnt how to serve both God *and* Mammon, it's the Pope. No, I think I must have translated it wrong . . . Ah, I've got it! Look at thc envelope!'

My father looked. His friend was pointing at the stamp.

'The stamp you put on was only enough for domestic purposes! To send a letter to Italy costs more than that! That's what they're trying to tell you—that you need to pay more! *Non Satis Pecunia* doesn't just mean "money is not enough"—it also means "not enough money". It must be the Latin way of saying "postage due".

There must be a cardinal at the Vatican in charge of postage who has rejected this letter on financial grounds and of course Latin is still the *lingua franca* of the Vatican, if nowhere else on earth, so he's written "postage due" in Latin.'

None of this endeared the Catholics to my father, though he was somewhat mollified when the local priest told him the next day that he could do all the dancing he liked on the Sunday, as long as he had done all his religious duties beforehand.

'There was no problem with that,' he told me. 'I have always done all my religious duties beforehand. That is the great advantage of being an agnostic. You are always in a perfect state of unpreparedness.'

'And did Mother agree to dance with you of a Sunday?' I said.

'She did. All except the samba.'

'She refused to dance the samba?'

'Yes.'

'Why?'

'She could never get the hang of it.'

And I thought that was that, until my father said, 'Oh, I forgot to say—we later adopted *Non Satis Pecunia* as the unofficial family motto. Not only did "Not enough money" almost always fit our position perfectly, but we felt it had received the blessing of the Pope. Indeed, indirectly it had been the Pope's own suggestion. I did once write to thank him for it, but of course we never heard back.'

How Grandfather Survived the War

My father never talked about his father at all. I asked him why once.

'Because nobody's ever asked me about him, of course,' he said, looking surprised.

'Well, tell me about him,' I said.

'Willingly,' he said. 'Like almost all grandfathers, he was in the thick of the Great War, but in a most unusual way. Thing was, my father worked for a firm in the Midlands in the first years of the century. Unfortunately, it wasn't the British Midlands. It was the Midlands of Germany. Anyway, as the war approached, there was great pressure on him to join up and fight. From the Germans. To prove that he wasn't a spy. So he did—he joined the German Army.'

'My God!' I said. 'Your father took up arms against his own country! I don't believe it!'

'Steady on! Be fair! He couldn't be sure he was actually going to fight against England. Germany tends to invade places like Belgium and France much more than Britain, and he had no objection to helping smash the French.'

'Yes, but . . .'

'I know what you're going to say. How could he bear to eat all those sausages and dumplings? But you're wrong. The German Army was the first one in the world to offer its men a vegetarian alternative. Sauerkraut, actually. No, what made life difficult for him was that his German wasn't too good and he kept not understanding orders and . . . well, finally he just left.'

'You mean, he deserted?'

'Let's just say that he came back to England with his family,' said my father, 'and joined the British Army. Ended up in the Royal Welch Fusiliers. A regiment with a proud history. To begin with, his exploits in the German Army were of value to the officers, who debriefed him endlessly on life as a German soldier. Unfortunately, he couldn't remember much beyond the catering side of things and there was only so much information about sauerkraut that the British Army needed to know. What finally turned them against him was that he didn't speak Welsh and lots of people in the R.W.F. didn't speak English, only Welsh, so he found himself a bit of an outcast in the ranks.'

'Just like in the German Army,' I said.

'Aye,' he said. 'Now, we shall never know exactly what drove my father to leave the R.W.F. It might have been . . .'

'Do you mean he deserted again?' I said.

'It might have been the thought of fighting against his erstwhile Boche brothers-in-arms,' said my father, ignoring me. 'It may have been the endless droning of war poets at night in the trenches which drove him mad—Robert Graves was in the same regiment, of course. People talk about shell shock. They never mention sonnet shock. Anyway, my father went on leave and didn't come back.'

'Went on the run, you mean.'

'Nothing cowardly about my father, as his next move showed. He joined the Red Cross.'

'Humanitarian move,' I said.

'Very clever move,' said my father. 'Who would

70

ever think of looking for a missing person in the Red Cross? And of course the Red Cross were in the thick of it. Being shot at by both sides. He met Hemingway in the Great War, you know. Both were working in the Red Cross.'

'How did they get on?'

'Hated each other,' said my father, tersely. 'Hemingway was a big bully and kept challenging him to boxing matches, which the poets never had done at least, and he made life impossible for my father and finally he couldn't take it any longer and he and the Red Cross went their separate ways. Anyway, when the war ended he was uncomfortably aware that he was probably the only soldier still wanted for desertion by both sides, and that if he didn't take measures he might end up being shot as a deserter. Armies go on looking for deserters after wars end, you know. There isn't much else for them to do after an armistice, actually.'

My father fell silent.

'So what happened?'

'Oh, he changed his name and his identity and started a new life. But they never give up, you know. They're cunning devils. And in 1924 they finally got him. We came home one day and found my father, stretched out on the floor . . .'

'Dead?' I said.

'Suffering from diabetes,' he said. 'The Red Cross had finally caught up with him and dealt with him in the only way they knew how. Medically.'

'But . . .'

We were called for supper at that moment, and my father never referred to my grandfather again.

71

Aunt Jane and Queen Mary

Ever since I could remember, Aunt Jane had been such a familiar part of the family scene that I was never quite sure if she was an aunt on my father's side or my mother's side. She got on very well with my mother, so I assumed she was on my father's side, which turned out to be the case.

'Tell us about the time you met the late Queen Mary', said my mother to Aunt Jane one day. 'I don't think the children have ever heard that one.'

'Oh, I don't think anyone would be interested in that,' said Aunty Jane.

'The late Queen Mary?' I said. 'You met Queen Mary after she had died?'

'You cheeky boy!' she said, slapping my wrist. 'To pay for that, I shall tell you how I met Queen Mary. Queen Mary, you know, was the wife of King George V.'

'The late George V?' I said.

She aimed another slap at my wrist but I knew it was coming and moved my arm away, thus getting a slap on my knee.

'People don't remember much about Queen Mary these days,' said Aunt Jane, 'except that her hairdo was not unlike a large baked Alaska. How she ever got a crown to stay on top of her hair, I shall never know. It was probably lashed down by tiny mooring ropes, tied in position each morning by teams of personal maids.'

'Did she wear a crown every day?' asked my mother.

'Oh, yes,' said Aunt Jane. 'She was famous for

that. But the thing she was really famous for was taking other people's possessions.'

'She stole things?' said my brother.

'No, no, no,' said Aunt Jane. 'But whenever she really wanted something which belonged to someone else, she would admire it extravagantly and so meaningfully that people felt obliged to hand it over as a gift.'

'That's blackmail,' said my brother Ralph.

'Blackmail is a nasty word, Inspector,' I said.

'Blackmail is a nasty thing, Sergeant,' said Ralph.

This was one of the little routines which Ralph and I indulged in and which we thought very funny, though nobody else did. The fact that only two people in a world population of several billion laughed at it should have told us something.

'When I was a young girl, you stupid boys,' said Aunt Jane, who was used to ignoring us, 'my mother loved the idea of royalty. She would read about the Royal Family for hours on end and fantasise about meeting them, or even just seeing them from a distance. And then one day she discovered that Queen Mary was coming to visit our local school, so of course she insisted that we went and stood on the corner of the school drive to wave to her when she arrived. We got there about half an hour too early but eventually the royal car arrived, a big black one with a royal standard flying, and Mother made me wave the rather nice Union Jack which we'd brought from home specially. Much to our surprise, the royal car came to a complete halt and Queen Mary got out and came over to us.

' "That's a nice flag you've got there, little girl,"

73

she said.

'I curtseyed and said "Thank you" very shyly.

'Then I just stood there.

' "It's a very nice flag indeed," said Queen Mary. "Very, VERY nice."

'Then a lady-in-waiting who had followed the Queen from the car went over to my mother and whispered in her ear. My mother nodded and leant over to me.

' "Give the Queen your flag, darling," she said.

' "No, I won't," I said.

' "The Queen wants you to give her your flag," said my mother insistently and rather nervously.

' "No, I don't want to! It's my flag!" I said. "Anyway, she's got her own flag! Look!"

'And I pointed at the royal standard on the car. But while I was doing so I had taken one hand off my own flag and Queen Mary suddenly grabbed it from me and started walking back to the car. Not knowing any better, I lost my temper and ran after her and started trying to grab the flag back from her while the lady-in-waiting fluttered all around in a panic, saying that I was committing *lèse-majesté*.'

'*Lèse-majesté* is a nasty word, Inspector,' I said.

'*Lèse-majesté* is a nasty thing, Sergeant,' said Ralph, and we went off into roars of laughter. Aunt Jane took umbrage and it was years before we finally learnt what happened between her and Queen Mary.

(Many books would leave you at that point, in suspense, but I am going to cut straight to the moment when, years later, she did tell us what happened.)

'Queen Mary's flag? Oh, we wrestled for a

74

moment and then the flag tore down the middle, so we had half each. I felt I had won, really, because I had the half with the stick on it. The Queen looked at me for a moment with real fury and then went back to her car and drove on. A little later a new flag was sent anonymously to me through the post, presumably from the Palace. But the one that I treasured was the half flag trophy from my wrestling match with Queen Mary.

'In my teens I used to dream sometimes of reuniting my half with the other half. Literally, I used to dream of it. Queen Mary used to be in the dream, too. We would solemnly sew the flag back together into one piece. Then we would fight for it all over again . . .

'Then one day I thought how silly all this was.'

'And you threw the flag away?' I said.

'No,' she said. 'I wrote to the Palace explaining what had happened and enclosing enough postage stamps to cover the cost of returning the half of the flag that Queen Mary still had. It never occurred to me that Queen Mary hadn't kept her half as avidly as I had kept mine.'

'And what happened?'

'I got a printed form letter back from the Palace, thanking me for my gift and saying that it had been given to one of Queen Mary's favourite charities. I then realised that nobody had even read my letter and had just assumed that my stamps were some kind of offering, so I determined to have nothing more to do with the Royal Family after that and became as firm an anti-monarchist as Mother was a fervent royalist.'

Mother's Deathbed

As I've already mentioned, from time to time Mother would retire to her bedroom to get ready for death.

'Where's your mother?' Father would shout, if he came home early.

'She's dying,' Ralph or I would say.

'Oh, Lord, not gone to meet her Maker again, has she?' he would groan.

She never did die, of course. (Well, she did once, but that was many years later.) When it all started, she wasn't even thinking of dying. She just used to get tired in the afternoon and, as she didn't know the word 'siesta', she pretended she had a headache. From headache to terminal headache was a short progression.

'I am going to lie down for a while,' she would say to us children. 'Don't make a noise. I have got a bad headache.'

'What's a good headache?' Ralph said to me once. I laughed, but I think he meant it seriously.

We did our best to keep quiet when she lay down, though it isn't easy for young children. Being boys, we used to indulge in a lot of hand-to-hand wrestling or what might otherwise be called 'trying to kill each other'. This was obviously quite noisy, especially if one of us got hurt and howled. So we tried to develop a form of fighting which involved very little noise.

'We'll have to invent silent wrestling,' said Ralph.

'There's no such thing,' I said.

76

'Yes, there is. Imagine wrestling with the sound turned down,' said Ralph. 'You know wrestling on TV? The way the wrestlers always beat the ground and complain and grunt and sometimes shriek? Well, why not do all that but as if it were a silent film? Or as if the sound had gone all wrong? Mouths open but no noise coming out?'

So silent wrestling was what we did and what we called it. It was a new game, invented by us. It was just the same as ordinary wrestling but with no soundtrack. Oh, and the other difference was that you didn't win by beating the other person into submission; you simply lost a point every time you made a noise. This meant that instead of concentrating on getting your opponent in a headlock or half-nelson, you tried to pinch him instead. Or tickle him. Laughing counted as a noise.

There must be hundreds of games born like this, from special circumstances in enclosed spaces. Variants of well-known games to fit local conditions. I once worked in an office where we developed a game of indoor cricket for four players which gave us endless hours of amusement until we were all fired for playing indoor cricket during office hours.

Maybe that is even how the Eton Wall Game came about.

'Sorry, Mr Poindexter, but there aren't any spare pitches this afternoon. Tell you what, though, why not take your thirty chaps and a ball and go to that muddy patch over by the big wall there and see if you can't work out some kind of game . . .'

They say that the Battle of Waterloo was won on

the playing fields of Eton. I doubt it. But I wouldn't be surprised to learn that the trench tactics of the Great War were worked out in the Eton Wall Game . . .

Where was I?

Oh, yes.

Not making a noise while Mother died.

She didn't come up with the idea that she was dying straightaway. I think the migraines were genuine enough, and that was why she went to lie down some afternoons. But when she started saying things like, 'I feel like death today,' and 'I've got a killing headache,' pretty soon she moved on to the idea of dying itself. Which, let's face it, is more impressive than having a migraine. If you have a bad headache, you can more or less continue life as normal, but if you're dying it's a lot harder to carry on with a daily routine.

'I am going to lie down for a while, boys,' she would say. 'If I am spared, I will make your tea later.'

'And if you are not spared?' Ralph said once.

'Then you'll have to get your own tea.'

As she always seemed to survive her own deathbed, we came to take it for granted that she would rise again, but I do remember once asking her anxiously if she ever really felt close to death.

'We are always close to death,' she said. 'In the midst of life we are in death. We must always be ready for death.'

'Yes, I know all that, Mother, but that's just Church talk. Nobody *really* feels close to death. I mean, I don't want you to die . . .'

'That's very sweet of you, dear,' she said. 'I don't want to die either, but when it is my time to go, I hope I am ready for it.'

'Oh, I hope I am not,' I said. 'I can't imagine anything worse than lying down, surrounded by candles, waiting to die. I'd much rather be hit by something like a cannonball when I wasn't expecting it and be instantly dead!'

'You want to die young, then, do you?'

I thought about it.

'No, I'd rather live till I was old and then get hit by a cannonball.'

'Not me,' she said. 'I'd rather die in my bed.'

'Well,' I said, 'what if you were lying in your bed one afternoon, ready for death, and a cannonball came through the window and killed you?'

'Gosh!' she said. 'That would be quite exciting! Well, I think I would be headline news in the local paper at the very least!'

'Local Lady Slain In Freak Civil War Re-Enactment Skirmish!' I said.

'Something like that,' said Mother.

And off she would go. These deathbed moments seemed to have a rcinvigorating effect on her, almost as if her brush with death had given her a renewed appetite for life.

'I sometimes envy hcr her near-death experiences,' said Fathcr once, when he came home and she was upstairs, dying. 'She's like a new woman afterwards. The only near-death experience I have ever had was life. I can't say it was much fun.'

'But you have no desire to meet your Maker?' said Ralph.

'Not in the least,' said Father. 'But I would quite like to meet my Designer and ask him for an apology.'

'Your Designer?' said Ralph. 'What do you mean by that?'

'Well, I have no quarrels with the way I was made,' said Father. 'But I have never thought that I was very well designed.'

He was in fact fairly solid in appearance but had never grown quite to the height he felt he deserved, nor got quite the ears he wanted.

'You know how in novels they sometimes describe the character as "a well-built man in his forties"? I would have to be described as "a well-built but badly designed man in his forties". That is why I would like to meet my Designer. Ask him what the hell he was up to. Why he couldn't have got the proportions a bit better . . .'

Not many people can be said to look forward to their own deaths, but Mother certainly did. Twice a week, sometimes. She claimed that she was so grateful to wake up and find she wasn't dead that the relief more than made up for the apprehension. She also claimed that when she finally came to die, she would be a lot more ready for it than anyone else. Mark you, she actually lived to a ripe old age and died in her sleep, so I am not sure if all that training was valuable or not. On the other hand, I recently read some research into sleep which showed that people who practise the art of the *siesta* live longer than most other people, so perhaps by having regular deathbed scenes our mother was actually prolonging her life.

'If she really thought she was going to die,' whispered Ralph to me one afternoon when we had got tired of wrestling and were looking for something else quiet to do, 'she would bid us a solemn farewell before she went upstairs. Or she

80

would gather her family round her bedside and give us some famous last words. Or at the very least tell us where the money was hidden.'

'What money?'

'The little fortune she has been keeping all these years, bequeathed to her by her Uncle Rodrigo who lived a wicked life in Costa Rica and repented at the very end, sending all his nieces and nephews a bag of gold.'

I am afraid that was how Ralph talked sometimes, living in a fantasy world of melodrama, or possibly re-enacting the last bad play he had read.

'But she never does,' he went on. 'So you can tell she is not really dying.'

He sounded almost disappointed, as if Mother's survival had deprived us all of a great final curtain scene.

It was about this time that Ralph himself got a part in a school play. He had been pestering the drama teacher so hard to give him a role in a school play that, although they were normally reserved for the final-year pupils, he was given a small part. A very small part. The school was doing one of those Agatha Christie-type thrillers where everyone in a country house is equally suspected of a murder so that all the actors can have a decent part. Except the corpse. Which was Ralph's part. He got a couple of lines early on and was then found dead. But it was Ralph's first ever part in a school play and he was determined to make the most of it, which he had a chance to do as he was on stage for twenty minutes after he died.

'Now, obviously I can't move and get laughs,' he said, 'but I can at least lie abnormally still. When there's an actor playing dead on stage people always stare at him a lot, hoping to spot his breathing. I'm going to disappoint them. I'm going to be the best corpse they've ever seen. But I'm going to have to rehearse very hard.'

Rehearsing for being a corpse, it seemed, took the form of lying around the house for long periods, as still as possible.

'What's it like?' I asked. 'Being dead, I mean.'

Ralph said that keeping absolutely still was incredibly difficult.

'Wanting to sneeze is the worst thing,' he reported. 'But there's also itching. And going numb. And being stepped on by stupid brothers.'

It was true. I had come round the sofa quite fast one day and not noticed him lying there until it was too late. I had walked on him. Fairly softly, I thought. He had reacted rather more violently than I had thought necessary.

'If you had *really* got into the character of a dead person,' I said, defensively, 'you wouldn't have noticed me stepping on you. Corpses don't notice people stepping on them. They ignore everything. They certainly don't jump up and hit you. What if one of the actors in the school play steps on you by accident? Are you going to jump up and try and knock him out, like you did me?'

Actually, although I made fun of him, I was very impressed that Ralph had a part at all. Like all people who can't act to save themselves, I have a great admiration for those who can, even if they are your elder brother. I was impressed by his devotion to his craft, even if it meant lying around the house inert. I was impressed by the way he had pestered people till he got a part.

And Mother was impressed too, though she was deeply upset by one thing which had never occurred to him.

'Ralph, I cannot believe that you have landed the part of a corpse,' she said, 'and that you lie around every day rehearsing the part but *you have never come to me for advice*!'

'But you don't act!' Ralph said.

'No, dear, but I die a lot!' she said firmly. 'How often does someone who gets a part as a corpse have the chance of turning to a member of the family with considerable experience of dying?'

The next time I found Ralph lying on the floor I asked him if he had got any good advice from Mother. He said nothing. I repeated the question. No reply. He was getting the idea. Good lad. I thought about kicking him but decided not to. Five minutes later he sprang up and said that he had indeed got some good advice.

'I asked her what dying was like and she said, "Well, you know how when you drown, the whole of your life is meant to flash past your eyes?" "Yes," I said. "I don't know if it does," she said, "as I have never even nearly drowned, but I do know that when you are dying on dry land scenes from your life come past your eyes at an ordinary pace." She said that on a good afternoon's dying she could get through five or ten years of her life. Well, I thought I'd try it. Of course, when you're only my age, you haven't got nearly so much life to remember . . .'

'Still, your memory would be much better,' I said.

'That's true. Anyway, as it gets pretty boring being a corpse, I thought I would try this, and it really works—you can replay the film of your life over and over again! So now what I do when I am rehearsing is rerun my life.'

'Am I in it?' I asked.

'Only the boring bits,' he said. 'And now, if you'll excuse me, I've got five more minutes of rehearsal.'

He went back into a coma again.

A few minutes later Father came back home from work.

'Where are the others?' he said.

'Mother's dying in the bedroom,' I said. 'And Ralph's on the sitting-room floor.'

'What's he doing there?'

'Dying.'

Father looked at me closely.

'And how are *you* feeling, my boy?'

'I'm fine!'

'Good. Let's have a cup of tea.'

There were four performances of Ralph's school play. We went to the first night. He did his lines very well and fell over very well, but his acting as a corpse was superb. He never moved at all.

'You'd think he was really dead,' said the people behind us.

Even I was a bit worried, he lay so still. But then, as the Scotland Yard policeman arrived and started to take evidence, we heard a very worrying noise.

It was snoring.

Ralph had got into the part so well and enjoyed his autobiographical movie rerun so much—or been so bored by it—that he had dropped off to sleep on stage.

The actors quickly became aware that they had

a snoring corpse in their midst.

There was only one thing to do.

One of the actors gave him a little kick as he passed.

Ralph leapt to his feet, clenching his fist and asking the actor what he thought he was up to.

As soon as he realised where he was and that it wasn't a dream he fell back, dead again.

It got the biggest laugh of the evening.

'The other three performances were fine,' he told us later. 'The first night was the only time I fell asleep. The rest of the time I was awake and motionless the whole time.'

'You're sure?' I said. 'Maybe the other times you fell asleep and only *dreamt* you were awake!'

'No,' he said, 'I wasn't asleep. I was really dead.'

Years later, when we were grown up, I heard Ralph talking to some other people about death. He brought the conversation to a dead stop when he said, 'It was my mother who taught me how to die with dignity.'

The others looked so solemn at this that I, the only person present who knew what he was talking about, burst into loud and raucous laughter.

It did not do my reputation any good.

Mother's Friends

My mother had a regular meeting of female friends which was held at our house, usually twice a month. They would spend most of the time debating whose house to meet at when they reassembled in a fortnight and after much discussion would always decide to come back to our house after all.

Nothing very odd about that. A lot of meetings do little else except discuss the next meeting or dismember the last one. But in another way it was a very unusual meeting—at least it was unusual if you have ever attended women's coffee mornings. Usually, women get together to play bridge, or have coffee, or swap baby clothes, or even to sell each other things, and then after a while it all degenerates into a general gossipy session in which they offer criticism of their husbands.

It was quite the other way around with Mother and her friends. They got together for the primary purpose of criticising their husbands. Then, if there was any time left over, they would get on to the bridge, whist, recipe swapping, etc. Of course, they didn't actually say it was for the purpose of criticising husbands. They said it was problem-sharing. But that is what it came down to.

'Item number one on the agenda,' I remember my mother saying once, 'is whether anyone has had any good ideas about what to do about Mary Whitgift's husband.'

Mary Whitgift was a small, freckled woman who always seemed to me to be on the verge of tears, an impression reinforced by her freckles, as they tended to look like tear smudges. Her husband was apparently suspected by all present, but especially by Mary Whitgift, of playing, quote, fast and loose, unquote. What this actually involved was never spelled out to my satisfaction.

'I can't imagine Harry Whitgift playing away from home,' said my father to my mother at supper one evening. 'Are you sure you are not imagining it all?'

So Mr Whitgift was not only playing fast and loose, he was also playing away from home! Well, it sounded innocent enough to me, but Mother and friends obviously didn't think so. What could it all mean? I picked up as much as I could from listening to my mother and father talking about her women friends' troubles. Father didn't take much of it in, but Ralph and I loved the gossip while pretending not to be listening. It was Ralph's big regret that he was too old to be admitted to the women's meetings, but for a while I was still considered young enough to be innocent and harmless, so I got a ringside seat among the women and Ralph saw me as what we would now call a mole.

'What were they talking about today?' he would ask me.

'Mrs Potter says that Mr Potter is too persistent,' I said.

'Persistent about what?'

'I don't know. They just think that Mr Potter is too persistent.'

'I see. Is this very bad?'

'No, I don't think so. They think it is very funny. At least, they laugh a lot about it. Sometimes someone will say, "Has he been persistent again this week?" and they all go off into big laughter.'

This is probably the only chance I was ever to get in my life to sit among a lot of women and find out what they talk about when men are not there, so I am sorry now that I did not pay more attention to the details. I seem to remember, though, that one of the women said how funny it was that they were on at Mr Potter because he was too persistent

87

and on at Mr Whitgift because he wasn't persistent enough. There seemed to be a clue there. Playing fast and loose seemed to be the opposite of being persistent. It wasn't much of a clue for a boy of my age, though.

'Have you tried reading a newspaper?' said Mrs Green one day.

'What about keeping the radio on?' said my mother.

'I find that humming loudly, slightly out of tune, works quite well,' said somebody else.

These were not solutions to playing fast and loose, or being persistent, but to another problem entirely: the problem of a husband who talked non-stop at breakfast time. This was Mr Wallace, who apparently was a chatterbox. Being a chatterbox was bad enough, but being a chatterbox at breakfast, said Mrs Wallace, was unforgivable. Breakfast was a time of silence and meditation and planning, a time when she liked to sort her thoughts out, make plans for the day ahead and organise excuses for the things she should have done yesterday but hadn't. Mr Wallace seemed to be in the habit of nattering throughout this period, telling her bits from the paper, things he had heard on the radio, things chaps at work had said. It was like having someone next to you at a church service talking the whole way through it.

'It's worse than the radio,' she said. 'You can ignore the radio. But you have to listen to him a bit, just in case there is something important among all the rubbish. Not that there ever is. Sometimes I could scream.'

'Then why *don't* you scream?' said the one who had recommended humming loudly. 'That would give him a shock! It might even cure him. Just scream!'

There then followed a debate on whether shock tactics ever improved a man. Someone said they had once thrown their husband's supper away because he was so late for it. Someone else said they had hired a gardener to mow a lawn which the husband had repeatedly promised to cut. Someone else said they had heard of a wife who had sold her husband's car while he was at work, though they couldn't remember quite why. Everyone agreed that, even if shock tactics didn't change a husband, they certainly made a wife feel a lot better. Mrs Wallace said she would seriously think about screaming at breakfast.

'So, what were mother's friends worried about today?' Ralph asked me.

I told him about Mr Wallace's breakfast-time behaviour, but Ralph did not think that was very interesting.

'What about Mr Whitgift playing fast and loose?'

'They didn't talk about that today. Have you worked out what playing fast and loose is yet? Is it some kind of game?'

'It might be,' said Ralph guardedly. 'There are some games with names like that. Hit and run. Hare and hounds.'

'Hide and seek,' I said.

Ralph scoffed at this suggestion.

'I don't think grown-ups would be playing hide and seek,' he said. 'And if they did, I don't think they would get into trouble for it. I do know that husbands get in trouble for playing games too often. You hear women saying that their husband

89

seems to prefer the golf course to being at home, or that they wish their husband came shopping instead of going to the football match. But playing fast and loose . . .'

At the next mothers' meeting Mrs Whitgift said she had news on the playing fast and loose front. She reported that she had actually accused Mr Whitgift of playing fast and loose and he had got very angry and denied it, but she was convinced he was, and she cried a little and everyone said, 'There, there,' and comforted her, and Mother suddenly noticed me and shooed me out of the room, and I went and told Ralph.

'It's time we did a little detective work,' said Ralph. 'Let's go and keep an eye on Mr Whitgift.'

'How do you mean, keep an eye on him?'

'Well, follow him, see what he does.'

'How are we going to follow him?'

'In disguise.'

'In a car?'

'No,' said Ralph. 'On foot.'

'What happens if he gets in a car and drives?'

'We jump on the back bumper and cling there.'

Ralph had seen more films than me.

'Anyway,' said Ralph, 'you find out where he lives and I'll do the rest.'

I found out the address from Mother's phone book and we went round there the next afternoon.

'Hold on—we're not in disguise,' I pointed out.

'We don't have to be,' said Ralph. 'I've been thinking it over and I've realised that Mr Whitgift doesn't know who we are, so there's no point in disguising ourselves.'

To be on the safe side we didn't try to hide outside the Whitgifts' house, but loitered forty yards away at the end of the street, where it joined a main road. We had beginner's luck here, because just when we were starting to get bored with the whole thing (there seemed absolutely no sign of life in the Whitgifts' house) a car drew up near us and Mr Whitgift got out. The car was being driven by a woman wearing tennis clothes. They said goodbye very cheerfully, he walked down the road to his home carrying a bag and she drove off.

'That's it!' said Ralph. 'He must have just come back from playing fast and loose! That woman was in games clothes! He's probably already changed out of his games clothes so that Mrs Whitgift won't know when he gets home that he's been playing! And that's why he got out of the car there and not outside his house! But we still don't know what fast and loose is. And we don't know who the woman driving the car was.'

'Yes, we do,' I said.

'No, we don't,' he said.

'Well, *I* do,' I said.

'How could you possibly have found out already?'

'I've always known,' I said. 'She's one of Mother's friends. She comes to the meeting. She's Mrs Potter.'

'Brilliant!' said Ralph. 'That's brilliant! You're brilliant! Now all we have to do is go and tell Mother that we have solved the mystery.'

You'd think that Mother would have been delighted, but when we found her in the kitchen and told her that we had found out that Mr Whitgift was playing fast and loose with Mrs Potter she took it very badly.

At least, she seemed far from being pleased.

She sat us down and made us go through the whole story. How I had been listening at the meeting. How I had told Ralph about Mr Whitgift playing fast and loose. How Ralph and I had gone to do some detective work. How we had seen them together. How the only thing we didn't know was what kind of a game 'fast and loose' was.

'Do you know how it is played, Mother?' I asked.

I didn't expect that she would. She was rotten at games. She never came to school matches. But she said she knew what it was. She said it would be too hard to explain the rules, though.

'It is a sort of game played by men and women,' she said. 'Just for fun. Though it's quite dangerous.'

'In tennis clothes?' asked Ralph.

'Tennis is sometimes involved,' said Mother.

She would say no more.

After that, I was not allowed to sit in on Mother's friends' meetings any longer.

I don't think Mrs Whitgift came to them again after that, and I don't think Mrs Potter did either.

The only time I heard either of them referred to again was once when Mother and Father were exchanging gossip at supper time.

'I hear that Mary Whitgift is not playing to the rules,' said Mother. 'She is demanding total custody of the children. She's not playing ball.'

'You shouldn't use children as shuttlecocks,' said Father. 'It's not cricket. You shouldn't move the goalposts.'

'Not even if it's a level playing field,' said Mother.

Ralph and I looked at each other, baffled.

There were just too many games in life to keep up with.

Dog Days

For as long as we could remember, Ralph and I had always wanted a dog. I wanted a dog so I could have someone to play with who wasn't Ralph. He wanted someone to play with who wasn't me. We both had friends to play with, of course, but they had to go home when it got dark and a dog would always be there, round the clock.

We asked our father if we could get a dog.

He said no.

We asked our mother.

She said no.

This would have been when we were still quite young, before they sent us away to school. I realise now that this is the best possible age to have a dog or cat. This is for two reasons (I hope all young parents are taking note). One is that at that age a child identifies strongly with the pet, certainly thinking of it as an ally against the parents. The other is that by the time the child is getting through its teens the dog or cat will be getting old and will die, thus introducing the teenager to the mystery and heartbreak of death at a bearable level.

(Some households even hold a private funeral, selecting a plot at the bottom of the garden under the trees, burying the late lamented and often putting up a headstone saying simply 'Twinky' or 'Fido'. When families sell houses and move on, they always leave the grave and the headstone behind, which is why new occupants are sometimes taken aback to find a mysterious memorial in the undergrowth. Who was Jocko? Or Stripey? Is it a family pet lying there? A faithful old dog? Or perhaps . . . someone? An old family retainer? A relative? I knew a man once who moved into a large country house with a small white cross in the shrubbery bearing the name 'Rover'. 'We had to dig up Rover's grave when we replanted the shrubbery,' he told me, 'and we were more than surprised to find an entire four-door saloon car buried there.')

Then, about four years later, Ralph and I came home at the end of one term and found that Mother had bought a dog after all. Why she had waited so long I do not know, though, looking back, I suppose she felt lonely when we were away at school and a dog was company, if not indeed an extra child.

It was a little white Scottish terrier. We didn't really like it. We went to our mother and said it wasn't the kind of dog we wanted and could she take it back. She said it was too late. That was what we had got. We had better learn to like it.

'If only she had consulted us,' said Ralph bitterly. 'She would have known that we didn't want a little yappy dog.'

'Well, I don't think we ever did discuss the matter,' I said. 'You never told me what kind of dog you wanted.'

'Yes, I did,' he said. 'I wanted a dog like Jumble.'

'Jumble?' I said. 'What's Jumble?'

'You *know*,' said Ralph. 'He was the dog in the

94

Just William stories. A mongrel. Best kind of dog you can get. Mum should have got a mongrel.'

I had forgotten that Ralph had been mad about the William stories. He told me once he would like to have modelled himself on William Brown and I suppose that if only he had had a gang like the Outlaws, and a dog like Jumble, and an anarchist spirit, and an older sister like Ethel, and an older brother like Robert, and a hostile world against which to plot, then he would have been in heaven and ready to emulate William. Unfortunately, he had none of them. On the other hand, Ralph's plans usually came off, whereas William's never did except by accident or by the author fixing the outcome. I myself always felt that William's ambition was not matched by his organisational powers. Whatever you thought of his ideas, I thought his planning was rubbish.

'That's the whole point!' said Ralph, when I told him what I felt. 'The whole point is that William's plans always go wrong and that's why they're so funny! Even when they go right, they go right by accident, so they're still funny!'

I suppose that's where Ralph and I took different paths. When things went wrong, he thought it was funny, whereas I just thought that things had gone wrong and wanted to know why they had gone wrong. I had some sort of primitive scientific spirit and Ralph had a primitive sense of humour. If Ralph had been sitting under the apple tree instead of Isaac Newton and the apple had fallen on his head, he would have laughed like a drain and tried to work out a way of getting it to do the same on someone else's head and we'd never have known abut gravity.

(Since I have grown up, I have come to think that that's one of the main problems with Britain. We prize humour more than science. You hear people saying, 'Trouble with him is he's got no sense of humour,' but you don't often hear anyone saying, 'Trouble is, he's got no sense of scientific inquiry.')

'Well, that was then,' I said. 'You don't want to be William any more, so you don't need his dog any more. What we should have got is a Labrador.'

'A Labrador?' said Ralph. 'A great big galumphing Labrador? What on earth for?'

'Good hunting dog,' I said. 'That means it can be taught things. Mongrels can't be taught things.'

' 'Course they can. Mixing races produces very intelligent specimens.'

Did we really have this conversation? I am sure we did. Young teenagers are very good at regurgitating half-understood theories. What was interesting, though, was that although Ralph and I had both agreed on how much we wanted a dog, we had totally different ideas of what kind of a dog we wanted. He had wanted a dog out of literature. I wanted a dog I could train. We had never discussed it. And so we had ended up with a wee white Scottie dog.

'What shall we call it?' said my mother.

'Please please please please please please don't call it Scottie,' said Ralph.

My brother had a horror of the obvious.

'All right,' said my mother.

'Or Mac, or Dougal, or Hamish, or . . .' said my brother, trying to go through all the naff Scottish names he could think of.

'Or Sandy,' I said, trying to help.

96

'Or Wullie,' said Ralph.

'Why should we call it Woolly?' said my mother.

'Or Jock,' I said.

'In that case,' said my mother, 'I have a good idea for his name. It's Scottish without being obvious.'

We looked at her expectantly.

'Let's call him Bonnie!'

We looked at her disappointedly.

'After Bonnie Prince Charlie?' said Ralph.

'No, no!' said Mother. 'Because his family came from Edinburgh!'

We looked at her, baffled.

'The main river in Glasgow is the Clyde, I think I'm right in saying. So as he comes from Edinburgh, it should be Bonnie. Bonnie and Clyde!'

We looked at each other, reunited. There is nothing like a clunking remark from a parent to bring children together.

*   *   *

I actually got quite fond of Bonnie, as you might expect. He ran as fast as his little legs would take him, and never gave up, and fetched sticks, and never gave them to you, and growled playfully if you tried to take it from him, and bit you playfully if you succeeded, often quite hard. He also liked to lie on his back and be rubbed. Occasionally I would oblige and run my hands over its bare underneath, being careful to avoid its sexual organs, though I don't suppose Bonnie noticed.

The first thing you notice when you stroke a dog lying on its back is its anatomy and how similar all mammals' bodies are to each other. The same ribcages, the same system of knees on legs, the same arrangement of limbs. I used to feel Bonnie's legs as if I were some sort of experimental surgeon, working out where the bones and muscles all were, and occasionally I realised that what was under my fingers was very like the joints on a butcher's slab. I once caught myself thinking how tasty Bonnie might be if roasted and then thinking that there was something very sick about this train of thought. Though to this day I find it hard to rub a dog's underneath without thinking of white hairy pork chops . . .

(The one area in which mammals seem to vary a lot, incidentally, is in the disposal of nipples. We humans have just the two, high up on our chests. Dogs have at least half a dozen, arranged in pairs down the chest, like buttons on a greatcoat. Cows have a pack of four, but, rather oddly, all bunched together way down the body between their back legs. Essay question number one: how do you think the history of fashion might be different if female humans had their bosoms between their legs?)

'Is that ours?' said my father one day at supper as Bonnie crossed the kitchen and went out into the hall.

'Is what ours?' said my mother.

'That dog.'

'Yes. Hadn't you ever noticed it before?'

'No.'

My father took another mouthful then corrected himself.

'Yes, come to think of it, I had noticed it before, but I had always imagined it was from next door or just visiting, because I knew we hadn't got a dog.'

'Well, we have now.'

There was another mouthful, then, 'Well, if we have got a dog, what is it called? Scottie?'

'No!' cried Ralph. 'It is not called Scottie! It must never be called Scottie! No dog should ever be called Scottie! It is bad luck to call a Scottie Scottie!'

'We could call it Macbeth, then,' said my father and roared with laughter. Nobody else did.

'Is that funny, dear?' said my mother.

'You know how in the theatre it is always considered bad luck to refer to *Macbeth* by name? And that actors always call it 'the Scottish play'? Well, it seems that we have the reverse case here. If it is bad luck to call the dog Scottie, why do we not call it Macbeth instead?'

He chuckled powerfully again. Ralph and I looked at each other. Father's approach to humour was sometimes extremely mechanical. Jokes only worked with him if he could see the cogs and wires involved in their workings. I used to wonder if his humour was more German than English. Later, when I got to know some Germans, I realised I had probably been unfair to Germany.

'Does Macbeth do any tricks?' asked my father.

'No,' we said.

'Should do,' said my father. 'No point having a dog unless you teach it something.'

'Why teach it tricks?' said my mother. 'I always think that's a bit undignified. Couldn't we just leave it to its instincts?'

'Of course we couldn't!' roared my father. 'Do you house-train a dog by leaving it to its instincts? Do you teach a sheep-dog to round up sheep by leaving it to its instincts? Is it a greyhound's

natural instinct to run after an electric hare? We
have done cats and dogs the disservice of
domesticating them, which means that we have
agreed to look after them and feed them and
protect them and in return we have to teach them
what to do! We have denatured them. Dogs cannot
live in the wild any more. So we must teach them
how to live out of nature. No, I shall believe that
Macbeth is worth his keep when you have taught
him to do something!'

'Bonnie,' said my mother, but he wasn't
listening.

Later, when my brother and I were taking
Bonnie for a walk, we discussed what tricks to
teach him. Ralph, not unnaturally, was all for
teaching him something flamboyant and
theatrical—standing on his hindlegs, tight-rope
walking, something like that.

'What is the *point*?' I said. 'When is a dog ever
going to need to stand on his hind legs? What is
the point of tight-rope walking? Where in nature
will he ever find a tight-rope?'

'Nowhere,' said Ralph. 'Weren't you listening to
our father? We don't live in nature now. We live in
a circus. Better train him to do circus tricks. When
people come round, he can do his tricks and
people will go away mightily impressed. Maybe
they will throw us money. Anyway, human beings
don't encounter tight-ropes in nature and *they*
learn tight-rope walking!'

'Well, I think it's stupid,' I said. 'I think we
ought to teach him the basics first. The commands
for sit and come—things like that.'

'Have it your own way,' said Ralph. '*You* teach
him the kindergarten skills. I'll do something a

little different, if you *don't* mind.'

What that something a little different was, I had no idea, because I never saw Ralph teaching him anything. He never saw me either, come to that, because I used to keep my training sessions with Bonnie for our walks. Ralph and I took it in turns to take the dog for a walk and when I was out with him, just him and me, I used to spend half the time teaching him a few basics. Very basic, actually. And very few. But soon enough I taught him to sit, by saying 'Sit!' and pushing his bottom down at the same time, and I got him to obey the order 'Stay!' and the order 'Come!'

'How are you getting on?' asked Ralph one day.

'Well, I can more or less get him to obey the orders to stay, sit and come,' I said. 'But anything else seems impossible.'

'What else have you tried?'

'I've tried to get him to obey the order to get out of the bathroom while I go to the lavatory. But he won't.'

It was true. He liked following us around the house, wherever we went. He had occasionally taken to following me into the bathroom and sitting next to me while I sat on the throne and read a book, which for me was always the main purpose of going to the loo. I tried to shoo him out because it was so embarrassing, him sitting there watching me. Then I realised that I was the only one who was embarrassed and that embarrassment is an emotion unknown to animals. But as I was still embarrassed, I still tried to shoo him out and failed. If I did manage to push him out, he merely sat outside the door, whining and scratching at it. Which was just as embarrassing.

'How are *you* getting on?' I asked.

'Oh, I am getting on fine,' he said, but more he would not say. I sometimes tried to guess what sort of thing Ralph would try to teach a dog to do, but with Ralph anything was possible as long as it was outlandish. He had started to read all about the eccentric figures of the history of art—French poets who took lobsters for walks on pink ribbons, writers who slept all night in an open coffin, that sort of thing—and I wondered if he would ever tackle that sort of gesture himself or be content just to read about it. Or, as a compromise, get Bonnie to do it.

One day at supper our father suddenly asked us if we had trained Bonnie to do any tricks yet.

'Yes,' I said.

'Yes,' said Ralph.

'Have you indeed?' said Father, taken aback. 'And when can we hope to see these in action?'

'Whenever you like,' I said.

'Ready and willing,' said Ralph.

'All systems go,' I said.

'Just say the word,' said Ralph.

'England expects,' I said.

'Chocks away,' said Ralph.

I don't know if I mentioned that Ralph and I had developed a game which involved repeating each other's sentiments in more or less equivalent phrases until one side ran out of ideas.

'At your command,' I said.

'Just say the word,' said Ralph.

'You've said that already,' I said.

'Damn, so I have,' said Ralph.

'Will you please *please* stop this bloody nonsense and come to your senses!' said my father, who couldn't stand our brotherly games. That was half the reason we did them in the first place. 'Who is going to put Macbeth through his paces first?'

I said I would and ten minutes later we were out on the lawn. I was on one side with Bonnie the dog. My father, mother and Ralph were on the other, watching closely.

'I haven't really taught him tricks, as such,' I said. 'It's all very well teaching a dog fancy tricks, but before you teach a dog fancy tricks you have to teach him the basics. So I thought I would go for the elementary grounding . . .'

'Just get on with it,' roared my father.

I got on with it. I walked with Bonnie and told him to sit. He sat. I told him to stay and walked away. He stayed, even though he was looking after me longingly. 'Come!' I said and he dashed towards me.

'There you are,' I said. 'The big three basics. Sit, stay and come.'

'Very good,' said my father. 'Safe and conventional, but at least you did it. Ralph?'

Ralph strolled forward while I retreated to my parents' side. He leant down and patted Bonnie. Then he stood up straight and addressed the throng.

'In my little demonstration of dog-training,' he told us, 'I shall use methods which date from as far back as the 1920s.'

'Dog-training methods?' said my father.

'No,' said my brother. 'Artistic methods. The 1920s were the years of Dadaism and surrealism. Suddenly, people didn't know what to expect any more. The old certainties were gone. Modernism could turn things on their head and often did. Was

103

it for effect? Or did they believe in it?'

'Oh, for God's sake, get on with it!' said my father.

'It is therefore in this spirit, the spirit of the first wave of modernism, that I present a session of dog-training,' said Ralph. 'First of all, I shall get the dog to sit.'

He turned to Bonnie. Bonnie was standing, looking eagerly at him.

'Come!' shouted Ralph.

The dog sat.

'Stay!' commanded Ralph.

The dog stood up.

'Sit!' cried Ralph.

The dog bounded over to him.

'There you are!' said Ralph. 'Wasn't that wonderful?'

'Not exactly,' said my father. 'The dog got every command wrong. It was a total failure.'

'No!' said Ralph. 'He got it all right! Didn't he?'

He turned to me for confirmation.

'Yes,' I said, nodding slowly. I knew Ralph better than the others did. 'I think I know what has happened. Ralph has trained him to do the wrong actions to the wrong commands. It's an act of . . .'

'Dadaism!' said Ralph. 'The first time Dadaism and dogs have ever been combined.'

It turned out that Ralph had taken great pains to teach Bonnie to sit when told to come, to get up when told to sit and so on.

'Don't you *see*?' he asked my father. 'The words are quite arbitrary. It doesn't matter what a word sounds like as long as it's the same word every time. You could teach a dog to beg by telling it to die, as long as the dog thought that "die" was in fact the order to "beg".'

'Yes, I see that.'

'So what I just demonstrated was an obedience which sounded and looked like an act of extreme disobedience. The Dadaists would have enjoyed that!'

'I haven't the faintest idea who the Dadaists are,' said my father. 'But I wonder if they could have solved one small problem. When *you* told the dog to sit, it came to you. When *your brother* told it to sit, it sat. It had two different responses to the same command. One was Dadaist and one was logical. How do you explain that?'

'Well,' said Ralph slowly, 'I would imagine that the dog has learnt to respond to the word "sit" in one way when it hears it in my voice, and in another when it hears it in his voice. It's probably not the same word to him, but two different words.'

'Extraordinary,' mused my father. 'I've never known anything like it.'

'I have,' I said.

'Have you indeed?' he said. 'Tell me about it.'

'We call the dog Bonnie. You call it Macbeth. But it answers to both names. It's almost as if he understands that both of them are his names. The only difference is the user.'

'Extraordinary,' said my father again. 'It's almost as if the dog is learning two different languages from two different people. And of course there are times when dogs do learn different languages. A French dog not only learns to respond to an order like *"Venez!"* or *"Restez!"* but it has to learn to respond to a French accent. If an Englishman told it to *venir* or *rester*, it might not respond. It might not understand his accent.'

'How very French of a dog not to understand an Englishman,' said Ralph.

'I tell you one experiment we might try,' I said. 'Why don't we get a Frenchman in to say "Sit!" to Bonnie and see what happens!'

'I've got a better idea,' said my father. 'Why don't *I* tell him to sit and see what happens? After all, we know that he responds in two different ways to the word already, from the two people who have been training him. Let's see what happens when someone who has *not* been training him tells him to sit.'

Everyone thought that this was a good idea. Even my mother, who had been displaying scant interest, moved in close to see what would happen.

The dog sat there.

'I can't tell it to sit while it's sitting,' said my father. 'Make it stand up.'

'You can't do that,' said Ralph. 'I have already trained it to stand up when I tell it to sit. If it's standing up already when you tell it to sit and it does nothing, it might be because it thinks you're me and is obeying me. But we can't tell for sure.'

'Yes, we can,' I said. 'Why don't we throw it up in the air and Dad can yell "Sit!" when it's in mid-air ? That way, it won't be doing anything when the order is issued. Except flying.'

'Gliding,' said Ralph.

'Well, gliding,' I said.

'Falling,' said my father.

'Well, falling,' I said. 'If we do that, then we shall know when it lands how it reacts to Dad telling it to sit.'

'I think you're all mad,' said my mother, but she

didn't look too displeased with the idea.

And so it was agreed.

I lifted the dog.

I threw the dog up. Just before it landed, father yelled 'Sit!'

As soon as it landed, it ran to my mother's side and crouched against her.

'Is it sitting?' said my father. 'I can't see from here. Your mother's dress is in the way.'

'It's sort of crouching,' said Ralph.

'Or leaning,' I said.

'No, it's not,' said my mother. 'It's not crouching or leaning or sitting or standing. It's cowering! It has recognised me as the only sane and friendly one among you and has come to me for sanctuary.'

'Well, I think we have to say that that experiment was inconclusive,' said my father, unabashed. 'I think we also have to say that if it had been Mrs Pavlov conducting the famous Pavlovian experiments with dogs, they would have been inconclusive too. As soon as the dinner bell rang, Mrs Pavlov would have fed them.'

'No more experiments from now on,' said mother firmly. 'This dog is going to live the life of a dog, not of a laboratory specimen.'

In which she was not entirely right, as she later came to bewail the fact that Bonnie was white and therefore showed up dirt terribly.

And this led to the infamous experiment in which Bonnie was dyed black for a while to see whether:

a) the mud would show (it didn't)

b) the dye would run (it did)

c) he would change his character with a new colour (he did)

107

d) he would react strangely to his new name of Blackie (he ignored it).

But that is another story, as indeed is the denouement in which, although Blackie did not really show mud, dirt or coal dust, he did look terrible the day he got whitewash all over himself, and my mother wished he were white again.

The G-word

My brother came home from school one day and said to my mother, 'Miss Withers used the g-word in class today!'

'Good Lord!' said my mother. 'How terrible!'

'Yes,' said my brother. 'We were all shocked.'

I felt mildly shocked too, though I didn't know what the g-word was. I felt very encouraged, though, that Ralph knew. As he was my elder brother, I expected him to know everything and this was further evidence that he was omniscient. The only difficult bit, I usually found, was getting him to share his omniscience with me.

'What *is* the g-word?' I asked him later.

'G-word?' said Ralph. 'I don't think there is one.'

'Then how could Miss Withers use it?'

'I don't think she did.'

'Then how . . . ?'

'Look,' said Ralph. 'Grown-ups are always referring to swear words by their initial letters, aren't they? The f-word and the b-word and the c-word, and so on. To begin with, I used to think that every letter in the alphabet had a swear word attached, but in fact it seems to be just F and C and B. So I thought I might make up for all that by inventing one.'

'So what *is* the g-word you've invented?'

'That's the point, you dolt,' said Ralph. 'There doesn't have to be one. All I have to do is say that there is one. And grown-ups will never admit that they don't know what it is, especially to a child.'

When my father came home, my mother told him that Ralph had told her that Miss Withers had said the g-word in class and everyone had been very shocked.

'I see,' said my father. 'I see. I see . . .'

You could see his mind racing through all the English obscenities and swear words. My father was quite good at crosswords and it only took him ten seconds or less to establish that there was, in fact, no gross word in English beginning with G.

'Remind me,' said Father. 'What does Miss Withers teach?'

'Geography,' said Ralph.

'That's not the g-word,' he added.

'Mmmmm,' said my father. 'So what is it?'

'What is what?'

'The g-word.'

I realise now I was very lucky in having the kind of father who would admit to not knowing the g-word.

'I couldn't possibly say it,' said Ralph, looking shyly at the floor.

'I respect you for that,' said my father, gazing at Ralph dreamily. 'I respect you for finding yourself unable to tell me what this terrible word beginning with G is. I admire your delicacy and demureness, your sensitivity and sweet nature. On the other hand, if you don't tell me immediately what the g-word is, I shall tear your arm off and beat you to death with it.'

He often said this. He never did it. But he usually got his way.

'Oh, God,' said Ralph under his breath, realising he had no back-up plan.

'God, eh?' said my father. 'So that's the g-word, is it?'

'Yes,' said Ralph, grasping at the back-up plan which had suddenly been handed him on a plate.

'So,' said my father. 'Miss Withers has been blaspheming in a geography lesson, has she?'

'Yes,' said Ralph. 'She certainly has.'

'Good for her,' said my father. 'If I taught geography, I'd have to let off steam now and again.'

'But that's not all!' said Ralph, desperate not to lose the tactical high ground which he had occupied not a moment before. 'She also said the n-word!'

'Do you mean "Knickers"?' said my father.

'Yes!' said Ralph.

'Your spelling is dreadful,' said my father. 'Knickers is not the n-word. It's the k-word.'

'Oh, bugger,' said Ralph, without thinking.

'Ralph!' said my mother.

'Did you say the b-word?' said my father strictly.

'Y-E-S,' said Ralph.

'Well, D-O-N-apostrophe-T,' said my father.

'W-H-Y-N-O-T?' spelled Ralph.

I left the room at this point.

When a family starts spelling out a conversation to themselves, life is being lived at half speed.

Little did I know it, but they had invented

text-messaging fifty years before anyone else did it.

The Blessed Virgin Mary

One of the advantages of having an agnostic father and a Roman Catholic mother was that Ralph and I felt that religion was not entirely a settled matter and was still worth discussing, even though I have since found out that most siblings very rarely talk about matters like God, faith and heaven. We must have been different, because I remember once even asking Ralph if he was religious.

He thought about it for a moment.

'I think I am religious, yes,' he said. 'But not about religion.'

'About what, then?'

'Oh, you know. The theatre, films, the arts. That sort of thing.'

He was quite right, of course, but I still think that of the two of us, he was the more likely to follow mother's path to Catholicism. I liked to think that I was too scientifically minded (or, what was probably more accurate at the time, too down-to-earth and ploddingly factual) to be drawn to that sort of thing, but Ralph loved . . . well, if not religion, at least the drama of religion. Being theatrically inclined, he was very drawn to Catholicism as a performance art, in the same way that a lot of people are mad about musicals who don't particularly like straight plays. Or people who like opera but don't really like music.

'I can see why Oscar Wilde was converted on his death bed to Catholicism,' he said to me once. 'He

111

must have loved all that incense and holy water. He probably thought of all the smells in a Catholic church as an extension of all his perfumes and aftershaves. And Catholic churches are always so over-decorated in the Victorian manner, like a turn of the century drawing room. Very lush, very plush, very Oscar.'

'In that case, why did he wait till he was dying to join the Church?' I asked. 'Why didn't he get in there from day one?'

Ralph thought about this.

'Good point,' he said. 'I think maybe when he was dying he suddenly realised he had left it rather late to make arrangements to meet all the best people in the next world. Maybe it was a social move as much as anything.'

'All the best people?' I said. 'You mean like Mother's saints?'

'Yes . . .' said Ralph, doubtfully. 'Put like that, it does sound dreadful.'

Our mother was on familiar terms with a lot of saints—at least she referred to them quite frequently and occasionally prayed to them individually. Ralph and I felt that they all sounded pretty much the same and all sounded really boring.

'One saint is bound to be much like another,' he said to me. 'They've all come out of the same life experience. They start out bad and interesting, but then the light of Christ shines upon them and they suddenly see the errors of their ways and become good and boring. Then they get martyred and go to heaven.'

'And when they get to heaven,' I said, 'all they find is lots of other saints, all telling the same

112

stories about persecution and martyrdom. Showing each other their martyrdom wounds and scars.'

'There must be millions of them, too,' said Ralph. 'Not just the famous ones. All those ones that have places named after them. St Neot, St Ive, St Pancras, St Asaph.'

'Saint Tropez,' I said.

'Who *are* they all?' said Ralph.

'San Francisco,' I said.

'Yes, yes, we get the idea,' said Ralph. 'So there you have it. Lots of saints standing around in haloes and robes, swapping tales of martyrdom and boasting about the place named after them.'

'St Mirren,' I said.

'Yes, yes,' said Ralph.

'Santa Monica,' I said.

Ralph leapt on me, punching my head and pulling my hair, which was one of his ways of indicating that a conversation had now closed for business. But this particular exchange came back to us several weeks later when we were out walking together. We had taken the dog out for exercise, as a way of getting out of some more onerous household duty, and had turned the corner of a remote part of the common when we both became aware of a woman standing in front of us. There was something striking about the woman. It may have been her very old-fashioned clothes. It may have been her expression, which was an incredibly sweet smile. Or it may have been the fact that she was hovering in the air, about two feet off the ground.

'Oh, my God,' said Ralph.

'Oh, my God,' I said.

She went on smiling sweetly and beckoned to us

to come closer.

'Do not be afraid, children,' she said.

When I say 'she said', I am not sure that either of us actually heard her speak or saw her lips move. It was almost as if she was talking to us internally and when we compared notes afterwards we found we thought we had both had entirely different conversations with her.

To me she said sweetly, 'Do you know who I am?'

I said that I had read accounts of the appearance of Mary, Mother of God, to people, and that she was a bit like that.

She said that that was who she was.

I asked her what happened if I didn't believe in her.

She smiled and said it made no difference. She was who she was.

I said that she normally only appeared to young children in Spanish-speaking Catholic countries and that she was way off her beaten track.

(This may seem a cheeky way of addressing the Blessed Virgin Mary, but I must stress that she was in no way frightening and her warm presence encouraged this kind of informality. As someone who didn't even believe in her, I was very impressed by her.)

She said I was wrong. She quite often appeared in a non-Catholic context, but then people refused to believe she was a vision. She had recently appeared to some children in Glasgow and had been pelted with stones which luckily had gone straight through her. It was only the Catholics who ever reported sightings of her, so that was why people got the impression that she only appeared

114

to Catholics.

I said I had never quite worked out why she appeared in visions in the first place. Why would she want to return to the earth at all?

She became a little agitated at this and said that she had to get out and about sometimes, that life in heaven could get on top of you. She preferred on the whole to appear to non-Catholics because there was no fuss then. She could tell that Ralph and I were not the kind to rush home, tell our parents and come back to set up a souvenir stall. She said she would be grateful if I told her that I wasn't going to tell anyone.

Meanwhile, he told me later, Ralph's conversation was going quite differently. The first thing that had struck him about her, he said, was her clothes. (Costume, he called it. Typical of a future theatre director.) Having studied Renaissance painting, he knew immediately that she was wearing the kind of garments which the Virgin Mary wore in fourteenth-century paintings.

'You know who I am?' she asked him too.

'I certainly do,' he said. 'I have seen you in many paintings.'

'You are a very clever boy,' she said.

'But I do not understand why you are dressed like that,' he said. 'You are not a fourteenth-century person. You are a first-century AD sort of person. So why . . . ?'

'Alas,' she said to him, 'if I were to wear the clothes I really wore on earth, nobody would recognise me. My image is now firmly established with medieval garb. So I have to stick to it because that is how everyone sees me. Do you even know what Biblical fashions looked like? To go to the other extreme, can you imagine if I appeared in a vision in modern clothes?'

'That would be very controversial,' said Ralph, trying to imagine her in a mini-skirt and, probably luckily, failing.

'It would also be totally unsuccessful,' she said. 'Besides, medieval clothes are very comfortable. I am not unhappy to wear them.'

'May I ask you a question?' said Ralph.

'Please do.'

'Why are you hovering two feet above the ground? Is it to stress your miraculous nature?'

She smiled.

'Of course not. It is to seem important. This is something we were taught very early on. In the same way that figures of authority on earth, like Popes or kings or even managing directors, have learnt always to be higher up than their subjects, and preferably with the sun behind them, so I have learnt when appearing in a vision that people are much more impressed if I am higher than they are. Do you have any more questions?'

'Yes. Why are heavenly visions always of you, of the Mother of God, never of any of the saints or disciples? Why are you the only one that appears in visions?'

He told me that he sensed an immense weariness when she answered this.

She sighed and said, 'The saints never want to appear in visions. They are far too happy in heaven standing around in groups and talking about martyrdom. They form little cabals, you know. All the ones who were burnt tend to congregate together, and those who were stoned . . .'

She sighed again.

116

'Sometimes you just want to get out and meet different people. That's why I appear on earth so often. Compared to everyone else, that is.'

'Do you see your son very often?' said Ralph sympathetically, or at least that is what he claimed to have said sympathetically.

She sighed once more.

'I think he has more in common with his father. He spends a lot of time with him. Well, yes, my son and I do see each other, but . . .'

At the end of the last sigh she faded completely away.

Ralph and I looked at each other.

We were lost for words.

Then she reappeared.

'Normally I am keen for people to report that they have seen me in a vision,' she said, 'but I think in this case you must not tell anyone that you have seen me. Do you understand?'

We nodded, dumbly.

She vanished.

Then she reappeared.

'Because if you do, nobody will believe you.'

Then she went and never came back.

And she was right, because we told everyone and nobody even began to believe us.

Autograph Collecting

When I was a boy, we had a craze for collecting autographs, but it was slightly diluted by the fact that none of us at school had the signature of anyone really famous. One boy had a football programme given him by his dad which had been signed by a famous footballer, but unfortunately he was a famous footballer of a previous era and nobody had ever heard of him.

'His dad should have sold it when he was still famous,' said my brother Ralph. 'Now it's worthless.'

Ralph had spent several years besotted with the glamour of show business, but by the age of thirteen or fourteen had already passed through that stage and was now keenly aware only of the business possibilities behind the glamour. So I was not surprised when a week or so later he announced in the playground at break that he had the autograph of a famous person for sale.

'Who is it?'

'Frankie Vaughan.'

Frankie Vaughan was very big in the 1950s. He was England's answer to American singers like Perry Como and Dean Martin—fat-voiced and classy and doomed to be drowned in the tidal wave of rock 'n' roll which was about to come along. We didn't know that then, and nor did Frankie Vaughan, and nor did our mums and dads who loved Frankie Vaughan for reasons we couldn't fathom.

'Let's see.'

Ralph produced a sheet of paper and carefully exposed the bottom of it. Sure enough, there was a florid signature which seemed to say 'Frankie Vaughan', though as the playground cynic Jimmy Sugden pointed out, it might well have been 'Freddy Naylor' or 'Fruity Valance'.

'That's the proof that it's genuine,' said Ralph. 'Famous people have to do their signature so often that it gets a bit automatic. That's the proof.'

But people wanted more proof than that and Ralph, to do him credit, triumphantly produced it. It was a copy of a showbiz magazine in which Frankie Vaughan wrote a monthly letter to his fans and signed it with a facsimile of his signature. It certainly looked uncannily similar to Ralph's autograph.

'Anyone can have my autograph for a pound,' said Ralph.

'Let's have a look,' said Jimmy Sugden and grabbed the sheet of paper from him. 'Why would Frankie Vaughan sign a piece of paper for you?'

'Hey!' cried Ralph, but it was too late. Triumphantly, Jimmy Sugden displayed the sheet of paper to everyone and showed that there were a dozen Frankie Vaughan signatures on the same sheet, some better than others, some incomplete and all obviously done by Ralph.

'*You* did these!' said Jimmy. 'You copied his signature!'

Ralph was never totally mortified by these experiences.

'All right,' he said. 'Five bob for the whole sheet.'

There were no takers.

Later, when we got home, Ralph told me that he had spent at least two days perfecting Frankie Vaughan's signature.

'I'm not going to let that go to waste,' he said. 'Doing Frankie Vaughan's signature is a skill. If only I could see a way of using it . . .'

The next day he showed me a letter he had written to Frankie Vaughan.

'Dear Frankie Vaughan,' it read, 'you must have

to waste hours of your life every week signing photographs and programmes and letters for fans. Why not hire me to do it for you? I so admire you that I have mastered the art of writing your autograph. Many people might be tempted to put this skill to evil ends, but I only want to do it for you. Here is your signature. What do you think? Yours sincerely.'

'What do you think?' said Ralph.

'I think it's very good, but I don't think you are likely to hear from him,' I said.

I was right.

Although he sent it to the Frankie Vaughan column at the magazine, there was no answer.

So he got hold of the address of the Frankie Vaughan Fan Club and the name of the secretary of the fan club and wrote her a letter.

It was rather a different letter from the one he had sent to Frankie himself.

'Dear Sue,' it said, 'as you know, I am often too busy to write as many autographs for my many fans as I would like and I think it is about time that it was organised properly. I have discovered a young man who writes my signature as well as I do and suggest that you employ him for the purpose. I can thoroughly recommend him as industrious and reliable. His name and address is (here followed Ralph's name and address) and I would like you to get in touch with him. Of course, you will have to pay him, but it will be well worth it. Love, Frankie Vaughan.'

All this typed painstakingly on my father's typewriter and signed with Ralph's best Frankie Vaughan imitation.

The fan club never replied directly, but several

120

days later a policeman came to call at our house.

He talked to Father for a while in his room, then Ralph was called in.

The policeman said they took a very dim view of Ralph imitating Frankie Vaughan's autograph and said that in fact forging someone's signature was against the law.

'You mean,' said Ralph, 'that just imitating someone's signature is illegal? Just practising it? Just trying to see if you can do it?'

'No,' said the policeman, 'but trying to use it for gain and profit is. You were trying to get a job by using his signature. I have to say that to my eyes you made a really good job of it, but it didn't fool the Frankie Vaughan Fan Club.'

'As a matter of interest, how did they spot it was a fake?' asked my father.

'Like most famous singers, apparently, Frankie Vaughan never ever gets in touch with his fan club,' said the policeman drily. 'And if he did, he wouldn't sign himself "Frankie Vaughan". He'd sign himself "Frankie".'

My brother and I were outside in the garden as the policeman left. When the policeman saw us, he changed course and come over to us.

'Seeing as how I let you off so lightly, Ralph,' he said, 'you can do something for me.'

'Me?' said Ralph. 'What?'

'Sign this.'

He took a record from out of his case. It was the latest Frankie Vaughan LP.

'Just write "from Frankie Vaughan" on it,' he said. 'The wife loves him. She'll be over the moon to have it signed by the man himself.'

Ralph signed it with a flourish.

The policeman departed.

It was at that moment that, for the first time, I began to have my own private doubts about the police force. Ralph, however, later told me that it was this incident which gave him a respect for the police he had never had before.

How to Write a Thank You Letter

One year I couldn't help noticing that my brother Ralph got more Christmas presents than I did.

Only one more than I did, but that was enough.

He got a present from Uncle Henry and I didn't.

I was furious.

Why him and not me?

I was so furious that instead of sulking I had it out with Ralph. They say that in marriage it's better to talk about problems than to keep silent. Of course, nobody is married to someone like Ralph.

'Well, perhaps the reason Uncle Henry sent me a present and not you is that he knows of my existence and not yours,' said Ralph. 'Or, more likely, perhaps he likes me and doesn't like you. Perhaps Uncle Henry thinks you have got enough possessions already and doesn't want you to have too many. Perhaps he thinks you're a spoilt brat . . .'

I leapt on him.

'Why are you two boys fighting again?' said my father, coming in.

'Because Uncle Henry sent him a present and didn't send me one,' I said.

122

'The secret of getting presents is sending thank you letters,' said my father. 'And the main thing is to write a thank you letter as soon as possible. It doesn't matter what you say. Speed is all. The donor will remember speed of response and give you another present next time. It's an investment for the future.'

'Well,' said my mother doubtfully, 'I'm not sure that speed is the *most* important thing. I'm happy to get a thank you letter at any time. In fact, sometimes children write to me two or three weeks later and I'm never cross that they've waited so long. I'm just happy they've done it. In a way, it's really nice to get one when you're not expecting it.'

'As far as I can gather,' my brother said, 'you and Dad want us to write two thank you letters to each person. One straight after the event and one a lot later.'

'I think that would be excessive,' said my mother.

'Look!' I said. 'This is no good to me! Uncle Henry has never given me a present! So how can I say thank you?'

'The whole trouble with making the effort to write thank you letters,' said my father, as if I hadn't spoken, 'is that once you have got the present, the incentive to write back has gone. It's like being paid in advance. When someone gets the lolly in advance, they feel they don't really have to do the job. Well, getting a present first is the same sort of thing. Ideally, you should write the thank you letter before you get the present.'

'I think that would be excessive,' said my mother.

Later, when Ralph and I were friends again, I

asked him what he would do.

'Mum and Dad have given their advice,' I said, 'and pretty rotten it was too, so what's yours?'

'Funnily enough,' said Ralph, 'it's the same as Dad's. Write the thank you letter before you get the present.'

'That's stupid.'

'Well, it's what I did with Uncle Henry.'

'You *what*?'

'Yes, I did. Way before Christmas, when I was feeling very poor, I made a list of people I might get presents from. Uncle Henry was not on the list. I thought it would be nice for him to be on the list. So I wrote him a letter thanking him for a present from the Christmas before. I didn't refer to what the present was, as he hadn't sent me one. I reckoned that he would never remember that he hadn't sent me anything and it would never occur to him that any child would write a thank you letter for something he *hadn't* got and he'd be shaken enough to put me on his gift list and send me something this time.'

'That's stupid,' I said.

'Seems to have worked,' said Ralph.

'Are you going to write a thank you letter for this present?' I said.

'When I get round to it,' he said.

That gave me a chance. I suddenly saw that if I wrote a thank you letter to Uncle Henry *now*, I would be ahead of Ralph next year.

So I wrote a letter to Uncle Henry which went roughly like this:

124

Dear Uncle Henry,

Thanks very much for the present, it was very kind of you. We had a wonderful Christmas, except for the mistletoe catching fire. We went to the pantomime in the New Year and it was great, especially the bit where the pumpkin would not change into a stagecoach and the fairy godmother said a very rude word.

With love from your nephew.

Someone had once told me that grown-ups liked it if you put things in letters which had gone wrong, so that's why I mentioned the mistletoe and the pumpkin trick.

A little while later I got a letter from Uncle Henry which said:

Dear Nephew,

I was very pleased to get your thank you letter, especially as I had never sent you a present, as you well know, you cheeky little bugger. Still, one should always reward enterprise, so I enclose a £10 note to make up for me being mean at Christmas. If you feel like it, give half to your brother Ralph as I never sent him a present either. One day you must tell me how the mistletoe caught fire.

Your old Uncle Henry.

I had never thought of Uncle Henry as anything but a rather quiet and boring old chap before, but this rather changed my view of him. It also rather changed my view of Ralph.

'Ralph,' I said to him one day, 'just supposing, just *supposing*, you had never written to Uncle Henry. I'm just supposing. And supposing he had never sent you a Christmas present. Then who do you suppose that present from Uncle Henry at Christmas time was really from?'

Ralph looked at me closely. I obviously knew more than I was letting on. And I obviously knew there was something fishy about Uncle Henry's present. And he knew when it was time to come clean.

'It wasn't a present from Uncle Henry,' he confessed. 'Well, it was. But I gave it to myself and made pretend it came from Uncle Henry.'

'Why?'

'To make you jealous.'

I took this in for a moment, in silence. It was just the sort of thing that Ralph would like to do. I was surprised that he actually had the energy to do it, though.

'It must have been very disappointing not getting a present from Uncle Henry,' I said. 'So I hope this makes up for it a bit.'

And I gave him £2.

It wasn't quite the £5 that Uncle Henry had suggested.

But it was a lot more than I felt he deserved.

And it was worth it, to see the expression on Ralph's face. Which, I have to say, didn't go away until I told him the full story.

And that wasn't for another four or five weeks.

The Squirrel Problem

One day, my father decided that he should build a bird table so that Ralph and I could learn about wild birds. Unfortunately, because of other tasks getting in the way, it took him five years to make. Ralph and I filled in the interim by, among other things, looking at birds in the wild and by the time the bird table arrived and was shakily put up, we knew all about wild bird life, except perhaps in the context of a bird table.

And then, suddenly, after all those years, we had a small bird table in the garden to which small birds came. It was perhaps just as well that large birds did not come to it. It would have buckled under the strain.

'Now that we have a place to watch birds, the boys can learn the names of all the inhabitants of the bird kingdom,' said my father proudly.

'Why is it called the bird "kingdom"?' said Ralph, who had recently discovered Shakespeare. 'Who is the king of the birds? Who are the dukes and earls of the bird kingdom? What happens when the old king dies? Does the bird kingdom ever get invaded by would-be usurpers who would like to steal the crown jewels of the king of the birds?'

'No,' said my father shortly.

But he was wrong. A few weeks later we looked out of the window and saw a grey squirrel on the bird table. Having wrenched open the nut-holder and consumed the lot, he was now busy wolfing down the loose seeds. He must have thought it was

127

Christmas.

'Better tell Father that the bird kingdom has been invaded by a cruel tyrant who is e'en now breaking open the treasury of the country and wreaking damage most fearful,' said Ralph.

'You tell him,' I said.

'All right,' said Ralph. He shouted, 'Dad, there's a squirrel on the bird table!'

Our father appeared with an air-gun, but by the time he had located the pellets, broken open the gun, loaded it and opened the door, the squirrel was long gone.

'We have a problem here,' he said to me. 'The problem is to devise a source of food which the birds can get at and the squirrels can't. No use asking Ralph. He won't even think there's a problem. But if you have any ideas . . .'

I tried to visualise it.

'Short of levitating the bird table in mid-air, I can't imagine what such a device would be like,' I said. 'The ideal thing would be to have a bird table floating in space.'

'In space it would be easy enough,' said my father. 'That's all a thing can do in space. Float. But on earth, short of having some sort of flying device attached to it, a rocket maybe . . .'

'I know!' I cried. 'A hot-air balloon! Or helium balloon! With a bird table underneath instead of a gondola!'

My father shook his head.

'It would have to be a tethered balloon or it would fly away. And once you have a tether, you have something along which a squirrel can climb. The table must be attached to the planet somehow, however tenuously. And squirrels can

128

get along any known attachment.'

Instinctively I knew this to be true. My father and I had often watched squirrels come light-footedly over the telephone cables which linked our garden to the next, like tight-rope walkers at the peak of their form. We had seen them scale a tree like lightning. We had seen them jump from tree to tree.

'The only thing I can think of,' I said, 'is a platform in mid-air, something like the ping pong balls you get in fairgrounds hovering over an upwards jet of water or air.'

'Nice idea, but it would need too much energy,' he said, 'and besides, I wouldn't put it past an agile squirrel to ride the upwards jet to help him reach the food. No, if we can't prevent them getting to the bird table, maybe we can thwart them once they get there. Look, let's go down to my workshop and see what we can think of.'

And so we got started on one of our sessions, in which my father put forward constant ideas and I tried to see the problems with them and vice versa. After half an hour, the sheets of paper on his drawing board were covered with the sort of drawings which Leonardo da Vinci would have had all over his notebooks if Leonardo had ever bothered to try to tackle the problem of squirrels which steal from bird tables.

(As a fellow inventor, my father had only a guarded reverence for Leonardo. He felt the Italian, though clever enough, had wasted too much time on fanciful ideas ahead of their time, like helicopters and tanks, and too little on more pressing problems. 'What's the point of sketching a helicopter which won't work,' he said to me once, 'when he could have ensured complete immortality by inventing a flushing toilet which *did* work?')

The most promising idea he came up with was a plan for a reinforced nut dispenser, much like the ordinary one except that it had an extra double grille round it. The idea was that birds with their long beaks could still peck at the nuts, but squirrels couldn't get through to nibble them.

'Mark you,' said my father, 'some nut-loving birds, like chaffinches and bullfinches, are at a disadvantage. They have to have strong chunky nut-cracking beaks, so their beaks are therefore short.'

'Why couldn't they be long?' I asked.

'Belong to what?'

'No, why couldn't they have long beaks?'

'Question of evolution. Nut-loving birds develop short strong beaks. Fish-loving birds develop long thin beaks you can spear fish with. Birds of prey develop cruel, hooked, tearing beaks. Pelicans develop beaks with huge capacity so that they can store fish in them, like posh pieces of luggage.'

I thought about this.

'Does that mean that a bird with a short beak has to acquire a taste for nuts, or that a bird with a taste for nuts has to develop the right beak?'

'It means that the birds which have not adapted die out, and those which have, don't.'

I wish my father were still alive so that I could ask him what he thought would happen to seagulls. In my lifetime seagulls have more or less given up the will to fish and have come inland to live off rubbish dumps and landfill sites. Does this mean that their physical attributes—notably their cruel, curved beaks—will change to suit their new diet?

130

Will they evolve new beaks ideal for investigating half-empty cans of luncheon meat? Or, if my father was right, will the seagulls with the most suitable beaks for rubbish survive and breed?

(I am sure that young men with omnivorous notebooks are already crouched beside landfill sites, justifying their grants by studying this very notion. So I will leave it to them.)

We rigged up the anti-squirrel device with the extra grille to keep the squirrel out and it certainly deterred the squirrel, though it seemed to deter half the birds as well. Too much like hard work perhaps. The squirrel didn't give up, however, and still roamed around the bird table area, hoping perhaps that the birds would drop some nuts.

'When a squirrel finds a load of nuts in one place like this,' said my father, 'he must think that someone has waved a magic wand. In nature, nuts grow singly on trees and have to be extricated with a lot of effort. Here, suddenly, is Aladdin's cave. It's a bit like a slug finding a row of baby lettuces growing. And now we have locked him out of the Garden of Eden. We have let the squirrel see heaven and we won't let him in. But he can still look through the door at the forbidden goodies. No wonder he haunts the bird table.'

'Why don't you put some nuts out separately for the squirrel, then?' said my mother, who had heard this. 'I don't see why you should discriminate against one part of nature in favour of another. If birds need feeding, so do squirrels. Anyway, if the squirrel had his own nuts, he wouldn't come bothering the birds.'

To my surprise, my father thought this was a good idea and dragged me down to the workshop again to help design a nut-holder for squirrels.

'What we need,' he said, 'is a device which will let squirrels get at the nuts, but not too easily. If they can get the nuts easily, they will just take them all away and store them, then come back for the birds' nuts and we will be back to square one.'

We covered more sheets of paper with doodled plans for a squirrel nut dispenser. Of course, there are nut dispensers in nature as well. They are called trees. But I couldn't see any way in which we might copy a tree. Even Leonardo da Vinci would have found it hard to use a tree as a model for a nut dispenser . . .

'What on earth is that meant to be?' said my father, glancing over at the drawing I was doing. 'It looks more like a machine gun than anything. If a machine gun can be made out of wood.'

'That's what it is,' I said, blushing. 'I got sidetracked and I started wondering how Leonardo would have set about inventing a machine gun. That's why it's made out of wood. And why it's so . . . decorative,' I finished lamely, looking at the curly outline.

But instead of inveighing against the Italian charlatan as usual, my father went pensive.

'Hmm,' he said. 'You might have something there . . .'

The long and short of it was that he developed a device very like a slow machine gun which shot nuts when activated. The nuts came out one by one, like lazy bullets, through a rotating plate a bit reminiscent of the ones you get in the middle of mincers.

It worked perfectly.

We put it in the trees at the bottom of the

garden and the squirrel caught on immediately. It was a nut dispenser. He twiddled the little plate device and nuts came out. He ate the nuts. Then he twiddled again and more nuts came out. He ate them and started the process again. He was as happy as a little boy who has just discovered how a bubble-gum dispenser works and he left the bird table strictly alone after that.

Unfortunately, the birds discovered the squirrel's nut dispenser.

They also discovered that if you had a beak you could get the nuts through the delivery system without having to work it.

And they started systematically nicking the squirrel's nuts.

'Little buggers!' said my father when he realised what was going on. 'Why don't they stick to the bird table? Well, come on, lad! We've got a job ahead of us.'

'What job?'

'We've got to devise a squirrel nut dispenser which is inaccessible to birds.'

And he got more paper out and started more drawings. I'm afraid to say I left him to get on with it by himself. But if nothing else, I did begin to understand why Leonardo da Vinci was a one-man band. He must have been agony to work with.

A Proverb in Time Saves Nine

'Leastwise said, if not mended,' said my father once, if not a hundred times.

It was one of his favourite proverbs, even if it never caught on outside the family.

He was fond of it because he had rescued it at a time when it might never have been heard of again.

It was all part of his bold belief that you should never throw anything away because it might one day come in useful, and that is why we would often find 'useful' little domestic tools made out of forgotten objects which he had whipped up in his workroom.

'Darling,' my mother would say, holding up a tired toothbrush tied or even welded to a blunt screwdriver. 'What's this for?'

'It's a brush extension,' he would say. 'It's a brush with an additional handle.'

'Ye-e-es, but what's it *for*?'

'It's for brushing in places where a normal brush won't reach.'

'Such as . . . where?'

'Such as down behind radiators!' he would say triumphantly.

And it is true that you seldom come across a device able to clean behind radiators, were you to want to do such a thing, and that what my father had made would do the trick. Unfortunately, my father's devices were never made as strongly as they might have been and often came apart in action, so most of the radiators in our house had old toothbrushes jammed down the back, which had come loose and couldn't be reached by human arm or finger.

My mother used to ask him to devise a gadget for getting gadgets out from places like that, but he never got round to it.

When the central-heating engineer came now and then to do a bit of maintenance, he would notice after a while that most of the radiators had old toothbrushes stuffed away behind them, and as this is not the sort of thing that is easy to point out to your employers, he tended to turn to me for the answer.

'As a matter of interest, lad, do you know anything about all these little brushes down the backs of the rads?'

'Oh, those,' I would say. 'Well, new broom sweep clean but old brush still sweep in the morning.'

He would frown and say nothing. He probably didn't know it was another of my father's proverbs which, like the brushes, had been improvised from old bits of other proverbs. Among the others which I still remember from those far-off days are:

'Swing low, sweet chariot, and duck when it returns.'

'You can take a horse to water, but it's easier to take a bucket to the stable.'

'Spilt milk is spilt yoghurt in the morning.'

'One man's eggs is another man's basket.'

'There are two kinds of newness. One comes from being new, the other is the old sneaking in the back door.'

This last touched deeply on one of his most fervently held convictions that it was a mistake to be either traditionalist or progressive. He thought you should steal ideas from everywhere. He also approved of Dr Johnson, who, he had read somewhere, used to switch sides in mid-argument just to practise the art of debate. I once found him holding up one of the first of the new pocket calculators and crying, 'This new-fangled modern rubbish! I just love it!'

'What's wrong with it?' I asked him. 'Or to put it another way, what's so good about it?'

'It's going to destroy people's ability to calculate for a start,' he said. 'But for people like me who could never calculate in the first place, it's a godsend.'

To practise his debating skills he used to have endless arguments with my Catholic mother, trying to convert her to his agnosticism. He could have saved his breath. He wasn't just arguing against my mother, he was arguing against 2,000 years of entrenched superiority.

'I thought I was getting somewhere last week,' he told me once. 'I can't shake her faith in the Vatican, but I did get her to disapprove of the Pope for a while. An anti-Papal Catholic—that would be something, wouldn't it?'

But the next time they had an argument she had forgotten about her tiff with the Pope, and indeed started to bring my father round to her way of thinking. He broke off the conversation before she could convert him to Papism.

'That was a close shave,' he said to me, sweating slightly. 'She didn't quite bring me over to Rome, but we got within sight of the Alps. Oh, well, it takes both sorts to make a world.'

This was another of his proverbs. I once dared

136

to ask him what it meant.

'It's based on an experience your mother and I had in an old-fashioned British railway hotel,' he told me. 'At the end of the meal we had in the big, draughty dining room the waitress asked us if we wanted any cheese, and we asked her what kind of cheese they had, and she said, "Both kinds."'

'What did she mean by that?' I asked.

'That's what I asked her,' he said. '"What do you mean, both kinds?" And she said, "With silver paper or without."'

He roared with laughter. Later I asked my mother what it meant.

'In those days, dear, there were only two kinds of cheese: Cheddar or Danish blue.'

These days, when the waiter brings a platter of eight different cheeses and gives you a lecture on each one and by the time you've got to the smoked Lancashire you've forgotten which one the goat's cheese is, I sometimes envy the uncomplicated old days I never knew. But then, as my father used to say, 'Memory is a one-way street.'

I often wonder what he meant by that.

The Missing Maid

My mother had an imaginary maid called Annie, which is not really quite as odd as it sounds. After all, many children have imaginary friends they play with. Some men have imaginary business meetings to explain their lateness back from work. I myself had an imaginary grandparent for a while who kindly let me do things my parents had told me not to do. But, looking back, I do have to admit that my mother is the only person I have ever met who had an imaginary maid.

It started out as just a bit of a joke. My mother, who could remember the days when domestic servants were normal, always felt that she too deserved a bit of help in the house.

'When I was young, everyone had maids,' she said.

'Except for the maids,' said my father.

'Sorry?' said my mother.

'There is this myth that in the old days everyone had servants,' said my father. 'Not at all. Most people *were* servants. *They* didn't have servants.'

'Be that as it may,' said my mother, 'I wouldn't mind the occasional maid myself. She wouldn't have to be too efficient. Just willing. We could have a cup of tea together at eleven o'clock in the morning and she would tell me all about her bedridden mother.'

'What bedridden mother?'

'Maids always have bedridden mothers,' said my mother. 'That's why they go out to work.'

'To help pay for their treatment?'

'Partly. But mostly to get away from their bedridden mothers.'

My father had probably forgotten about this conversation by the next week when he was doing the drying up and discovered there was a cup missing.

'Hold on,' he said. 'We usually have the same number of hooks as cups to go on them. But I've hung up all the cups and there's still one empty hook. That means a missing cup.'

'I think it got broken,' said my mother.

'Oh? Who broke it?' said my father who, being a man, liked to apportion blame wherever possible.

'Annie,' said my mother.

'Annie? Who's Annie?'

'The maid.'

'What maid? We haven't got a maid!'

'I know,' said my mother, 'and I blame you! If we had a maid, maybe that cup wouldn't have got broken!'

'But . . .' said my father, which is as far as he got, because there was no logical way of continuing the conversation and my father, being a man, thought that conversations could only be conducted logically.

Two nights later, at supper, he asked for the mustard. It wasn't on the table. It wasn't in its normal place. Nobody could find it anywhere until it was spotted among all the jams and honeys.

'Who on earth put it there?' said my father.

'Annie, I expect,' said my mother.

And so Annie slowly became a living legend, an honorary alibi, the ghost who was responsible for all the little things that went wrong. Poor old Annie. She couldn't get anything right. She broke things, she put things away still dirty, she forgot to water plants, and once she even failed to take a vital phone call warning us that Aunt Emily was coming for the weekend. I don't remember her ever getting the credit for anything, only the blame.

I remember one day my father was looking for a screwdriver he had misplaced (he had been making a phone call at the time and had actually left the screwdriver inside the phone directory when he closed it) and when he finally located it, sitting in the phone book like some bulky bookmark, all he said was, 'Stupid girl!'

What this meant was that Father was now also using Annie as an excuse.

And what that meant was that she had finally been accepted as a full member of the family.

After that it was inevitable that there were further elaborations as to her existence. I remember once finding an overturned vase of flowers which Annie was clearly responsible for knocking over and, as my brother Ralph and I mopped up the mess, I remarked that I thought Annie was getting, if anything, clumsier than ever.

'Yes, poor girl,' said Ralph. 'Personally, I blame Charlie.'

'Charlie!' I said. 'Who on earth is he?'

'Annie's boyfriend,' said Ralph. 'He's leading her a bit of a dance at the moment. She doesn't know if she's coming or going with him. No wonder it's affecting her work.'

People in the theatre apparently always like to give their characters more background detail than the playwright has thought fit to provide. I think it's called the 'back story'. So Ralph was constantly fleshing out Annie's story with further details. I could never do that.

*   *   *

When summer came, for instance, and I went to get the croquet set out of the shed, I found that one mallet and two balls were missing. I told Ralph about it.

'I have a horrible feeling that we left it to Annie to put away last year,' he said. 'I'll have a word with her about it when I next see her.'

This was plainly going to be difficult, so I was taken aback when the next day he turned up with the missing croquet kit.

'She said she was really sorry but she put some of it under the stairs by mistake. Personally, I think it's all Charlie's fault.'

'Charlie?'

'Yes. You know they've just split up, don't you? It seems to have affected her badly.'

I knew Ralph well enough to realise that he had undoubtedly mislaid the croquet stuff himself and was covering up for it. But I was also impressed by the way Annie—who had started life as a simple gremlin—was sprouting subplots and complications. I even tried to invent one or two myself, but for some reason was never as adept at it as Ralph was. I remember once that he was puzzled because our two cats had gone off their food and were refusing their meals.

'Maybe Annie is feeding them on the quiet,' I said.

Ralph looked at me oddly.

'Why would she do that?' he said. 'You know very well that mother is so possessive she hates Annie to have anything to do with the cats. Anyway, Annie doesn't even like cats. They bring her out in a rash.'

I didn't know anything of the sort, but I respected people who did and so I kept off the subject of Annie after that.

Until the police came.

This was just after we had come back from our summer holidays and our mother was sorting out all the dirty washing we had brought back with us.

She had spread it all out on the kitchen floor (she had a touching belief that if laundry was ready to go into the washing machine, it didn't matter how much more dirty it got meanwhile) and had ordered us boys out of the room while she sorted it out. As it was a nice sunny day—as it always seems to be when you come back from holiday—we went out into the garden to play and while we were there the garden gate opened and a policeman came in.

'Hello, lads,' he said. 'Either of your parents at home?'

'Why, what have they done?' said Ralph. 'Oh, be merciful on them! Do not take them away! Do not leave me and my brother to fend for ourselves!'

Ralph's little display of theatricality was, quite rightly, totally ignored by the police. I sometimes wish I could do the same.

My mother stood among the swirling expanse of summer washing, like Venus Arising From The Laundry, and listened, unflustered, while he explained that there had been a break-in reported in our absence.

'What sort of break-in?' she asked.

'Well,' he said, 'someone reported that the larder window was broken.'

'I don't think it is,' she said.

'Well, yes, it is,' he said. 'We came and had a look last week and it was broken, and I had a look just now as I came in and it is still broken.'

'Well, well,' said my mother. 'The things you don't notice. Of course, we only got back from holiday yesterday and we haven't even been in the larder yet. So, what did you do about it?'

'Nothing,' said the policeman. 'There was

nothing we could do. There was no-one in the house. There was no way we could tell if anyone had effected entry or taken anything, so we determined to come back on your return and pursue our enquiries.'

Do policemen still talk like this? I realise now, looking back, that they had invented management speak long before British management ever thought of it.

'Of course,' said my mother, 'even if someone got in through the window, they wouldn't have got any further.'

'Why not?'

'Because we always try to keep the larder locked. It was certainly locked while we were away. In fact, it hasn't been unlocked yet.'

'Well,' said the policeman, 'let's go in the larder and see if anything is missing.'

'You'd better be careful,' said Ralph. 'He might still be in there.'

'Who might be in there?'

'The burglar. Perhaps he got in through the larder window and couldn't get out and has been there ever since, with nothing to eat but raw rice and jam. Perhaps he is listening to us even as we speak.'

'Most unlikely,' said the policeman, but I couldn't help noticing that he opened the door very carefully and went in very slowly and cautiously.

'All clear,' he reported, looking slightly relieved. 'Now, is there anything missing that you can see?'

'If it was missing, we wouldn't be able to see it . . .' started Ralph, but the policeman gave him such a withering look that his sentence faded right away.

My mother took a quick inventory.

'I think, but I can't be sure, that the big cake tin is missing. I am pretty sure I left it on the shelf where that gap is. I baked a cake just before we went away. It's not there now.'

'Perhaps Annie took it,' I said.

'Who's Annie?' asked the policeman.

The others looked at me, appalled that I had brought Annie into this but interested in seeing how I would explain her.

'She's . . . er . . . she's our maid, but she's not really,' I said.

'Part-time, is she?'

'Yes, sort of.'

'And would she have come in while you were away? Does she have a key to the house?'

We looked at each other. Would Annie have a key to the house?

'No,' said Ralph, just as I said, 'Yes' and my mother said, 'The thing about Annie is . . .', and we realised we had got ourselves into a one-way corridor which we could only get out of by reversing back up it.

'Well,' said the policeman, 'if you just let me have Annie's address, I can pay her a visit and ascertain how much she knows about all this, if anything. Or who she has been talking to.'

'Talking to?' said my mother.

'You'd be surprised how often a servant lets drop to someone else that her family is away, and the information gets in the wrong hands. So if you could let me have her address . . .'

'We don't have her address at the moment,' said my mother. 'She was moving house while we were away. She was going to let us have her new address

144

when we got back from holiday.'

Ralph and I looked at each other, impressed. This was a side of Mother we hadn't seen before. When a parent ticks you off for lying, as happens to all children, it comes as a shock the first time you realise that they can lie too.

'Well,' said the policeman, 'as soon as she lets you have it, get in touch and we'll have a word with her.'

'I certainly will,' said my mother. 'However long it takes.'

'Good,' he said. 'Then I'll be on my way.'

From the kitchen window we watched him go out into the garden and cross the lawn towards the garden gate. We saw the garden gate open before he got to it. We saw him meet our father as he came in through the gate and talk to him. We saw the policeman point at the larder window and the kitchen. We saw my father laugh and say something. We saw them have a little discussion and then we saw them both coming back to the house.

'Uh-oh,' said Ralph. 'I think Dad may have told him the truth about Annie.'

And so it proved. The policeman had asked him if he knew Annie's whereabouts and our father, thinking to defuse whatever the situation was, had told him that she didn't exist.

'We take a very dim view of people inventing false witnesses to blame crimes on,' the policeman said to us sternly when he was back in the kitchen.

'We didn't invent her to explain the crime,' said my mother. 'We invented her long ago to explain breakages round the house.'

'Yes,' said my father, who wasn't quite sure what

was going on but felt he ought to back the family, 'she was just imaginary. And very careless.'

'Nevertheless,' said the policeman, 'you have attempted to deceive the police. You have invented a false witness to the crime.'

'Ah, but what crime?' said Ralph.

'Attempted breaking and entering,' said the policeman.

'I think not,' said Ralph. 'If you look again at the contents of the larder, you will find one piece of evidence you have overlooked.'

'Oh, will I indeed? And what might that be?'

'This cricket ball under the bottom shelf,' said Ralph. 'The cricket ball which I hit with a bat the day we left on holiday. Which broke the window. And which I told nobody about, because I knew it would disrupt all our holiday arrangements if we had to send for window menders and all that business. And I knew the larder was locked and nobody could get in, so it didn't matter.'

'If you knew all along,' said the policeman, who had not much liked Ralph from the start and now seemed to like him less, 'why did you report it?'

'We didn't,' said Ralph. 'Nobody did. *You* assumed that a crime had been committed, not us. We may have invented the witness, but you invented the crime.'

There was a long silence.

'Well,' said the policeman, 'I think the best thing would be to forget all about this and behave as if nothing had happened. Which, it would appear, is exactly what *has* happened.'

'Good idea,' said my father.

'Quite right,' said my mother.

The policeman smiled stiffly and went out and

vanished through the garden gate. We all looked at each other. We laughed a lot and then got back to normal life, which consisted of Ralph being chastised for breaking the window and me owning up about taking the cake from the larder and all that sort of thing. In fact, life was so busy that I don't think anyone in the house ever referred to Annie again, and she vanished, as shadowy and imaginary a figure as she had been when she started.

Besides which, one doesn't want to employ a maid who may have been involved in a crime.

Hotel Sausages

When Charles Darwin worked out his theory of evolution,' said my father, 'he got one thing wrong. He missed out hotel breakfasts.'

'What does that mean?' I asked obligingly.

I say 'obligingly' for that was what he wanted me to say, and in any case I always looked forward to seeing which tortuous path his logic would take him down.

(I never heard him having these conversations with my mother and very rarely with Ralph. I once asked Ralph if he ever got caught in intellectual conversations with our father.

'What sort of intellectual conversation?' he said.

'Well, the kind where he says that Charles Darwin made one vital omission when he invented the theory of evolution—he forgot to account for hotel breakfasts. What would you say if he said that to you?'

147

'I wouldn't say anything,' said Ralph. 'I'd pretend he hadn't said it. God save us from idle speculation.'

That sums up Ralph perfectly. He couldn't bear idle speculation. Full-time, deliberate speculation in period costume was more his sort of thing.)

'Well,' said my father, 'if natural selection was at work in hotel breakfasts as it is in the rest of the natural world, they would surely have become better, or at least more geared up to survival. But in the old days they were much better, or that is how I remember them. They were generally cooked individually, so that you got everything fresh. The egg had just been fried and still had a crinkly, brown, lacy outside. The bacon was glistening like the brown shoulder of some glamorous film star, not dull and greasy like the eye of a long-dead fish. The sausage was meaty and appetising, like . . .'

'Right, I get the idea,' I said. 'And what is it like now?'

My experience of hotels was quite limited, as on holiday we tended to rent a house or stay in a boarding house. But my father sometimes travelled in the course of his work and must have stayed in many a far-flung hotel.

'It is more and more geared towards the convenience of the hotel people,' he said. 'Ideally they would like to have it all pre-cooked and just warm it up at the last moment. They would like you to do all the work. They would like you to choose it yourself, serve yourself and clear it away yourself. So what they do is shove out huge trays of fried eggs and bacon and sausages and other greasy things and leave them on a hot-plate to get

148

greasier and older till you come along to make your selection. By which time it all looks revolting. Except for . . .'

'For what?'

'Well, the tomatoes are usually not too bad. No matter how lazy hotels get, very few of them sink so low as to serve tinned tomatoes. So you always get a fresh tomato at breakfast, grilled or fried quite recently, and they're never too bad. Sometimes the mushrooms aren't too bad either. Everything else is usually greasy and horrible. Especially the sausages.'

'Why them?'

'I don't know. I think it's probably because hotels get the cheapest they can, and cheap sausages are always truly and startlingly boring. Sawdust. Pigswill. Bread padding. That's why I started taking my own.'

'Your own what?'

'Sausages. I decided that if hotels could never provide good sausages, I could make up for it by taking some good ones along and asking for them to be cooked by the breakfast chef and served up for my breakfast. It was a good idea, too.'

'I don't remember you ever doing that.'

'No, I haven't done it for a long time, not since your mother made me stop. That was after the incident at the Three Crowns in Gloucestershire.'

'What was the incident at the Three Crowns in Gloucestershire?'

'I'd rather not talk about it.'

'Tell me.'

'No.'

So the next time I was alone with Mother, I asked her about the incident at the Three Crowns

149

in Gloucestershire.

'I don't know what you're talking about, darling.'

'You know. Father and the sausages . . .'

'Oh, that! Who told you about that?'

'Father started telling me but couldn't go on.'

'Really? Yes, I suppose I can see why . . .'

For a moment I thought she was going to refuse to tell me too, and that it would always remain a mystery, but after a while she began the tale.

'This was before the war, when we were just married, and we had gone to Wales for a weekend in the car. Motoring, we used to call it then. In those days your father used to find the quality of hotel sausages so disappointing that he used to take his own packet of sausages with him, and get the hotel kitchen to cook them for him. Extremely embarrassing it was too. I had nothing to do with it.'

'You didn't even have one of his sausages?'

'No, I didn't! I stuck to the kipper, or perhaps the ham and eggs. But your father always insisted on having his own sausages cooked and, to be honest, he got away with it—the kitchen staff were so surprised at the request that they meekly followed his orders. Until we got to the Three Crowns.'

She went off into a small reverie for a moment.

'When your father's breakfast came, it had no sausages. He remonstrated with the waitress. The waitress went to inquire. She came back flustered. The sausages had apparently been sent in error as part of a breakfast ordered via room service. "To which room?" demanded your father. "To Room 116," revealed the quaking waitress. So off your

150

father went to Room 116.

'Now, of course I stayed in the dining room finishing my kipper and reading the paper because I didn't want to be part of any scene, so I didn't actually see what came next, but piecing together what your father has told me, this is what happened...'

Apparently my father had knocked indignantly on the door of Room 116, only to be taken aback by the immediate opening of the door and a young man saying, 'Ah, there you are—come in!'

My father went in the room and immediately spotted the breakfast tray sitting on a table with his sausages taking pride of place on it. But what attracted his attention even more was the sight of a young lady standing next to it wearing nothing but a dressing-gown and not wearing that very well. She smiled at my father wearily and said, 'We haven't got all day, you know,' swiftly followed by the young man coming back in and saying, 'You'd better go in the bathroom till we're ready,' and he pushed my father into the bathroom, closing the door behind him.

Now, when you are pushed into a bathroom by complete strangers, your immediate instinct is to come out of the bathroom and go on your way, but when you encounter someone who seems to know exactly what is happening and you haven't the faintest idea you also have another instinct to do what you are told, which is what my father did. A couple of minutes later the man shouted, 'All right, you can come in now!'

He went into the bedroom and found to his horror that both the man and the woman were now in bed together, wearing, as far as he could see, no

151

clothes and embracing each other.

'What . . . ?' said my father.

'Where . . . ?' said the man.

'Where what?' said my father.

'Where is your equipment?' said the young man.

'My equipment?' said my father.

How long this would have gone on for is hard to say, but at that very moment the door opened again and another man came in, carrying a tripod and a camera.

'Dreadfully sorry, folks,' he said, 'but I had to go and buy some film . . .'

His voice tailed away as he realised there were three people in the room.

'Is this a *ménage ‡ trois* set-up?' he said. 'That's hardly necessary, is it? Anyway, I don't think I could get you all in.'

My mother sighed.

'Do you know what had happened?'

'No,' I said. 'I don't think so. Had he stumbled across some sort of film set?'

'Hardly,' said my mother. 'He had stumbled across a divorce case set-up. In those days the only way you could get a divorce was through infidelity by one of the partners, and there had to be solid evidence that adultery had taken place. So, very often, the infidelity was staged. The husband hired a room with an actress, or a floozy, or an old friend and a photographer took a photo of the pair in bed and then they all got their clothes back on and went back to London.'

'Why couldn't they do it in London in the first place?'

'I don't know, but they never did. So obviously this pair were waiting for the photographer to turn up and when your father arrived they assumed he was the man with the camera. They got him to wait in the bathroom while they arranged themselves artistically in bed, then the real photographer arrived and it was all cleared up. Except, of course, the question then arose of what your father was doing there if he wasn't the photographer.'

'So he explained his mission to get his sausages back.

'Which was greeted by the others in dead silence.

'Because it sounded so unlikely.'

I could see that it was one of those wonderful situations where both sides think that what *they* are doing is normal and what the other side is doing is loony.

'And in dead silence the young man wrapped the sausages in a napkin and handed them to your father who said thank you and left the room, and as he went down the corridor he could hear the hoots of laughter behind him, and the first I knew of it was when I looked up from my kipper and saw your father, white as a sheet, collapse into his chair and say, "You'll never guess what I've just seen."'

Mother laughed.

'Of course, it wasn't what he had seen that had shocked him. It was the awareness of how absolutely ridiculous he had looked and of how following a course of action logically is not the same as being sensible. And that is when he gave up taking sausages to hotels.'

Figs and Uncle Walter

My Uncle Walter was a brilliant classical scholar. He had also, as a youth, been subject to long and debilitating attacks of some fashionable nervous complaint, which meant that he had missed long periods of his education.

'I used to get these attacks in some vital year like 560 BC,' he told me, 'or at least when our group had got as far as 560 BC, and by the time I was well enough to come back they'd got up to 450 BC or some impossibly modern date and I would have missed a hundred years. Well, you can't study classical history a century here, a century there, so although I was top of the class in the bits I did know, I was bottom of the class in the other bits.'

This had a dire effect on his circle of friends at school. It meant that he literally had to sit at one end of the class when he was top of the class and right at the other end of the class when he wasn't, thus mixing him with two totally different sets of chums.

'The ones at the top of the class were bright as hell and all pretty boring. The ones at the bottom of the class were not necessarily stupid, but they had decided that classical studies were not going to help them much in life and they preferred to do other things, so in the short periods I spent at the bottom of the class, I learnt how to play poker, do crosswords, perform magic tricks and so on.

'And yet, curiously enough, it was from one of those lower-caste friends that I acquired the line of

154

inquiry which has maintained my interest in the classics ever since.'

I kept quiet. I had heard the story before, but never tired of it.

'Humphreys was the boy's name and one day we were looking through a book of dirty Roman paintings—from Pompeii, I expect—when Humphreys said, "How do you suppose they keep their fig leaves on?"

' "Who?" I asked.

' "All those men you see as Roman statues," he said. "Their private parts are covered delicately with fig leaves. All very discreet. But in real life, how did they stop those fig leaves falling off?"

' "Well, I don't think they actually wore fig leaves in real life," I said. "I think that was just something they did on statues."

' "So in real life they were naked, without fig leaves?" he said. "Naked statues had to be covered up with fig leaves, but real-life Greeks and Romans could walk around naked? It's more important for *statues* to be decent?"

'And the more I thought about what Humphreys said, the more I realised that he had stumbled across one of the few areas of research that nobody had ever explored. Fig leaf culture. People talked about fig leaves and sniggered, but that was it. Yet there were some interesting problems there. Why did Roman men in statues cover their modesty with fig leaves? Why not some other type of leaf? And, more importantly, how did they get their fig leaves to stay on and not fall off? Eh, boy?'

This last was addressed to me or to any nephew within range. I always blushed and said nothing,

155

but my brother once said bravely, 'Perhaps they used elastic bands to fix them to their willies, Uncle Walter.'

Uncle Walter fixed him with his keen eye and said, 'Romans didn't have elastic bands. Don't think they had rubber, even.'

'Well, string, then,' said my brother recklessly. 'Or thread. They had thread, surely.'

'Have you ever tried fixing a fig leaf to your willy with string?' said Uncle Walter strictly. 'Well, have you, eh boy? Damned painful, I can tell you.'

And the thing was, we knew he knew, because it was an open family secret that he had spent a lot of time experimenting on himself to achieve the fig leaf effect. He used to wander along the corridors of his large house in Shropshire, dressed only in a toga which concealed his latest attempt to reconstruct the fig leaf effect, looking for his wife, Aunt Maud, to try it out on. Aunt Maud told me once that no matter where she was in the house, she was never quite sure that Uncle Walter might not come round the corner and insist on having her judgement there and then. Once, Uncle Walter had come up behind her in the conservatory, coughed, and said, as he opened his toga, 'What do you think of this then?' Only it hadn't been her at all, but a visitor called Mrs Arbuthnot who had come to look at their orchids and who then fled from the house screaming.

'Stupid woman,' said Uncle Walter. 'Has she never seen a fig leaf before?'

In order to pursue his classical studies, Uncle Walter needed a fairly constant supply of fig leaves and had planted a whole selection of fig trees on any south-facing aspect he could find. They grew well and by the time Uncle Walter died, he had bred a magnificent collection of fig trees. I met Aunt Maud again not so very long ago and asked if she was keeping busy.

'I certainly am,' she said. 'Here, take a jar of this.'

And she handed me a small jar of, according to the label, 'Aunt Maud's Fig Chutney'.

'Fig chutney, fig jam, figgy pudding—you name it, we do it,' she said. 'We shift about £400-worth a week.'

There was a picture of a Greek statue on the label, a warrior with upraised sword. The man wore nothing but a fig leaf. It seemed to be tied on with pink ribbon.

Ears

'I'll give you an example of decadence,' said my father suddenly one day.

I was alarmed. I thought for a moment he meant he was going to drink himself silly or write bad poetry or run off with a woman of the night. But he didn't mean that at all. He only meant he was going to embark on another of his theories.

'Nowadays, the ear is used almost entirely as a place to hang decorations from,' he said. 'People pierce their ears and hang earrings from them, or put studs in them. Nobody ever did that in the old days except gypsies, pirates and . . . and . . .'

He searched around wildly for a third example to fill out his triptych.

'Women?' I said.

'Yes,' he agreed reluctantly. 'But, generally, in those days the ear was used as a useful place to store things. Carpenters kept their pencils behind their ears. Workers put spare cigarettes behind their ears. Golfers put tees behind their ears. I knew a man once who kept a toothpick behind his ear. When did you last see someone keep something behind his ear?'

He looked at me challengingly.

'What do you use to help you read?' I said.

'Reading glasses,' he said.

'And where do you keep those?'

'In my pocket.'

'Where do you keep them when you're reading?'

'On my nose.'

'And where are they supported from?'

'Oh, stop being such a clever dick!' said my father, in the tone he sometimes used when he felt instinctively in the right and didn't want to argue. 'Spectacles are not *kept* behind the ear! They merely lean on the ear a little. And in any case spectacles will be replaced one day by everyone wearing contact lenses and ears will have no further use at all. That, I submit, is a good example of modern decadence; turning a thoroughly useful appendage into a mere display unit.'

I said nothing. He was absolutely right. But I would sometimes rather say nothing than agree with him.

'I used to know a man who even kept a pet mouse behind his ear,' said my father. 'Yes, a small, white, pet mouse. He usually wore a hat, so nobody noticed.'

'How stupid,' I said.

'You might think so,' said my father, 'but he didn't think so, for the very good reason that it saved his life. It became a vital piece of evidence in his murder trial. I'll tell you about it one day.'

But he never did.

Stargazing

Ralph was a Boy Scout for a while. I wanted to be a Boy Scout too, but because I was too young to join, I tried to convince myself that it was probably a waste of time. One day I asked Ralph if he had ever actually learnt anything from being a Boy Scout.

'Nothing so far, really,' he said. 'No, hold on. One thing. The other day they were showing us how to find north. They said that if you were going across country and had lost your direction, you could always follow the North Star and then you would be going north.'

'That's clever,' I said.

'I don't think it's very clever,' said Ralph. 'In fact, I think it may be stupid. Who in their right minds would be going across country by night? You travel by day. And by day you can't see the North Star. And even if you were travelling by night and you could see the North Star what help would it be if you were going south? You'd have the North Star behind you. You'd have to keep looking over your shoulder and then you'd probably fall over something and break your leg. So, what's the point?'

I sometimes wondered if Ralph talked to the

159

Scoutmaster in the same way, but I didn't say so.

'So,' I said, 'if you can't see the North Star by day, how can you tell which way north is when you're travelling in daytime?'

'You can't. Except by asking someone. Which isn't a very good way either.'

'Why not?'

'Because most people don't know which way north is.'

'How do you know they don't?'

He looked at me and decided to put on a funny voice to test me.

'Excuse me, I'm a traveller passing through by day. Can you tell me which way north is?'

And of course I couldn't.

'Do *you* know which way it is?' I asked.

'Of course I do. That's north over there.'

And he pointed out of the kitchen window.

'No, it's not,' said my father, who happened to be passing by. 'That's east. North is up there.'

And he pointed to the larder.

'How do you know?' said Ralph.

'Because that's the direction we set off in to go to visit your auntie in Manchester,' said my father. 'Also, it's where the North Star is.'

'Aha!' said Ralph. 'But how do you know where the North Star is by day?'

'You don't. You learn it by night and then you remember where it is by day. I just happen to remember that at night you can see the North Star out of this window.'

'And what happens if the North Star changes position?'

'It doesn't. It never does. That's why it's called the North Star. All other stars change position, but

160

not the North Star. Look, if it's fine tonight, I'll take you both out and show you the main stars. I suppose I really should have done this years ago . . .'

And sure enough after supper he dragged us out on to the lawn, and it was a fine night and in those days you could see the stars clearly because we didn't have light pollution, my children, and there were no satellites to confuse you, and not many planes either.

'That's the North Star up there,' he said, 'and the small constellation hanging down from it is the Kite, and nearby there is the Wheelbarrow—you see the one shaped like a wheelbarrow?—and that one up there is called the Boomerang, and that is the Scarecrow, and that's the Double U . . .'

'Hang on, hang on!' said Ralph. 'I've never heard of any of these constellations. The Wheelbarrow . . . the Scarecrow . . . Where are the famous ones like the Plough and Orion's Belt? The ones I've actually heard of? The ones they talk about at Scouts?'

'Oh, those terrible old names!' said my father. 'I don't use those! They're so misleading. Do you see the Wheelbarrow, for instance . . . ?'

We could just see him in the dark, silhouetted against the sky, pointing. We looked up where he was pointing. We could see the wheelbarrow. We said we could.

'Now, that, believe it or not, is sometimes called the Plough. But do you think it looks like a plough?'

'No,' I said.

'I don't know,' said Ralph. 'I am not really up on ploughs.'

161

'Then what is the point of calling it after a plough!' said my father. 'If it doesn't look like a plough *and* if most people don't know what ploughs look like, what's the point! I once asked a farmer if he thought it looked like a plough and he said he didn't, though his grandfather had had a plough which looked a bit like that, but not much. It does, however, look quite like a wheelbarrow. So I call it the Wheelbarrow.'

'You can't just give a constellation another name!' said Ralph.

'Of course you can!' said Father. 'In fact, the ancients did it as well. They didn't just call it the Plough, they also called it the Great Bear. And they called the one hanging down from the North Star the Little Bear. Ursa Major and Ursa Minor. Like boys at a prep school. So the ancients thought that the same constellation looked like a bear *and* a plough. But ploughs don't look like bears at all, do they? And nothing in the sky looks like a bear at all!'

Honesty compelled us to admit that when it came to spotting likenesses to constellations, our father had it over the ancients every time.

'There you are, you see!' he said triumphantly.

'But,' said Ralph, 'but, but, but, but . . .'

It was the noise he made when there was a gaping hole in someone's argument and he couldn't quite spot it. If I can sum up the feelings of the three of us in the dark at that moment, they were probably something like this:

FATHER: I am giving these boys a more advanced grounding in astronomy than any other boys in the world are getting.

RALPH: I sometimes think our father has gone

162

completely potty.

ME: I shall be interested to see who wins this one.

'Actually,' said Ralph, 'I don't think it does look like a wheelbarrow. Wheelbarrows don't have curved handles.'

It was a shrewd move. Instead of attacking on a broad front, i.e. by trying to destroy my father's entire argument, he had chosen to insert his blade into a perceived weak area, i.e. by trying to worry him.

We all stared at the Plough in the dark.

'I think you may be right,' said my father, rather nobly, I thought. 'Well, I shall have to think of a new name. How about the Pram?'

Nowadays he wouldn't have plumped for that because people hardly use prams any more, only buggies, and people can hardly remember what prams look like any more than ploughs. He would have gone for the Supermarket Trolley, I think. But back then we thought he had more or less got it right.

'All right,' said Ralph. 'The Pram. But how are you going to get everyone else to call it the Pram?'

'And the one over there,' said my father, ignoring him, 'the one I call the Double U, is called by a lot of people Cassiopeia. Now, Cassiopeia was some old Greek character who did something wrong and got turned into a star, or so the old Greek story goes, but I ask you, does it look like anyone has ever looked in the history of the world? No, it doesn't. It looks like a double U. That's all it looks like.'

'I think it's a bit pointless giving the stars names at all,' said Ralph. 'The only one that's any use at

163

all is the North Star. Let that have a name. Forget the rest.'

There was a long pause in the dark.

'You may be right,' said my father, and we went inside again as it was getting cold.

Two years later Ralph left the Boy Scouts and I joined at the same time, but they never told us anything about the stars at all. In fact, we spent the whole of the first lesson learning which was the right way up to hoist the Union Jack, which was so boring that I never went back again, and thus I missed Arkela's introductory talk on sex, which was said to be sensational.

The Champagne Bottle Problem

My father rather resented having to buy things which he could perfectly well have made himself. He also resented throwing away things which he felt could be useful. He combined both resentments once very neatly by building a wastepaper basket out of things which people had thrown away.

'There you are,' he said. 'Every bit of that wastepaper basket has previously been thrown away and has now been resurrected. Refuse receiving refuse. Very poetic.'

He inaugurated the wastepaper basket with a bottle of champagne. Not a full bottle of champagne. That would have been a waste. An empty one which had been lying around the kitchen for years in case anyone needed it as a candle holder, though nobody ever had.

'I declare this wastepaper basket well and truly open,' he said, throwing the empty champagne bottle into it. The impact shattered his handiwork and it fell to bits. Chagrined, he threw the bits of the wastepaper basket into the kitchen bin, but kept the empty champagne bottle.

'You never know when you might need a candle holder,' he said. 'Or indeed an empty champagne bottle.'

'Why would you ever need an empty champagne bottle, Dad?' I asked.

He opened his mouth immediately, but not in time to stop me adding, 'Apart, of course, from the obvious eventuality of starting your own champagne factory.'

He closed his mouth again, so I knew then that that was what he too had been going to say. He then opened it again and said, 'You might wish to send a message in a bottle. Champagne bottles would be ideal for that. The average bottle kicking around in the surf you wouldn't look twice at—just think of all the times you've seen a bottle rolling around in the waves and all you thought was, "Oh, what dreadful litter"—but a champagne bottle you'd always look at twice just in case it was full. Then you'd spot the message.'

And there the matter might have rested if my mother hadn't looked up from her sewing—she was doing souvenir Turin Shrouds for the local Catholic church at the time—and said, 'Champagne bottles are made of dark glass.'

'So what?' said my father.

'Well, you wouldn't see the message through the glass of a champagne bottle. You can't see anything through the glass of a champagne bottle.

165

Think of all those times you've wondered if there was any champagne left in the bottle and you've held it up to the light and even then you can't really see if there's any champagne left. I think a champagne bottle would be the worst possible container for a message, even if you could get the cork back in.'

There was a pause here. A respectful pause while we all waited to see how my father would come back to this devastating critique.

'That's true,' he said. 'Unless the message was written on . . . on . . .'

'On what?'

'I'm not sure,' said my father.

And there we left it, mentally chalking it up to Mother as a win on points, until my father burst in about a week later holding a roll of oddly shiny-looking paper.

'Know what this is?' he asked.

'Of course we do!' cried my mother. 'It's your will! Oh, do, do, do, read it to us!'

(She didn't really talk like that, but she had recently been reading some Georgette Heyer and said she had been influenced. 'What is the use of reading a book if you are not influenced by it?' she once said to me. 'I think it is rather rude not to be influenced by what you read.')

'It is some paper I have designed for writing messages on to put in champagne bottles,' he said. 'It is phosphorescent, and therefore the glow of the message will be seen glimmering in a ghostly fashion through the glaucous glass.'

He put some paper into the empty champagne bottle and he was absolutely right. You could see the writing through the glass.

166

'And how are you going to get the cork back in the bottle?' my mother said. 'Nobody can ever get a cork back into a champagne bottle.'

My father went very quiet and retired to his workshop where presently we heard the noise of breaking glass, but he must have failed in his attempt to produce a gadget, as he never mentioned it again.

Advice from Father

One day at school I asked a boy if he had done his prep yet and he said to me, 'No, I haven't. Never put off to tomorrow what you can do the day after tomorrow.'

I looked at him without smiling. What he had said was quite funny, but it was not the sort of thing this boy had ever said before. It was almost as if he had changed his character before my eyes.

'That was some advice my father gave me,' he added.

This shocked me, because I didn't think my father had ever given me any advice. Oh, yes, I had followed his example a lot, and picked things up from him and listened to what my mother said was good about him and imitated things he had said, but I didn't think he had ever given me any advice directly.

So when I got home and saw him tinkering away in his workshop on something, I went in and said hello and then said that I thought he had never *given* me any advice.

'Haven't I?' he said. 'Do you want some advice?'

'Yes, please,' I said.

'Then sit down and wait till your father thinks of something helpful.'

I sat down.

'Was that it?'

'Was what it?'

'Was that the advice you were going to give me? "Sit down and wait till your father thinks of something helpful?" '

'No. No, it wasn't.'

He turned to face me.

'Never believe anything you hear, and only half of what you see,' he said.

I thought about this and was about to argue back when he spoke again.

'Be careful to look inside your gumboots before you put them on.'

That made sense, I thought. I had once stepped on a dead mouse in my boot. It was horrible. I opened my mouth again. But it was too late.

'Nobody ever leaves money in the street meaning to go back for it. All cinemas are bigger inside than they are outside. Adding "as the bishop said to the actress" after an innocent statement will make it dirty but not, usually, funny. It is better to give than to receive, for then you do not have to write a thank you letter. When in doubt, have a banana. Croquet always brings out the worst in people.'

By this time, I had given up even trying to stem the flow.

'Always carry a corkscrew with you, for one day you will meet a man carrying a bottle of wine who has no corkscrew. Do not applaud a vicar's sermon; it only encourages them. When a man tries to sell you insurance, ask him what *he* is insured against. Everyone would be vegetarian if we left the heads on the animals we eat. Do not expect postmen to write letters. Blessed are half-brothers and sisters, for they shall have six grandparents.

'Ignore what Shakespeare says and do *not* imitate the action of the tiger, or you will be arrested, and quite right too.

'All envelopes are reusable but no letters are. This does not, however, mean that envelopes are more precious than letters.

'Never go out with a girl who is better than you are at arm wrestling.

'Beware of old ladies in queues, for they start out behind you and end up in front of you.

'Don't look up apparently empty chimneys. Avoid actresses. No, avoid women who *think* they are actresses. In fact, avoid *all* forms of amateur dramatics. Do not be afraid to prune ivy. When someone insults you, think very seriously for a moment whether he is right or not.

'There is no point offending an enemy. He is offended already. You would be better off offending a friend.

'No man is an island, though some are cut off at high tide.

'The leader of a group is often the worst musician in it, for if he were not the leader he would not get into any group.

'Man is the only animal who has ever thought it worthwhile to design and manufacture facsimile dog turds.

'People say that American tourists get everywhere, but you can never find one when you want one.

'Always order drinks for the interval. It will provide an incentive not to leave the theatre during the first act.

'Don't treat a head waiter as if he were God. He knows he is already.

'All art aspires to the state of bric-a-brac.

'Never accept second helpings of sloe gin.

'The bicycle saddle is the worst designed seat in the world. You would not ask anyone to sit on it to work, yet professional cyclists sit on one eight hours a day, every day, in the Tour de France. No wonder they have to take drugs . . .'

'Thank you, Dad!' I cried. 'Thank you! Thanks for all that advice.'

'One further piece,' he said. 'Never ask anyone for advice. You only run the risk of getting some.'

The next time I was in the playground, I asked the same boy again if he had done his prep yet. He said he had.

'Big mistake,' I said. 'The more we learn, the more we have to forget.'

He looked at me oddly.

'Did your father tell you that?'

'Yes,' I said.

Later I realised that in fact he had never said anything of the kind. I must have made it up myself. I must have profited from listening to my father's advice to get in on the racket myself. That was, in fact, the very day I began to give advice myself. And a fat lot of good it did me, because giving advice never helps the giver unless he listens to what he is saying, which he never does. Take it from me.

Aunt Emily's Funeral

I have noticed in life that funerals are often very cheerful affairs, at least after the dear departed has been dealt with and forgotten about. But sometimes Father would let the whole thing prey on his mind.

'Call that a tribute?' he would say. 'The vicar obviously didn't know the man he was burying. The speeches of thanks were maudlin. And the hymns were the same old hymns. Did you listen to the hymns?'

'No,' my mother would say. 'There was no need to listen to them. I knew them already. I was just singing them, not listening to them.'

'Well, if you had listened to them you would have realised how incredibly cheerful they all are. "Goody, goody, old George has died and gone over to the other side," that's the message! Then we spend the rest of the service saying how sorry we are that he has gone. Well, all in all, I'm glad George is dead. At least it spared him the tedium of being at his own funeral.'

Even when he approved of a funeral, it left him in no better mood. I remember him coming back from a funeral of an old friend where they had told lots of funny stories about the old chap and there were lots of heart-warming reminiscences about a great bloke.

'Fat lot of good it is *now*!' he said. 'Why didn't we all tell him how much we appreciated him when he was alive?'

'Didn't you?'

'No. We insulted him. That's the nearest the Englishman can get to showing affection for a friend. Making fun of him. I wish now I'd told him how much I really liked him.'

'Wouldn't that be a bit difficult?' said my mother. 'How would you approach someone and tell them that, as you can't say it after their death, you'd like to tell them now how much you appreciate their being alive? Wouldn't they feel a bit threatened? Rather too near death for comfort?'

'Depends how you do it,' said my father. 'Take you, for example.'

'Me?' said Mother, looking a bit alarmed.

'Yes, you. I'm going to miss you a great deal when you're gone. More than anyone else in the world, as a matter of fact.'

My mother looked pleased for a moment. Then she came to her senses.

'You will certainly miss me,' she said. 'In fact, considering the standard of your cooking, you'll probably starve to death unless you marry again quickly. But it won't happen that way. Women live longer than men, about seven years longer on average, so it will most likely be the other way round and you'll probably go first.'

'Well, if I do, will you miss me?' asked my father. 'Are there any hilarious but touching stories you'd like to tell about me now, before I go?'

'No,' said my mother.

'Not even the one about me and the pheasant?'

'No.'

My father let it rest there, but occasionally he would return to the subject, dropping hints about the kind of funeral he would like.

'It's no use telling me what kind of funeral you want,' my mother said eventually. 'You've already established that funerals come too late for dead people. They need to happen when they're alive, according to you.'

If she thought that would silence my father, she didn't know my father. Six months later he suddenly said, 'I've been giving some thought to the Aunt Emily problem.'

'Is there an Aunt Emily problem?' said my mother.

'There certainly is.'

'I can't think why,' said my mother. 'Of all our aunt population, she presents the least threat.'

There was a lot in this. Aunt Emily (who was our aunt by marriage because she was married to Uncle Jim) was the cheeriest of all our aunts. She never tittered, she always roared with laughter. She saw the bright side of everything. She tended to forget our birthdays and then remember them a week or two later and over-compensate by giving us better presents than we would have got had she remembered. She would drop in occasionally unannounced and we always felt much uplifted by her visits.

'There are some people in life who give energy,' said my mother once, 'and there are others who drain it from you. Aunt Emily is a giver of energy.'

'What are you, Mum?' I asked her.

'Your mother is more of a night storage heater than anything else,' said my father. 'You think she's switched off, but all the time she's accumulating energy for useless daytime tasks.'

'So what is the Aunt Emily problem?' said my mother. 'Apart from the smoking, that is.'

Emily was not our only smoking relative, but she was the only one who seemed to enjoy it. Other people took surreptitious drags from their cigarettes. She took great puffs. Other relations coughed quiet, discreet baby coughs. Aunt Emily had wonderful great coughing fits and went purple in the face.

'Well,' said my father, 'I have been working out how best to celebrate Aunt Emily in her lifetime and I thought we might give her a mock memorial service tonight after supper. Just a short service, nothing posh.'

'Is she dead?' said my brother, who hadn't been around at our last funeral discussion.

'No. But I have decided that people shouldn't have to wait until their funerals for all their friends to get up and say nice things about them. So we're going to try out an anthumous ceremony for Aunt Emily in which we can dwell on all the nice things we'd like to say about her.'

'Wouldn't it make more sense if she were here?' said my brother. 'Then she would *really* know how we feel about her.'

'It's just a run-through,' said my father. 'Nothing elaborate. See how it goes.'

'Can I say something?' said my brother.

'Yes, of course,' said my father.

He waited for him to say it. Nothing was forthcoming.

'Well, what do you want to say?'

'Not *now*,' said my brother. 'Tonight. I'd like to say something in aid of Aunt Emily tonight. At the run-through.'

'Very good!' said my father. 'Anyone else?'

I shook my head. I wasn't the performing type.

Mother shook her head. She wasn't either.

'You've got to say something, darling,' said my father. 'I thought you liked Emily!'

'I do,' said my mother. 'That's why I don't want her dead.'

'We're not wanting her dead!' said my father. 'We're wanting her appreciated. I want us to focus on Emily and work out why we like her. And then say why.'

'Well, I like her because she's about the only relative we've got who always helps with the washing up when she comes here with Jim . . .'

'Hold it! Keep it for tonight! Don't say a thing now!'

That night, after supper, we sat round the cleared-up table and waited for Dad to begin what he refused to call a 'service' but which he couldn't think of any other word for.

'I'd like to start the ball rolling by saying that Aunt Emily is one person we are always glad to see,' said my father.

'I'd like to say that she is the only one who always helps with the washing up when she comes here to . . .' started my mother.

'I haven't finished yet!' roared my father.

'I'm sorry,' said my mother. 'It sounded as if you'd finished.'

'I've hardly begun,' he said.

'Look, I haven't got all evening,' said my brother. 'I've got loads of homework to do. Can I do my bit next and then leave?'

'No!' exclaimed my father. 'Wait your turn!'

'I thought this was meant to be a united family tribute to Aunt Emily,' I said. 'It's more like a free-for-all. I'm not sure I'd care to have this kind of tribute if I were dying.'

'She's *not* dying!' said my father.

'I'm going to do my bit whether you want me to or not,' said my brother, standing up. He took a piece of paper out of his pocket and started reading.

> 'Aunt Emily, Aunt Emily,
> Coming across the park.
> With your little Marlboro
> Glowing in the dark!
>
> See the inch of ash there,
> Ready to fall off,
> Hear the rich vibration
> Of your smoker's cough!
>
> See your stained forefinger
> Like mahogany!
> That's how I'll remember you,
> Dear Aunty Emily!'

There was a short silence, then Mother said, 'I think it's very nice that you bothered to write something, dear, even if it did dwell on her smoking somewhat.'

'I'd like to say something about Aunt Emily in the war,' said my father. 'Not many of you may know this, but Emily had a distinguished war. She was an Army driver, you know. So many men had been casualties that women were often enlisted to do jobs that men normally did. By the end of the War you found women in all sorts of jobs, and often doing them as well as men did.'

'Better,' said my mother. 'Especially driving.

Don't forget that women are statistically better drivers than men.'

'Not necessarily in wartime,' said my father. 'Women are less of an insurance risk on the roads in peacetime because they take things easily and don't get drawn into overtaking or road rage, but there's a certain competitive edge needed for wartime driving. If you've got to get a message through or deliver something vital, you don't hang around in the slow lane or do lots of hand signals. That's why there were no female pilots in the Battle of Britain, or female bomber pilots, come to that. They wouldn't have had the heart to shoot down the enemy, bless them, or bomb a nice tidy German town.'

'I was driven by Aunt Emily once,' I said, 'and she didn't kill anyone, although she nearly got a man on a zebra crossing. Perhaps she thought he was a German.'

'On the other hand . . .' said my father, and then his voice trailed away. I looked at him. He was looking over my shoulder, open-mouthed. I looked round at where he was looking. It was Aunt Emily, standing in the doorway.

'We didn't hear you come in,' said my mother.

It didn't seem quite enough, in the circumstances.

'Hello, Emily,' said my father. 'How long have you been standing there?'

'Oh, since Ralph recited his affecting little poem,' she said. 'Do I gather this is some sort of memorial service for me? Am I meant to be dead?'

'No, no, no, no!' said my father. 'You're *all* getting the wrong idea about this! Listen . . .'

And he explained as best he could that it was

actually the precise opposite of a funeral, that what he had intended was to honour the living.

'Before I drop dead of a smoker's cough, is that it?' she said. 'Go on. Say so, if that's what you think. That's what Ralph seemed to think.'

'Actually, I'm quite fond of your smoker's cough,' said Ralph. 'It's got great character. It's like what I always imagined a bittern's boom sounded like. Or maybe a steamer's fog-horn on Lake Titicaca.'

We sat her down and gave her a whisky and a cigarette and pretty soon she cheered up and became the old Aunt Emily again. Indeed, she saw the bright side of it and, after her second whisky, insisted on making a speech in praise of herself in which she told several stories against herself which even my father had never heard before.

The funny thing was that several weeks after she had come in unannounced, she gave up smoking. And she never smoked again and, somewhat to Ralph's chagrin, though not to anyone else's, she lost her rasping smoker's cough.

'Do you know something?' my father said. 'I think being at her own funeral has added years to her life. Well, who shall we do next?'

Hot-water Bottles

When people talk about domestic science, it's usually shorthand for cookery lessons at school, if anyone still has cookery lessons at school. But my father meant something quite different by it. By domestic science he meant a kind of science which was subtly different from any other kind of science.

'I mean the kind of science that we use in the home and nowhere else. The kind of science that scientists never discover because they are confined to the laboratory.'

'How do you mean?' I asked.

'Well, it's all very well discovering that every action has an opposite and equal reaction, but what use is that to the average person in the average home?'

'I don't know,' I said. 'It might teach me not to try to push a fridge back into place if I only had a slippery, soapy kitchen floor to get a purchase on.'

'I think common sense might tell you the same thing,' he said tartly. 'No, I am thinking of things like getting out of the bath and immediately drying yourself.'

'Isn't that a good idea?'

'No, it isn't.'

'Why isn't it?' I said.

'Because the bathroom is the hardest place in the house to get dry in!' he said. 'By the time you've finished a bath or shower, the air in the bathroom is saturated. When you get out of a bath, you're getting into air that is sopping wet. It is holding as much water vapour as it can. It is turning everything clsc wet. You know what windows look like in a bathroom when you've just had a bath?'

'They are all steamed up.'

'Exactly. Except that it's not steam, it's moisture. So when you pick up your towel and try to dry yourself in a bathroom, you have got the dice loaded against you. As much as you try to dry yourself, the bathroom air is trying to get you—

and the towel—wet. So what you have to do is go through to your bedroom, which is full of dry air, and dry yourself there!'

'And get seen by the neighbours because the windows aren't covered with condensation.'

'I hope you are not going to start worrying about what the neighbours think?'

'No . . .' I said.

My father had complete disdain for the neighbours and their opinions. If they had come round and told him that our house was on fire, he would have sneered at them for their petty bourgeois prejudices. My mother was perpetually having to clear up after his gaffes and faux pas with nearby residents.

'Now, the matter of drying yourself after a bath is easily solved,' he said. 'The laws of domestic science can clear it up. I have just solved it for you. But there are some things which are not so easy. I am thinking, above all, of the great hot-water bottle problem.'

'Is there a great hot-water bottle problem?'

'There certainly is. Let me explain. When you take a hot- water bottle to bed, it is hotter than you. You snuggle up to it. You derive warmth from it. With any luck, a great feeling of comfort will steal over you and you will drift off to sleep. But what happens when you are asleep?'

'It leaks and you dream you are wetting the bed and you wake up and it's true . . .'

This had actually once happened to me, just at the age when I had finally put all memories of really wetting the bed behind me.

'No, no,' said my father. 'Not if you screw the top on properly. No, what happens when you are

180

asleep is that the hot-water bottle gets gradually colder until it reaches a state in which it is no warmer than you.'

'I know,' I said. 'And by the time morning comes, it's stone cold. At least, it's hardly warm at all.'

'And do you know why it's still a bit warm?' said my father. 'It's because when the hot-water bottle gets cooler than your body heat, *it* starts drawing warmth from *you*. It stands to reason. When you get two bodies next to each other, the colder one draws heat from the warmer one. Therefore, for most of the night the hot-water bottle is making you *colder* by borrowing your warmth to stop its own cooling process. That's why we wake up feeling so cold when we've taken a hot-water bottle to bed the previous night.'

'I'd never thought of that,' I said.

'No-one's thought of that,' he said. 'No-one except me. And I am the only person in the world who is doing anything about it.'

'What are you doing about it?'

He said nothing but opened a drawer and pulled out a small device which looked like a length of cord attached to an alarm clock with a malignant growth on the back.

'Do you see this?'

'Yes.'

'What do you think it is?'

'Well, it looks like a length of cord attached to an alarm clock with a malignant growth on the back.'

'Why malignant?' he said.

'All growths are pretty nasty,' I said.

'No, they're not,' he said. 'Mistletoe is a

181

parasitical growth on a tree, but there's nothing nasty about it, is there?'

'Yes there is,' I said. 'I always think it looks a bit sinister growing in trees, like some kind of baleful disease. I have never liked mistletoe.'

My father took a deep breath. Because he and I were so alike in some ways, our conversations could quite often drift off the point as we tried to score off each other, like two evenly matched tennis players getting bogged down in a long rally.

'Never mind about mistletoe,' he said, with an effort. 'What we have here is a device to combat hot-water bottle syndrome.'

'How does it work?'

'Well, you attach one end of the cord to the hot-water bottle. You anchor the clock to the bottom of the bed. During the night, the winding of the clock, magnified by this gearing—or what you call a malignant growth—will gradually pull the hot-water bottle out of the sleeping zone, like a winch pulling a fishing boat up on to the shore, so that when it is cold in the morning it will no longer be touching you. It will be at the bottom of the bed, out of harm's way.'

'Have you tested it yet?'

'No.'

'Do you think it will work?'

'Yes. Would you like to try it?'

'No, thank you, Father.'

'Then I will try it myself. Tonight.'

'Are you sure the workings of an alarm clock will be enough to pull a heavy hot-water bottle?'

'Sure. There is the gearing, don't forget.'

Before I went to bed that night, I met my father in the kitchen carrying a hot-water bottle. He

182

smiled and tapped it and said, 'Tonight's the night.'

It didn't seem to worry him that it was quite a warm night, not at all the sort of night for a hot-water bottle. I went to bed myself and read for a while and then, with heavy eyelids, turned off my light and fell asleep.

I was woken by screaming.

Someone in the darkened house was roaring and screaming, as if afraid for their life.

I rushed out on to the landing.

The noise came from my parents' room.

I rushed in there.

My mother was asleep in her bed.

My father was thrashing around in his bed.

He was wrestling with a length of cord, kicking at a hot water bottle and apparently beating an alarm clock to death.

'Are you all right?' I asked.

'I am fine,' he said. 'But I am afraid the experiment has been a failure.'

'Why?'

'Well, if you must know, while I was asleep the cord which was attached to the clock and its gearing must have got wound round my toe, or toes, because I woke up in considerable pain to find my leg being stretched and pulled to the bottom of the bed.'

'You mean, instead of the hot-water bottle being pulled clear, it was trying to pull *you*?'

'That is so,' said my father stiffly. 'A mere detail.'

'A mere detail? It might have killed you!'

'I hardly think so.'

'Well, it might have cut off all the blood to your

183

big toe. And you might have had to have it amputated!'

Scientific honesty forced my father to say, 'It's just possible. Anyway, there are obviously one or two bugs that need to be ironed out and I will get to work on those later. Meanwhile, let us be glad that your mother has not awoken. Incidentally, I think there is no need to tell her what has happened. It would only hamper my research.'

As quite often happened, my father tired of the idea and never got back to work on his hot-water bottle syndrome cure at all. In fact, the only reference that was made to it at all in later times came from my mother, at a time when my father was working on a device to permit the reuse of dental floss after it had been used for the first time.

'This is no more likely to succeed than his hot-water bottle retriever,' she said. 'Still, at least he won't be in danger of pulling his toes off with dental floss.'

'Were you awake that night, then?' I said, thinking back to the failed experiment.

'Of course,' she said. 'But I would always rather feign sleep than have one of your father's experiments explained to me.'

I could see her point.

Lawn Mowers

My father hated having to own something if he only used it very rarely.

'Even something like a picnic basket is a scandalous under-use of resources when you come to think of it,' he said. 'We rarely have picnics. Almost all the time our picnic set is lying unused and wasted. It's an unproductive asset.'

'But think how useful it is when we do need it,' said Mother. 'Maybe just two or three times a year, but when that time comes, we would be lost without it. Imagine going on a picnic without a picnic set!'

'All right, I've give you another example,' said my father, looking around the room wildly for another example and lighting on the bookshelves. 'That Latin-English dictionary. When did we last use that? How can it possibly be said to pay its way?'

'It's not there to pay its way!' said my mother. 'It's there just in case, like a fire engine or a fire extinguisher. Just because we haven't used a fire extinguisher in five years, do you think we should get rid of them? Because they're not paying their way?'

'No, but . . .'

'If you're going to use this pretend economic language,' she said, 'then I would say in defence of the Latin dictionary that we have already made the investment and are making no further payments. It requires no maintenance, no upkeep. We don't need dictionary engineers coming every twelve months to check it over. It doesn't need spare bags like a vacuum cleaner.'

'No, but . . .'

'It doesn't need rewiring,' she continued remorselessly. 'We don't have to get it serviced, like a lawn mower.'

'Lawn mower!' said my father, jumping in. 'A perfect example of what I'm talking about! How often do you use a lawn mower? Half a dozen times in the summer at most? And yet we're told that everyone has to have one! It's a bit like a farmer having to have a combine harvester. Useful once a year, but the rest of the time it's just a big lump of machinery taking up space in a barn. The lawn is big enough to justify me having a mower, but it isn't big enough to justify me having it *all the time*.'

'I don't think many farmers do actually own their own combine harvesters,' said my mother. 'I think they get it from a contractor and just hire it for the short season.'

'Still, think of the trouble of them going to get the damn thing and having to take it back again . . .'

'I don't think they actually do. I think the contractor comes into your fields with his own machine and does it for you, then goes away again.'

'Really? Hmm . . . I wonder if . . .'

Three days later, at supper, he said, 'It's no good. I can't find one. I've asked everywhere.'

'Find what?'

'A man who comes and mows your lawn for you.'

'Don't be ridiculous,' said my mother. 'There are plenty of them. They're called gardeners.'

'Ah,' said my father, 'but gardeners don't bring their own machines. They expect *you* to have one of your own waiting for them. What I was looking for was a man who had his own machine and would bring it with him.'

'There's no such thing,' said my mother.

I heartily wished there was, because Ralph and I were judged old enough by now to take a turn with the lawn mowing and we hated it. The machine we owned was one of those old-fashioned ones without an engine which you had to push (as I write these words, I find myself hardly able to believe that we used to depend on such things). You grunted and groaned and leant hard against the handle, and you could never let up for a moment because, as soon as you relaxed, it stopped, and it was horrible.

'Which one of you's turn is it to mow the lawn next?' our father would say, using the sort of grammar we use when we talk, not when we write. And we would simultaneously point at each other.

'Well, sort it out between you. But make sure the lawn is cut by tea-time.'

And then one day he came home looking triumphant, and sounding triumphant too, because as soon as he came in, he said, 'I think I've cracked it! I think I've found a solution to the problem!'

'What problem's that, dear?' said my mother, knowing that what seemed a problem to him was mostly not a problem to other people, and vice versa.

'The lawn mower problem. I was talking to Mr Findlay . . .'

'Who's Mr Findlay?'

'He lives at Number 35 down the road. The

house with the blue shutters. Anyway, he was mowing his lawn when I came past just now and I got talking to him and it turns out that he suffers from the same problem as I do.'

'Wind?'

'No, no! The lawn mower problem! He resents having a machine which is scarcely ever used!'

'I see . . .'

'So we have decided to pool our resources.'

'I don't see . . .'

It turned out that Mr Findlay's machine was rather better than ours, so they had decided to sell ours and halve the proceeds, then share the use of Mr Findlay's lawn mower. It would be kept at Findlay's place and moved up to ours whenever we needed it.

'What an extraordinary arrangement,' said my mother.

'It makes great sense,' said my father. 'At last the machine will reach something like its true potential. And we can share the cost of servicing it.'

'I still think it sounds a pretty outlandish scheme.'

'Not to Mr Findlay,' said my father. 'He says it was quite normal in the Middle Ages.'

'What does he know about the Middle Ages?' said Ralph.

'Quite a lot,' said my father smugly. 'He's a lecturer on medieval history at the university. Apparently, in the Middle Ages, when peasants worked the land side by side and worked for their masters as much as for themselves, the sharing of farm equipment was the rule rather than the exception. He says it's rather nice to think that he and I are going back in time to the simplicities of six hundred years ago. And I agree.'

And it seemed to work for a while. Mr Findlay mowed his lawn with his petrol-driven monster and taught Father how to use it, and Father would borrow it but not trust us to use it, so everyone benefited. Until the day when he came home frowning and said that he would be using the lawn mower that evening.

'But you've only just mowed the lawn,' said my mother.

'Not our lawn,' said my father. 'I'm, well, mowing Mr Findlay's lawn.'

'Mowing Mr Findlay's lawn!?'

'Mr Findlay is going to be away for two weeks, so I said I would keep the grass at bay, just this once.'

'But grass doesn't grow that fast in two weeks.'

'Well, the thing is that . . .'

Father was squirming slightly. It was such an unusual thing to see him embarrassed that we all stopped what we were doing and listened to him.

'The thing is that, apparently, when they shared tools and equipment in medieval times, the owner of the tools could ask for certain favours from his fellow peasants. Mr Findlay has been explaining it to me. It's actually all fascinating stuff.'

'Look,' said Ralph, 'Mr Findlay is not a medieval peasant and nor are you.'

'And nor are any of us,' said Father, 'but we all still hang on to Magna Carta.'

'There's nothing in Magna Carta about mowing other people's lawns,' said Ralph.

And Father looked it up just in case there was, but there wasn't, and after that Mr Findlay got

Father to do one or two other jobs for him, such as a bit of digging and some apple-picking, saying that it was all exactly what they did in the Middle Ages—if one man borrowed another man's tools, then he owed him certain favours.

'Yes,' said Mother, 'but this is all rather far-fetched historical fa la la. It's not contractual or anything, except by ancient custom. It's not as if you've actually signed anything.'

My father muttered something.

'What's that?' said my mother sharply.

It turned out that, more for fun than anything else, my father had signed some agreement. Mr Findlay had said it was an ancient custom. My mother said it was an outrage. My father said there wasn't anything they could do. My mother said, 'Oh, yes there is!' My father said, 'What?' My mother said, 'Get a good lawyer.'

'Well, he'd have to be a good medieval lawyer, wouldn't he?' said my father. 'And they don't grow on trees. When did you last hear of anyone being taken to court on medieval charges?'

'And being found innocent,' said Ralph gloomily.

'Look!' said my mother. 'I've got an idea! In the Middle Ages, Britain was still a Catholic country, wasn't it? So all we need is to get hold of a person with a Catholic background, a knowledge of medieval law and history and a smattering of Latin!'

'Yes, that's all we need,' said Father. 'And where are we going to find someone like that?'

'Father Brady!' said my mother triumphantly. 'Father Brady fits the bill perfectly!'

'Father Brady!' said my father. 'What in God's

name do we need a priest for?'

The mention of the Catholic Church to my father was like a pink rag to a bull. That is, he was irritated but not infuriated, not angry but wary. Father Brady was the more senior of the priests attached to the Catholic church which mother sometimes attended.

'This is his little hobby,' said Mother. 'Catholic history. The way it used to be. Some English Catholics look back to pre-Reformation days in the way that some others hanker for the old days of the Empire. He's a bit like that.'

'Well, I don't know . . .' said Father doubtfully.

But he had nothing to lose. It wasn't exactly as if he was in thrall to Mr Findlay, but Mr Findlay did seem to have some peculiar sway over Father, and so they decided to invite Mr Findlay round for tea one day and just by chance get Father Brady along as well.

I had often seen Mr Findlay from a distance, but I had never seen him close up before. From a distance he looked small and slightly spiteful. From close to, he looked exactly the same. He had a little smile which flickered over his features like a flame on a gas cooker which isn't sure if it wants to go out or not. He took a cup of tea and shook two tiny sweeteners into it, then mother started asking him about his work at the university. Yes, he specialised in the Middle Ages. Yes, he was interested in medieval law. Yes, he was interested in where Church law and state law met and sometimes conflicted with each other. Yes, he was writing a book about the legal implications of the Crusades. Yes, he was quite taken aback when Father Brady came in and also sat down for a cup of tea . . .

'I heard you talking about the Crusades. You're not thinking of sending our friend on a Crusade too, are you?' said Father Brady, nodding at Father.

'I'm sorry?' said Mr Findlay.

'Well, I hear you're very keen on medieval obligations. Have you not held him to some duties in the field as a result of your ownership of the lawn mower?'

'Oh, that,' said Mr Findlay with his quicksilver smile. 'Yes, we thought it might be quite fun to enter into a medieval arrangement as an experiment to see if it worked. He seemed very keen.'

It rang true. It was just the sort of thing that Father would be keen on—trying something experimental to see if it worked. And not giving up even when it plainly wasn't working.

'Well, it's hardly experimental, is it?' said Father Brady. 'These arrangements were tested extensively throughout the Middle Ages, and you might say that they were eventually thought to fail because they were replaced by other arrangements.'

'Oh, but you mustn't think that something has failed just because they move on to something else,' smiled Mr Findlay. 'Would you say that English was a finer language than Latin? Is the Anglican Church an improvement on the old Catholic ascendancy?'

The two of them looked at each other with respect and dislike.

'I gather you persuaded him to sign some sort of form,' said Father Brady. 'That seems a little

192

demanding, does it not?'

'Not unusual in medieval times, I think.'

'In what language is it written?'

'In English, of course,' said Mr Findlay, taken aback.

'Tut tut,' said Father Brady. 'I think only Latin would have done, in a medieval agreement.'

'Ah, but would a Saxon farmer have been able to understand Latin?'

'Perhaps not,' said Father Brady. 'But would he have been able to write or read at all?'

Looking back, I think that what Ralph and I were witnessing, from our silent position by the door, was a re-enactment of the old struggle between the temporary feudal powers (represented by Mr Findlay) and the Catholic Church (represented by the Catholic Church). I remember little about the ensuing power struggle, except that it ended with a deep division between Findlay and Brady about what a certain word was in Latin. (I think it may have been the Latin for 'lawn'. Or indeed for 'mowing'.) Mr Findlay plumped for one word, Father Brady for another.

'If only we had a Latin dictionary here,' said Father Brady pleasantly. 'We could settle the whole thing.'

'Oh, but we have!' said my father, leaping towards the bookshelf. 'You never know when you might need one, that's my motto.'

We consulted the dictionary and Father Brady won the day. This seemed to represent victory. The bit of paper that Father had signed was produced and torn up. Mr Findlay grudgingly agreed to lend Father the mower when necessary. There was no more talk of medieval practices.

Father did not go on a Crusade. And for many weeks thereafter he made no criticisms of the Catholic Church at all, and even sprang to its defence on occasion.

Leonardo da Vinci and Me

We had a French teacher at school called Potty Turner. That wasn't his real name, of course. He was really called Mr Turner. (Have you noticed that all teachers are called Mister, Miss or Missus until proved otherwise? The reason that teachers are given nicknames is because they have no first names. Only Mister, Miss and Missus. You can't go on calling them Mister, Miss and Missus for ever so you have to move on to nicknames. If teachers were allowed to be addressed by their first names, they wouldn't get nicknames like Snotty, Dotty, Potty and Froggy.)

Mr Turner had, apparently, got his nickname because he had once organised a school French trip to Poitiers and the correct French pronunciation of Poitiers had got simplified by the children to 'Potty' and had then been transferred to him. Subsequent generations of French students at the school knew nothing about the trip to Poitiers and imagined that he was Potty Turner because he was slightly potty. And as all teachers are slightly potty in some way or other, it sort of made sense.

'Anyway,' he told me years later, when I was grown up and had bumped into him quite by accident in the bar on a cross-Channel ferry, 'you're very grateful to have a mild nickname when you know that you could have been landed with something really vile. Do you remember Crippen Croft, who took the Lower Sixth for maths?'

'Before my time,' I said. 'Why was he called that?'

'Because it was popularly assumed that he was beating his wife.'

'Good heavens! Why did people get that idea?'

'Probably because he was beating his wife. What they didn't know was that she quite enjoyed it.'

'Oh . . . Did all the teachers know about their nicknames?'

'Of course. Even Crippen Croft. In the common room we often referred to each other by the nicknames the boys had given us.'

It was extraordinary talking to a teacher as if he was human. I had always thought of Potty Turner as larger than life. Now, he was just like me. In fact, he wasn't even larger than me. Somewhat smaller, actually.

'Are you going to France for your holidays, Sir?'

He looked at me quizzically.

'You don't have to call me "Sir" any more, you know,' he said. 'You've left school now.'

'Yes, but . . . but I'm not sure what to call you.'

'Tut tut,' he said. 'You've got such a choice. Mr Turner. Ian. Potty. Herbert . . .'

'Herbert?' I said. 'Where do you get that from?'

'It's the name I was given.'

'What about Ian?'

'It's the name I wish my parents had given me.'

There was a pause, then he said, 'I am going to France for my holidays, for two reasons. One is to speak a bit of French with people who are older than sixteen-year-old English schoolboys and can speak it better than I can, and the other is to go to a place where nobody knows I am a schoolteacher.'

Another pause.

'Which is not easy. There is something about being a teacher which is hard to shake off. I have never quite analysed it, but it must be something to do with body language . . .'

Another pause.

'I once went for my holidays to Switzerland, to get away from school and boys and chalk, and one day I got up to the top of a high mountain pass where I stood for a while, drinking in the vast view. And I was joined by an elderly Austrian gentleman and we stood side by side in silence, until he suddenly said—in English, mark you—"So, what school do you teach at?"'

More pause.

'It took me years to get over that dreadful moment. What was it about me . . . ?'

I think I know now what it is about teachers, but I didn't know then, so I didn't say anything. And then, far from me embarrassing him, he did what teachers do best and suddenly embarrassed me by saying, 'By the way, do you remember the Leonardo da Vinci incident?'

Good God.

I hadn't.

But I did now.

Blasted Potty Turner.

This thing about Leonardo da Vinci went back to a time when Potty had stood up and said to us in a French class one day, 'Now, I think it's about time I took a rest and got *you* to do some teaching.'

Horrified silence.

'No, don't worry, children—I'm not going to hand over the class to anarchy. But everyone should know what it's like to be a teacher, and you should all have the experience at least once of getting up in front of the form and giving a little lecture. So what I am going to ask each of you to do is prepare a little talk, no more than ten minutes' long, on some French topic, however loosely connected with France. Then when we've got a spare moment, or we're all confined to the classroom by a cholera outbreak, or we've being held hostage by a mad axeman, we can fill in the time with these little talks. All right?'

A relieved silence that it was no worse.

'You'd better all tell me in advance what your chosen subject is, in case there is any overlap. One talk on Robespierre would be bad enough. Two would be a nightmare.'

'I was quite hoping to do something about the French Revolution, Sir,' said Oldroyd. 'Is there anyone else you could recommend?'

'How about Dr Guillotin?' said Potty.

'Dr . . . ?'

'Man who invented the guillotine. Named after him. Humane and painless method of killing. Well worth investigating.'

By the time it came to me, all the subjects I had thought of choosing had gone.

'I can't think of anything, Sir.'

'How about Leonardo da Vinci, then?'

'Sir?'

'The famous painter. Mona Lisa. You've heard of the Mona Lisa?'

'Yes, Sir, but I didn't know he was French. I thought he was Italian.'

'Technicalities, boy. Leonardo lived in France for a while. The Mona Lisa is in the Louvre. That's good enough. Anyway, if you don't learn about Leonardo da Vinci here, where will you learn? The man was a great scientist, but we don't teach the history of engineering or science in this school. Great painter, but does Mr Rowley ever teach you the history of art?'

Mr Rowley was a paint-speckled man who only had two aims in his class: to keep us quiet and to get on with painting his own pictures, which he exhibited in local competitions.

'No, Sir.'

'There you are, then. A small lecture on Leonardo da Vinci. He was an amazing man. He invented almost everything before we thought it had been invented. Who was it who called him a one-man China?'

'Please, Sir,' said Oldroyd, 'did he invent the guillotine before Guillotin did? Because if he did, my talk's going to be a waste of time.'

'We'll have to wait for our lecture on Leonardo from our friend here before we know for sure, won't we?' said Potty Turner, looking archly at me.

I looked up Leonardo da Vinci in all the reference books in the library and pieced together enough stuff to make a ten-minute talk on the man. Well, more like two hours, really. He was indeed an extraordinary man and I am glad that I was made to do that research on him, because otherwise I would never have found out everything I know about him, all of which I have now forgotten. I even, for the sake of thoroughness,

198

looked him up in Grove's huge five-volume *Dictionary of Music and Musicians* and, blow me down, he was there too, as a minor composer. Very minor composer. Oddly, they only mentioned his music. Didn't mention anything about his art or anything. So he sounded like a very, very unimportant person.

The one fact I couldn't handle was something I found in one of the big encyclopaedias, the *Britannica*, I think. At the very end of a long, long entry on the Italian polymath, after his life had been summarised and all his achievements repeated, it added almost as an afterthought: 'Leonardo is thought to have been homosexual.'

This stumped me.

You see, I had no idea what 'homosexual' meant.

In those days homosexuality was barely mentioned and certainly not by that name. Things had not moved on much since Oscar Wilde's day and, as we later learnt from George Melly's autobiography, in order to have any sex with people of your own gender in the 1950s, you had to either join the Navy and go to sea or infiltrate the surrealist movement.

Still, I wanted to be thorough, so I looked it up in a dictionary.

'Homosexual,' it said. 'Homosexual = of the same sex.'

Now, even I could see this made sense. Homo is Greek for 'same' and we all know what sexual means, so 'homosexual' must mean 'of the same sex'.

On the other hand, I couldn't see what it meant.

'Leonardo da Vinci is thought to have been "of

199

the same sex",' I said to myself.

It didn't sound right.

The same sex as what? The same sex as who?

Did it mean that he never changed sex, but remained a man throughout his career?

If only there was someone I could ask.

'How's the lecture on Leonardo going?' said Potty Turner one day in the corridor.

'Fine,' I said.

'Great man,' said Potty. 'It's always a sign of a great man when he is known by his Christian name alone. Leonardo . . . Michelangelo . . . Titian . . . Socrates . . . Homer . . .'

'And there's also Pele . . . Marilyn . . . Louis . . . Elvis . . .' I said.

'Trust you to bring the tone of the conversation down,' he said. 'Vile child.'

It didn't seem a good time to ask him about being homosexual.

'How's the lecture on Leonardo going?' asked Oldroyd one day.

'Fine,' I said. 'How's the lecture on Dr Guillotin?'

'So so,' said Oldroyd. 'One snag is that I've discovered he didn't actually invent the guillotine. The first one was built by a French carpenter and a German harpsichord maker called Tobias Schmidt.'

'*Harpsichord* maker?' I said. 'How did he get in on the act?'

'I'm not sure,' said Oldroyd. 'Maybe originally they weren't thinking of a descending blade, but they were planning to behead people with wires. You know, like a cheese cutter.'

'Or maybe he knew that harpsichords were

about to go out of fashion and be replaced by the piano?' I offered. 'So he was trying to think of other uses for the harpsichord? "Hey, try the new high-powered harpsichord for a thousand household tasks! It cuts the lawn! It takes the misery out of washday! And it removes your nosy neighbours' heads in an instant!'

'Mm,' said Oldroyd. 'I think that's a bit of a twentieth-century view of the marketing problems involved.'

'So how did Dr Guillotin get it named after him, if he didn't invent it?' I asked.

'Well, apparently he just put forward a proposal that there should be some sort of merciful mechanical device for taking heads off. He didn't say how it should be done. He just said it should be done. After all, it isn't always the inventor after whom things are named. Sometimes it's the patron.'

'Name one,' I said. 'Name one thing which was named after the guy who had the vague idea and not the guy who did the hard work. The Eiffel Tower? Designed and built by Eiffel. Suez Canal? Dug by Suez. Morse Code? Dreamt up by Samuel Morse. The Plimsoll Line . . . ?'

'Just a moment,' said Oldroyd. 'What do you mean, the Suez Canal was dug by Suez? There was no guy named Suez! It was built by Frederic de Lesseps! So why isn't it called the de Lesseps Canal?'

Were you a boy? Does this ring bells with you? Did you have conversations like this at school, with other cocksure but half-knowledgeable boys? Like a mixture between elegant fencing and vicious knee-kicking? I had forgotten all about it till that moment. Invigorating and pointless.

And not exactly allowing you much of a chance to ask the other boy what 'homosexual' really means.

So it was that I got up one day at Potty Turner's invitation to lecture the class on Leonardo da Vinci without quite having worked out my policy, and so it was that having got through ten minutes of lecturing my peers into a state of submission, I was emboldened to say at the end, 'Oh, and you might be interested to learn that Leonardo is thought to have been of the same sex.'

'Very good,' said Potty Turner. 'Any questions for your lecturer, boys?'

They only had one question. The same sex as what? I said he was thought to have been homosexual, which meant of the same sex. They hooted with laughter. It turned out that I was about the only boy in the world who didn't know what homosexual meant. For the next year or more, it was a running joke in the school. That I was of the same sex. That I was attracted to men. Especially Leonardo da Vinci. For some reason I could never make out, they thought that if I didn't know about homosexuality—if I was quite innocent of the subject—it meant that I was homosexual.

And attracted to long-dead Italian geniuses.

As these things do, it all faded away, especially when some other equally ludicrous rumour sprang up (I think the chaplain of the school was supposed to be having an affair with the wife of Mr Sams the history teacher) but I suffered for a while and I have never been able to respect the genius of Leonard da Vinci as much as I should. Even now, if I am at a dinner party and someone says, 'Well, of course Leonardo da Vinci invented all those things hundreds of years ago,' I always spring to his attack and say, 'Oh, him! He may have had the idea but none of them would have worked, everyone knows that. He was the Jeffrey Archer of invention, that man . . .' and people are surprised by my vehemence and fall silent.

If anyone says, why are you so anti-Leonardo? I can never tell them the real reason.

That he and I were once romantically linked.

And I came out of it very bruised.

'Yes,' I told Potty Turner on that cross-Channel ferry, 'yes, I remember the Leonardo da Vinci business. I had a hard time of it. And in a way, it was your fault, because you suggested the subject.'

'Yes,' said Potty Turner, as we stared out across the thin ripples of the English Channel, lit by a weak English sun. 'Yes, I did, I'm afraid. And I'm afraid I benefited from it too.'

'How so?' I said.

'It took the pressure off me,' he said. 'The boys thought you were gay, and you weren't. It never occurred to them that I might be, although I was.'

Good God.

It had never occurred to me either.

I turned and looked at him.

'Don't worry,' he said. 'I was never attracted to little boys. Or big boys, either. Only to men.'

Just then, someone came up to the ship's rail on the other side of Potty Turner and leant against it, and against him, familiarly. It was a man of about my age. I dimly recognised him.

'Hello,' said the stranger.

'Do I know you?' I said.

'You should do,' said Potty Turner. 'He once gave a magnificent lecture in your presence on Dr Guillotin.'

'Time for dinner, Ian,' said Oldroyd. 'Let's go, or we'll miss our table.'

'Good God,' I said.

Bird-nesting

'When I was a lad,' said my father, 'boys like you used to be out all day scrumping for apples and bird-nesting and all that sort of thing. You two never seem to get up to that sort of activity. I don't know what's wrong with you.'

'That's not fair,' I said. 'I go train-spotting.'

'Train-spotting!' said my father. 'What sort of hobby is train-spotting? What do you end up with at the end of it all except a lot of numbers in a book?'

I would never admit it, but he was absolutely right. I had been spotting trains for several years after the war, including the traumatic year of 1948, and all I had got to show for it was a small pile of Ian Allan train-spotter books with quite a lot of engine numbers underlined, because I had seen them and a lot more not underlined, because I hadn't.

The year 1948 was traumatic because that was when my father approached me and said, 'I've got bad news for you. The government has nationalised all the railways.'

'What does that mean? What is "nationalisation"?'

'It means that the government now owns all the railways.'

As it had never occurred to me to wonder who owned them in the first place, this came as no shock at all.

'So why is it bad news for me?'

'Because now they will have to change all the numbers.'

That was more like a shock. If British engines, including the ones I had already spotted, were given new numbers, it would mean starting all over again. I almost gave up there and then, but we train-spotters have got guts and determination and no initiative, and so I buckled down to the grim task of doing more train-spotting.

If you have never gone train-spotting, it has probably never occurred to you that almost all the time a train-spotter spends is spent not spotting. Perhaps in a big railway station, where trains are arriving and leaving all the time, it's a full-time job, but in and around the country station near where I grew up there would be long, long stretches with never a train in sight. That's when you either read a book or just started looking at your surroundings, and in my case I started to observe things. Wild flowers and birds, mostly. I even got a wild flower book and a bird guide to help the spotting, though I don't think I ever went so far as to underline their names when I spotted them. I remember once I thought I had spotted a green woodpecker in a tree, but before I could firmly identify it a train came along and frightened it away.

'Damned train!' I thought. Then I took its number.

'In his defence,' said Ralph, 'train-spotting does at least get him out of the house and keep him quiet.'

'I don't want him sitting quietly by a railway line!' said my father. 'What on earth good is that to anyone? I want him out scrumping apples and bird-nesting as we did in my day!'

'Are you encouraging him to steal?' said my mother, who was listening to all this as she darned some socks.

'It's not stealing!' said my father. 'Would you call picking mushrooms or blackberries stealing? It's all out there in the wild, ready to be picked!'

'It strikes me,' said Mother, 'that when people are uneasy about stealing they always give it another name to make it seem nicer. They don't say "stealing" apples. They say "scrumping" for apples. They don't say "stealing eggs from birds". They say "bird-nesting". They don't say "stealing other people's game birds". They call it "poaching". They don't say . . .'

'Yes, yes, we get the idea,' said my father.

'If you were a Chinese boy,' said Ralph, 'you probably really would go bird-nesting. You wouldn't be interested in bird's eggs. You'd only want their nests.'

'Why?' I asked.

'They eat bird's nests in China.'

I appealed to my father as the fount of all knowledge.

'Do they?'

He frowned.

'There is a certain kind of swift's nest which they do cook to release the birds' saliva . . .'

'Yes, yes, we get the idea,' said my mother in her

206

turn.

'So that's the situation,' said Ralph to me. 'Either you turn to petty crime or your father will feel you have let him down badly.'

'That's about the size of it,' said my father. 'Do a bit of poaching, lad, and we'll say no more about it.'

I was thinking about this conversation two days later. I was train-spotting again. I was sitting on the platform of our small country station, through which the big steam trains went on to big places far away without ever stopping, and thinking how unfair it was that I didn't feel the urge to steal eggs or raid other people's orchards. Well, I wasn't really thinking that at all. If you have never train-spotted you'll never have experienced the sense of timelessness that comes from it. It's a very tranquil experience, rather like going along a canal very slowly, or perhaps even more like fishing, just sitting there motionless, waiting, waiting, waiting . . . You stare down the railway lines, stretching away into infinity and converging into invisibility at the same time, hoping that a smoking monster will gradually appear at the vanishing point, but not caring much if it doesn't because it is so nice just sitting there . . .

And while I was sitting there on this sunny afternoon, the only person on the station except for a porter pottering around somewhere, I gradually became aware of a large basket sitting on the platform opposite. A big basket, like a laundry basket. One of those baskets with a flat lid. But an unusual basket because it was making slight noises. I got up lazily and crossed to the other platform. I went up to the basket. It was making murmuring noises. Humming noises. It was making noises like . . . well, as if it were alive, really. And it was moving very slightly as well. There was something in the basket which was alive and moving and possibly very, very dangerous.

So I kept clear but nearby, until, about ten minutes later, the station master came out (don't forget that in those long-gone days every station was staffed), looking at a big fob watch, and said out loud, though I was the only person to hear him, 'Well, three o'clock—better get it over with!' and he opened the basket. And about a hundred racing pigeons flew out. They flew up above the station, circled once and shot off north.

In those days, you see, the railways carried everything and would do little duties like release racing pigeons. So these pigeons had come by train from somewhere like Manchester or Halifax and the station master's duty was to release them at 3 pm, to start the race back home. Which he had.

And he went back into his little office and left me all alone on the sunny platform, and I went and looked into the empty basket.

But it wasn't empty.

There were still two pigeons left in the basket.

At the bottom.

Dead.

They must have been squashed to death by the others.

Almost without thinking, I got hold of the big bag in which I kept all my train books, picked up the two pigeons and put them in the bag.

Feeling rather like what I imagined a poacher felt, I tiptoed casually out of the station and went straight home.

My father was home early and was in the kitchen with my mother.

'Look, Father,' I said, emptying the bag. 'I've brought you a brace of birds.'

'Good God,' he said. 'The boy's been poaching. Where did you get these . . . ?'

'Ask no questions,' I said. 'And I'll tell you no lies.'

And to do him justice, he never did ask again, which was a shame because I was longing to tell him.

We had the pigeons for supper that night.

They were tasty, but a bit tough.

I suppose if you spent all your free time flying back to Manchester or Halifax you would get a bit muscle-bound.

Battlefield Visit

Mr Sams, our history teacher, was very keen on history but the odd thing was that he didn't really like it as history. He liked it much more as a form of drama. Oh, yes, he paid lip service to economic forces and the evolution of the steam age, or the discovery of America and invention of genocide, things like that, because he knew they would crop up in exams, but what really brought him alive was the personalities involved, and he seemed somehow to relive them in his own person.

When we did nineteenth-century diplomacy, for example, he visibly and audibly became a Victorian statesman, growing more measured and more august while he took us through the doings of

Gladstone and Bismark. Telling us of Brunel's final disillusioned years, he grew more bowed and crushed, before bouncing back while telling us about de Lesseps and Eiffel. When he did a talk on the English Civil War it was like a double act. You could see him trying to be Charles I and Cromwell alternately and he even crossed from one side of his desk to the other to indicate which side he was talking about.

(You sometimes hear arguments about whether history should be turned into dramatic re-enactments on TV, but it seems a bit old hat to me as I saw it all in Mr Sams's class years ago.)

We used to try to guess what the lesson was about based on the way he behaved when he came in and sometimes we would all write down our guesses and compare notes afterwards. I remember once he came into class clicking his fingers softly, with a slight dancing yet halting motion in the way he walked. I thought it was a sort of tango and put down 'Argentinean history'. Other people thought it was a camp walk and put down 'the trials of Oscar Wilde', or imagined he was seeing himself as the Prince of Wales dancing the night away with Wallis Simpson and put down 'abdication', but in fact he was going to tell us about the Greek War of Independence from Turkey. (This baffled us at first till one boy worked out that Mr Sams saw himself as Lord Byron. Byron hated the waltz. Byron had a limp. In some tortured train of thought, Mr Sams was trying to waltz like Byron.)

One day Mr Sams came in stroking his upper lip, which was so easy that nobody bothered to write anything down. Stroking lip = moustache.

Moustache = Hitler. QED. In fact, we were wrong, but only slightly wrong. It was the First World War he was going to tell us about and it was the Kaiser's moustache he was imagining. (Everyone thinks of Adolf Hitler as the man with a moustache, despite the fact that the Kaiser had a much bigger one. What we think of first with the Kaiser, or at least what I think of, is that weird helmet with the spike on top that he is always pictured in.)

'Some large-scale operations take years in the planning,' said Mr Sams. 'You read the bald statement that large quantities of people were moved from one place to another and you think, OK, but you forget all the transport that was involved, and the catering, and the accommodation . . .'

'Are you talking about the First World War, Sir?' said Oldroyd. 'I thought it just sort of happened. I thought everyone was taken by surprise.'

'No, I am not talking about the Great War,' said Mr Sams. 'I am talking about next term's history outing. As you probably know, the Great War is on the history syllabus, so I have finally persuaded the school to let me take you on a tour of the battlefields of the First World War. It will take about a week, although it will take me about a month to organise. One of the unlooked-for advantages of trench warfare, and of the inability of either side to make a crushing advance, is that most of the World War I sites are all in the same small area. That's why people go on Great War tours and nobody goes on field studies of the Boer War or the Second World War. If you did, you'd be all over the bloody place.

211

'So I have been planning an outing to Belgium next term where we shall get an insight into the terrible things that went on between 1914 and 1918, and why so many people died unnecessarily. Are there any questions?'

'Yes, Sir,' said Oldroyd. 'Couldn't we go to Gallipoli instead? It would be much warmer in Turkey.'

'No,' said Mr Sams. 'Any other questions?'

'Yes,' I said. 'Why did the Kaiser and his German soldiers wear all those pointed helmets in the First World War? What is the point of having a spike on top of your helmet? You're not going to attack anyone with it, are you? Or were they meant to charge the enemy head down? And spike him in the midriff?'

'There are a great many things in military life which seem baffling to us,' said Mr Sams, 'simply because they are left over from a previous tradition. Some of our officers went into the Great War still trailing swords. Some of them were riding horses. Some of our lot still had plumes on their helmets. I think we can allow the Germans a few spikes on theirs.'

'Maybe it was defensive, Sir,' said Oldroyd. 'Maybe it was to stop them being bashed on the head. If someone tried to hit them on the head with a stick, it would either be diverted by the spike or the wood would actually get stuck on the spike.'

'In all my studies into the Great War,' said Mr Sams, 'I do not remember there being any examples of people hitting each other on the head. Things had moved on since the Stone Age, Oldroyd.'

'Was there ever a Wood Age, Sir?' said Oldroyd.

The old enmity between the Germans and the French had nothing on the eternal skirmishing between Mr Sams and Oldroyd. It was a delight to the rest of us, and of course to them as well.

'No, Oldroyd, there was never a Wood Age,' said Mr Sams. 'Primitive man had to learn how to tame things like iron and stone and bronze, but wood was always there around him. It fell off the trees. A fallen branch is often the ideal shape for a club, so he could pick it up and beat his fellow man over the head with it without having to learn carpentry.'

'Yes, Sir, but tables and chairs . . .'

'The Wood Age is always with us,' said Mr Sams. 'When a thing is universal, we no longer notice it. Was there a Water Age? I think not. Was there a Leather Age? A Pottery Age? No. Any other questions?'

'Yes, Sir,' said a boy called Tinker. 'Can you and Oldroyd please sit together on the bus to the Great War so that the rest of us can get some sleep?'

In fact, as it turned out, Oldroyd sat next to me. We got on very well as a team. He asked Mr Sams all the probing questions and I laughed and suggested ideas for the next one. On the coach, though, we gave Mr Sams some peace. This was partly because Mr Sams had clearly done a good job of organising the expedition and partly because away from home we suddenly realised we depended on Mr Sams for our salvation. He was no longer someone in charge of a boring history lesson, he was now the leader of the tribe, and deserved our respect. What was the point of undermining the man who had the tickets, the

213

money and the timetable? Which, as Oldroyd pointed out to me, was probably what the British troops said about General Haig and the Germans said about whoever was in charge of them.

'Everything all right, you two?' said Mr Sams, as he walked down the coach somewhere en route to Dover for the crossing to Calais.

'Yes, thank you, Sir,' I said.

It wasn't my place to make sassy replies.

That was Oldroyd's job.

'Fine, considering,' said Oldroyd.

'Considering what?' said Mr Sams.

'Considering the terrible feeling I have that . . .'

'You're not going to be car-sick, are you?'

'No, Sir. I just get the feeling that we are sitting in this coach like paratroopers about to jump out and you are walking up and down, chatting us through it, like a sergeant-major encouraging his troops even though he knows a lot of them won't come back.'

'I think you're worrying unnecessarily, Oldroyd,' said Mr Sams. 'There's one huge difference between an Army officer and a history teacher. Nobody minds if an Army officer loses a few men. It's part of the job. But if a history teacher has as much as a single fatality, he's fired. He's lucky not to be put in prison for it. We might go so far as to say that a history teacher has to observe far higher standards than is expected of any officer in any army anywhere. And I am proud to say that we have never lost a boy on any of these expeditions.'

'Yes, Sir,' I said, 'but there is another difference. We're not going to war.'

In which I was wrong.

When we arrived at the hostel in Bruges which

had been booked for us, we found we were not the only school party to arrive for a tour of First World War battlefields. There was another one, as large as ours, which arrived two hours after we did.

'Excellent!' said Mr Sams. 'It's rather like having another regiment move up into the line beside you. I will go and liaise with them and see where they are from.'

I saw him talking to their teacher and I saw him coming back to our lines again. He looked more sombre than I expected.

'Bad news, Sir?' said Oldroyd. 'Have they got cholera? Dysentery? Shell shock?'

'Shell shock might be the best description,' said Mr Sams grimly. 'I have just discovered that they are a German school party.'

It never really occurs to you that both sides in a war have to study history and that the losers are just as likely to visit the scene of battle as the winners. Apparently these German boys and girls, who were about the same age as us, were studying the First World War as part of a peace studies course (don't ask me why) and had been brought here to study the full horror of war etc., etc.

'However, let us look on the bright side,' said Mr Sams. 'I have been talking to their teacher, a Mr Haffner, and he thinks it would be an excellent idea if we got together and had a session where we could talk things through, exchange ideas about our different views of the war, that sort of thing.'

And so we did, on the second day of our trip, after we had visited a couple of battlefields and seen inside a few old trenches, preserved for history, or more likely recreated for history. The only people who showed any interest at all in these

215

battle sites seemed to be the very old, who could more or less remember those days, or the very young, who were being taught to remember those days. The only middle-aged people we saw were either teachers or military anoraks racing around with guidebooks and old photos.

And the only warlike sound we heard was the barking of orders by teachers, keeping their classes together.

'I wonder if it occurs to any of them that being a teacher is virtually indistinguishable from being an NCO,' Oldroyd said to me. 'Look at them, wandering round with their little squads, trying not to lose any, making sure they don't desert . . .'

'Hold on,' I said. 'Where's Mr Sams?'

'Over there,' said Oldroyd. 'He's fraternising with the enemy.'

We could see in the distance the small, neat form of Mr Sams talking with the German teacher, a large, well-built man who was enjoying the distance from school to smoke a large cigar, which must still be thought quite normal in Germany. Mr Haffner was nodding slowly. Mr Sams was waving his arms round a bit. They were obviously discussing the evening's get-together.

'Extraordinary thing,' said Oldroyd, 'but from a distance Mr Sams has the air of a Hitler about him. All that nervous energy and arm-waving. Whereas Mr Haffner is very like . . .'

'My God, you're right!' I said. 'He looks just like Churchill! They're on the wrong sides! We've got Hitler and they've got Churchill!'

That evening, the communal discussion went quite well. We were made to mingle with the Germans and I found myself sitting next to a girl

216

called Ingrid who, as I can still recall, was amazingly pretty. She also spoke English quite well, which helped.

'We find all this stuff very boring,' she said. 'Girls are not interested in guns and bombs.'

'What about the German boys? I suppose they are not interested in wars they lost.'

'It is a bad thing for German boys to hear about the world wars,' she said, 'because they are sad that they were winning them all until the very end, then they lost. Also, they think that without the Americans you would always lose.'

I thought this over, and couldn't see any flaw in it.

'Are you interested in the war?' she asked.

'No,' I said. 'War is stupid. I quite like football.'

'Football is stupid also,' she said.

Mr Sams and Herr Haffner then opened up a discussion in which really only Mr Sams and Herr Haffner took part, as nobody else at this Anglo/German gathering seemed at all interested in rehashing or re-fighting any war. In despair, Mr Sams finally asked if any of us had any points we wished to raise, or questions to ask.

Oldroyd got to his feet, looking mischievous.

Mr Sams went a bit white.

'Sir,' he said, 'I wanted to raise a question about the images of war leaders. It's interesting that in the First War we have no very clear idea of who was actually leading the war effort on either side. We know the names of Hindenburg and Haig, but that's about it. No idea what they look like or anything. Now, in the Second World War people take on definite personalities. Rommel, Monty, de Gaulle, all heroic qualities. Hitler has his own very special personality, and so does Churchill. But having seen your and Mr Haffner's resemblance to those two great men, I am wondering whether sometimes nations don't get the wrong leaders. Mr Haffner has a Churchillian air about him, and I think in some ways Churchill was a very German figure. Calm, organised, methodical, unflappable. There was nothing at all German about Hitler. There wasn't much Italian about Mussolini—he had no style at all. And General Franco was much more like a small-town English solicitor than a Spaniard. So my question is do nations always get the wrong leaders? And if they do, is it for a good reason?'

Mr Sams, pale and flustered, looked as if he was about to slap Oldroyd down, but Herr Haffner got there first.

'That is a very good question,' he said. 'You are a very intelligent boy. Well done.'

Mr Sams looked incredulous.

'I too have sometimes wondered about the leaders we get,' Haffner went on, 'and I think it is no coincidence that they are all different from the national stereotype. It is a bit like the idea that the best books on a country are written by foreigners—de Tocqueville on America and so on. So maybe we find it easier to be led by someone who is not typical of us. If Napoleon had not been a Corsican, but had been typically French, if Hitler had not been Austrian . . . who knows?'

'Any other questions?' said Mr Sams.

'Yes,' I said. 'Did the German and British soldiers really play football against each other on Christmas Day in no man's land?'

Nobody knew. They had all heard the legend.

They had never seen any proof.

'Well, perhaps we could do it here,' I said. 'Recreate the legendary football match of Christmas Day 1916, I mean. Us against them.'

To my surprise, my idea was adopted and Sams and Haffner arranged that on the last day before we left we would have a friendly football match on the local school pitch, a Christmas Day 1916 special, to cement the bond of friendship between our two nations.

For the next few days we and the Germans got pretty friendly. We kept bumping into each other on battlefields, seeing each other at mealtimes and bonding together to make fun of the French. I flirted with Ingrid and we swore undying intentions to become pen pals. We even discussed war in detached and sensible ways.

Then came the football match.

I won't go into details.

But it was a disaster.

I don't mean that we were beaten by the Germans, though I think we were losing 2–1 when the match was abandoned.

I just mean that after about ten minutes things started getting rough, and general fighting broke out just after half-time.

'It is so sad,' said Ingrid. 'The war brought us together and now football has driven us apart. What is wrong with you men? You were very peaceful in the war and now you fight in football.'

'I will see you again after this whole wretched business is over,' I said. 'Promise you will wait for me.'

She promised. But, of course, she didn't wait for me and after a couple of letters I didn't write any more.

Mr Sams was very quiet on the way home.

'Looks like the England football manager on the way home from early dismissal in the World Cup,' said Oldroyd.

I never went on one of those trips again, though Mr Sams bravely went on going every year, leading expeditionary forces to the Low Countries, trying to recapture boys' interest in history. In my last term at school I bumped into him one day and we swapped memories about that disastrous football match.

'I bet you never let anything like that happen again,' I said. 'Steered clear of racial and nationalistic tensions whenever possible, I suppose.'

'I tried to,' said Mr Sams, 'but we had a bad experience with another school group last year. Had a punch-up even worse than the one we had in your year.'

'Bloody Germans, eh?' I said. 'They've still got a martial streak deep down, then.'

Mr Sams looked at me oddly.

'You're right about the nationalism,' he said. 'But they weren't Germans. They weren't from anywhere near Germany. They were from a school in Scotland.'

Walking the Line

'The Leith police dismisseth us,' my father would sometimes say out loud, without warning, to nobody in particular. Then he would say it again.

220

'The Leith police dismisseth us. Round and round the rugged rocks the ragged rascals ran. Red lorry, yellow lorry, red lorry, yellow lorry. The Leith police . . .'

Over and over again. He got quite good at them. These phrases are used by actors to achieve clarity, I believe. My father had a quite different view in mind. He wanted to avoid being sent to prison.

I am talking now about the days before the breathalyser and the blood and urine sample, and all the other things which the police have up their sleeves if they think you are too full of booze to be in charge of anything. Today a policeman can tell you scientifically whether a person is above the permitted level of alcohol in the blood by doing things to him which only glamorous hospital nurses were allowed to do in the olden times. But before all these scientific tests came in—and don't forget that the first breathalyser was not seen in Britain until 1967—before then they had to rely on rough and ready tests, like making you say tongue-twisters to see if you slurred your words.

'The last thing I want when I am coming home after a Masonic dinner, full of good cheer, is to be pulled over to the side of the road and made to recite idiotic sentences which tax the faculties even when you're sober,' said my father.

'You're not a Mason,' said my mother. 'You dislike the idea of the Masons. I wouldn't be surprised if the Masons didn't dislike the idea of you. So you wouldn't ever be coming back from a Masonic dinner.'

'I know,' said my father. 'But that is what I shall tell the police when I am stopped. As all the police are Masons, that will give me a 50/50 chance of being waved on. If however, they get the idea that I am coming back from the pub in a drunken state, they may make me say one of these tongue-twisters. So I have decided that if I practise them when I am sober until I can say them perfectly, I will stand a pretty good chance of being able to say them when a little tipsy. Or at least a much better chance than if I hadn't practised.'

'Explain that,' said my mother, who hadn't really been listening.

'Put it this way,' said my father. 'If I am stopped by the police one day on suspicion of drunkenness, they will ask me to say "The Leith police dismisseth us" several times. If I have never said this before, and most people haven't, I will make a mess of it and the police will think I am drunk. However, if I have previously said it lots of times while sober and got rather good at it, there is a good chance I will do it well even when auditioning for the police.'

'The Leith police dismitheth uth,' said my mother reflectively. 'No, the Leith poleeth dismisseth us. No, that's wrong! Look, I am stone cold sober and I can't say it!'

'Perhaps you could if you had a few beers inside you,' said my father unsympathetically. 'Or if you did some practising.'

Then he would wander off, muttering to himself, 'Peter Piper picked a peck of pickled peppers . . .' or however that particular one goes.

(I have tried to authenticate these tongue-twisters for this book, but it is very difficult to find any reference book which lists them. They are not poetry, even though they sound like a lot of modern poetry. They are not catchphrases, not

222

quotations, not humorous one-liners. So they are not listed. Yet they are among the most familiar lines in British culture. And yet also the most ignored. Go figure, as the Americans say. At least, I think they say something like that. I have tried to look up 'Go figure' in a book of American sayings, but I can't find one.)

As a matter of fact, my father was not a great pub-goer and it was most unlikely he would ever be stopped on the way back from the pub, as he wasn't much of a drinker either. He used to say that the only reason people ever drank was to recapture the delicious feeling induced by the first drink of the evening, that moment when sobriety is first displaced, and the more you tried to recapture it, the less likely it was to happen. Instead, the delicious moment receded and the delicious memory of it receded with it, and you just got drunk. The worst drink of the evening, he said, was always the last one.

What *he* enjoyed was the challenge of seeming sober. The challenge of being able to outwit the police, by preparing for their test.

'I may be the only person in Britain who is actually in training for being stopped by the police for being drunk,' he would say, proudly.

Then one day he met a man who had actually been stopped by the police on suspicion of drinking and given an impromptu, rough-and-ready test to see if he was tipsy.

'What tongue-twister did they make you say?' my father had asked eagerly.

'Oh, they didn't bother with tongue-twisters,' the man had told him. 'They made me walk along a line to see if I could get to the end without falling off.'

'And could you?'

'Of course,' said the man. 'In my youth I did a certain amount of circus work, including tight-wire walking. I could walk along any line in any condition. A good job, too. I was pretty drunk.'

This, of course, heralded a new phase in my father's existence. Not only did he now start practising walking along lines, he combined it with his previous regime, so we would find him tip-toeing along a straight line on the kitchen floor while uttering the immortal words, 'How much wood would a woodchuck chuck if a woodchuck could chuck wood?'

Then one night, when he had decided to walk round and visit a friend for a couple of hours, we got the shock of our lives. At about ten o'clock there was a knock on the door and a policeman stood there. He told us that Father had been picked up by the police and taken to the station. They had decided not to press charges and wanted Mother to go and pick him up in the car.

'I don't understand,' said Mother. 'What has he done wrong? He can't have been drunk in charge of a car, because the car's here.'

'He was wandering round in the middle of the road, endangering himself and traffic. We thought he was drunk at first, but he seems completely sober.'

At first my father wouldn't admit to my mother what he had been up to, then he confessed. He had been walking home when he had spotted a white line across the road. He had decided to use it for practice. He had been walking up and down it when a police car happened to come past and he was picked up for acting in a manner dangerous to traffic, or one of those portmanteau offences which the police use when they can't think of a real crime.

'What did you tell the police you were doing?' my mother asked him.

'I told them I was on the way back from a Masonic meeting,' my father said. 'As planned. Unfortunately, one of them was a Mason and knew that there were no meetings of the Masons that week in the area.'

He sighed.

'It was really embarrassing to be arrested while doing a drill to avoid arrest. So I came clean and told them what I was up to and they found that quite amusing and let me go. But as they let me go, one of the policemen said to me, "Between you and me, Sir, all that tongue-twister and walking along a line stuff—that's all out of date, now, Sir. We've got a new test." And he showed me how they now make people suspected of drinking do a very simple test. They make them hold their arms full length in front of them, then point the index fingers towards each other and see if they can make them meet.'

And so for the next three months, in any spare moment, he silently practised bringing his index fingers together at arm's length. Some other time I will tell you how this caused him to be violently set upon by a gentleman from Colombia, in whose country this is a very rude gesture indeed.

Wardrobe Adventures

People are affected in various ways by the Narnia stories. Some people see them as a heart-warming chronicle of the fight of good against evil.

Other people see them simply as a big adventure story.

Lots of people, I have no doubt, see it in the same way that C. S. Lewis himself imagined it, that is, as a Christian allegory of suffering, redemption and triumph.

But my father saw the Narnia saga as something quite different. He saw it as a terrible warning against the things that might happen to you in the back of a wardrobe.

'I've never felt quite the same about wardrobes since reading *The Lion, The Witch and The Wardrobe*,' he admitted to us once when he had just asked one of us to get some tennis shoes from the back of the wardrobe because he would rather not do it himself. 'It was such a terrible shock. One moment you have these not unpleasant children playing around in a strange room, the next moment they are exploring the back of the wardrobe and—bingo!—they find themselves in this dreary world of snow and mock-Christian charade, to which they are condemned for ever to return.'

'I've always quite liked the sound of the place,' said Ralph. 'It may be only mock-Christian, but it's actually more exciting than the Bible.'

'No, I have always hated the sound of Narnia,' said Father stoutly. 'It's always winter there and

226

there's no Christmas. Civilisation is always about to be overturned, and the children always have to become kings and queens to save everything and then wait for a lion to save them, and they always have to go through the back of a wardrobe to get there. It's like a mixture of Norse mythology, the *Just So* stories and the Habitat catalogue. Horrible.'

Once someone gets a phobia, it's hard to shift, and Father really did have some abiding fear of the back of wardrobes. I think it was mixed up with some awful childhood memory he once mentioned of being locked in a cupboard at an impressionable age, though whether this happened to him accidentally or on purpose I never found out. Anyway, this memory, mixed up with his thoughts about Narnia, combined to give him very odd feelings about confined spaces. I remember once we all went to see a Marx Brothers film, that one where they are on an ocean liner and Groucho, caught in the gangster's cabin canoodling with the gangster's moll, opens a door and vanishes, saying, 'As for me, I'm going back in the wardrobe, where women are women and men are only empty suits on a hanger,' or something like that, and everyone laughed, except Father who leapt up crying, 'You fool! Get out of there before it's too late!' and embarrassed us all mightily.

Well, if you have a phobia and can't get rid of it, you try to come to terms with it, and Father's method of coming to terms with the backs of wardrobes was to limit himself to only taking things out of the front or, if he thought something was at the back, sending someone else in to get it for him.

Mother would always do it for him if she was there, but one day when she was away and he suddenly wanted an old umbrella he seemed to remember having seen in the back of the wardrobe, he sent me in to get it.

'I'll send you in because you're smaller than Ralph. I'll rope you up, of course,' he said.

'Rope me up?'

'Like a mountaineer. I'll tie a rope around your middle and if you get into trouble I'll pull you back.'

I looked at Ralph. He looked at me. It is never too early to start learning to humour older people. Maybe that's what that Commandment about parents should really say. Not 'Honour thy father and mother,' but 'Humour thy father and mother . . .'

So I let him tie some twine round my waist.

'OK,' I said. 'I'll let you know if I'm in trouble.'

'We'll arrange a series of signals,' said my father. 'Pull once for a signal that you've found the umbrella, pull twice to ask to be brought back and pull three times for danger.'

'Hold on a moment!' said Ralph. 'Hold on a moment!'

I thought for a moment that Ralph was going to beg Father not to send me into the wardrobe.

I should have known better.

'Wouldn't it make sense to pull *once* for danger?' said Ralph. 'If he's in danger, he won't have time to pull three times. I mean, if he's being dragged into a frozen world beyond, where rival princes are battling for the rule of their own kingdom against disaffected serfs, or serpents have taken over the normal government and think he looks very tasty, he might only have time to pull once before vanishing, and there we would be, thinking he'd just found the umbrella, whereas in fact he'd been . . .'

Ralph obviously couldn't think of another way of describing my dreadful end.

'That's a good point,' said my father. 'So what shall we do?'

'I've got an idea,' I said. 'I'm only going to be three feet away, behind all these hanging clothes. Why don't I just talk to you?'

'Brilliant!' said my father.

'Let's arrange some signals,' said Ralph. 'If you need help, yell "Help!" If you find more than one umbrella, say "What colour was it?" And if you are dragged away by two men-at-arms who suddenly come through the back of the wardrobe, don't forget to say goodbye.'

'Just get in there and get the umbrella and come out again,' said my father.

So I did go in there and I did for a little while vanish from sight behind the clothes and it was so dark in there that for just a moment I felt scared, but this was quickly replaced by a strong temptation to untie the rope from around my waist and then give a scream and see what Father's reaction was when he pulled quickly at the twine and found nothing at the other end, but I am sorry to say that sense and decency prevailed and I found the umbrella and meekly came out with it.

'See anything?' said Ralph.

'No,' I said.

'No doors opening? No bleak wintry vistas? Nobody asking you to look after their kingdom for five minutes?'

'You may laugh,' said my father, 'but we all have our funny little ways. One day I shall find out what your funny little way is and I shall be sure to make endless fun of you.'

All credit to my father, he did gradually conquer his fear of the backs of wardrobes, though this only extended to the ones he knew well, i.e. the ones in our house. When we stayed with other people or in hotels, I was usually sent for to ferret around in the back of the strange wardrobe, though I only ever once found something out of the ordinary.

This was in a large old-fashioned hotel we spent the night in on the way to Scotland, though which city it was in I have no idea. My parents were in one room, me and Ralph in another (we were still young enough to share, or poor enough to have to share) and before I was even allowed to see our room, I had to go and check the wardrobe in the parental room.

'Do you actually want something out of the back?' I said, 'or is this just to check that it's all right?'

'Just a check,' said my father. 'Just to make sure. You know.'

It was a huge old-fashioned wardrobe, already quite full of pillows and blankets and things, and the back of the wardrobe was so far from the front I couldn't quite see it. While trying to reach it, I stumbled over a pillow and sort of fell against the back of the wardrobe, except that it wasn't the back. It was the wall. The wardrobe seemed to have been built without a back. I felt along the wall and, rather to my amazement, felt a handle in my hand. A door handle.

For a moment the hairs went up on the back of

my neck, but then I saw a logical explanation and the hairs all went down again obediently. It was a door. It was the connecting door to the next room, hidden by the wardrobe, which had purposely been placed against it to conceal it. I tried the handle. It worked. The door opened slightly. I peered through the crack. It was another room. There was a person sitting there, looking at me.

'Hello,' said Ralph.

It was our room, next door. I stepped into it, and quietly closed the door behind me.

'Well, well, well, well,' I said. 'Narnia isn't quite what I expected. In fact, it's very like the world I've just come from.'

'Would that be the world of wardrobes?' he inquired.

'It certainly would,' I said. 'A place where cruel fathers send you into dark places to look for they know not what.'

'Talking of fathers,' said Ralph, 'if you've just come through the back of his wardrobe, he'll be coming after you very soon.'

As he said this, we could clearly hear him shout my name. He sounded very worried. He would indeed be coming through any moment.

'Go in the bathroom,' said Ralph. 'Close the door behind you.'

Just as I had obeyed him, I heard my father erupt into the room.

'Where did your brother go?' he shouted.

'I thought he was in your room,' said Ralph. 'Didn't he go in there with you just now?'

'He was there a moment ago, but he came out through the back of the wardrobe through the connecting door into here and . . .'

'Didn't come this way,' said Ralph, 'and I've been here all the time.'

There was an awful pause. My father breathed heavily. Did he believe, just for a moment, that I had been swallowed up into some other space/time/storyboard continuum?

'He must have come through here,' said my father. 'He went into our wardrobe. He didn't come out. I followed him in. This is the only way out.'

'There must be another one,' said Ralph. 'He must have taken another exit, inside the wardrobe.'

My father went silent for a moment, then I could hear him rush back into the wardrobe. The bathroom door opened. Ralph quickly bundled me out, and put me where he had been sitting, then vanished into the bathroom. My father came out again.

'No, there's no . . .' he started and then saw me.

'Hello, Father,' I said. 'Where did you come from?'

'Where's Ralph?' he said, rather wildly.

'I've no idea,' I said. 'I've been here all the time.'

He roared at this and went back into his own room, via the wardrobe.

He never asked me to go into any other piece of furniture after this, nor did he ever refer to the episode again. For my own part, I think this may have been the first time I recognised that Ralph's future really was in the theatre.

Father Gives a Sex Talk

'There are four steps in sex education,' said my father suddenly to me one day as we were trying to design a new, improved bicycle saddle together. 'First, you discard all the gooseberry bush and stork nonsense and learn all about where babies really come from. Second, you realise one day that if that is where babies come from then your parents must at some remote time in the past have had sex together. And third, that means that at some remote time in the past your parents must, incredible as it may seem, have found each other attractive enough to have sex with.'

I had already passed through these three stages in sex education, though not entirely thanks to my father.

'What is the fourth stage?' I asked.

'The fourth stage is coming to the dreadful realisation that maybe those times are not so remote and maybe it is just possible that your parents still find each other attractive enough to occasionally have sex together.'

My father had always taught me to be honest about these things.

'And do you still?'

'I think so,' said my father, with the hint of a blush. 'You had better ask your mother. She has a better memory about these things than I have.'

I made a mental note to do this, when I felt strong enough.

'What is the fifth stage in sex education?'

'Did I say there was a fifth stage in sex

education?'

'No, but you once taught me that in every sequence of events, there is always one more event than the experts suspect. It was your missing planet theory.'

'Was it?'

'Yes. You said that however well we explain the motion of the planets, there is always some discrepancy in the calculations and it is always easier to account for this by putting it down to the effect of a missing planet than to do the calculations all over again.'

'Did I?'

'Yes. And you also observed that, more often than not, a missing planet did eventually turn up.'

'How extremely clever of me. I must make a note of that.'

There was a pause.

'So, what is the fifth stage in sex education?'

'The fifth stage in sex education,' said my father, 'is for parents to realise that their children realise that their parents still find each other attractive enough to have a sex life and to send the child off to the other parent if he wants any further information.'

That seemed to be that, so we went back to the job of redesigning the bicycle saddle. This was the result of one of my father's theories, namely that while it was quite possible to invent things which had never existed before, such as the stapler to replace the paper clip, it was equally possible to reinvent things which already existed but in a much better form.

'Look at chairs,' said my father. 'People are constantly coming up with new kinds of chairs which are better for you to sit on. But that's mainly because the ordinary kind is so bad. Chairs in the past have been made almost entirely for the convenience of the maker, not the sitter, resulting in thousands of bent spines and generations of bad postures. I predict that in the future chairs will undergo revolutionary change as we find that we have been sitting wrong all these years. Same thing with cooking. All cookery books are about how to make food taste nice. They are never about whether the food is good for you or not. I wouldn't be surprised if one day cooks don't start making a fortune out of recipes, and new foods, that taste dull, horrible even, but are terribly good for you.'

'Where do bicycle saddles come into all this?'

'Ah. Now, the bicycle has always been a very simple design. Once they figured out that the penny-farthing was a terrible mistake and that it was much more sensible to have two wheels the same size, they got the basic bicycle design worked out in Victorian days—gears, brakes, etc.—and it has never really changed much since. And one of the things that has never changed very much is the saddle, which, as we all know from experience, is a lot harder to sit on than the average chair.'

It was true. I hadn't really thought about it before. A bike saddle is a hard bit of leather, about the size and shape of an upside-down steam iron, though slightly contoured. The area-to-weight ratio is truly grim. Every square inch of saddle bears nearly a stone. The same goes for each square inch of your bum in contact with the saddle. If it's not much fun for the saddle, how much less so is it for the rider? No wonder it chafes and rubs and numbs and anaesthetises . . .

(I didn't think of any of this at the time. It was my father who said all this. But when it's you who are writing the story, you can often seem much wiser than you really are by repeating other people's words as if they were your own. The whole art of journalism, I believe, is based on this technique.)

'The one great achievement of the bicycle saddle was to introduce equality of the sexes,' continued my father. 'It had never really happened with horse riding. It apparently seemed not right and proper for a woman to spread her legs across a horse because it suggested that they might spread their legs at other times, so women were made to keep their legs together and ride side-saddle. What a palaver! How can you ride side-saddle efficiently? You can't grip properly, you can't balance properly, you can't get any decent speed without falling off. No wonder horse-riding accident and death statistics were twice as bad for women as men in Victorian times!'

'Were they really?'

'I'd be surprised if they weren't,' he said, which meant he didn't know. Many years later, when I was doing some historical research into Victorian times, I decided, while I was at it, to have a look at statistics of nineteenth-century horse-riding accidents. There weren't any. Statistics, I mean. Why should there be?

'Anyway, Victorian women were incredibly lucky that they weren't made to ride bicycles side-saddle as well, but I suppose the earliest manufacturers realised that even if they wanted to there was no way they could design a bike to be ridden sideways on. You can get away with sitting sideways on a horse, but a bicycle *has* to be ridden with central weight distribution. So far, so good.

'The amazing thing to me is that, even when they had decided against bicycling side-saddle, still nobody designed a different saddle for women. After all, men and women are shaped quite differently at that point where saddle meets body, aren't we? Know what I mean?'

'Well . . .'

I hesitated. I hadn't been aware that women's bottoms were shaped differently from men's.

'Here's a book that explains it very well. Take it away and have a good look at it. Afterwards you can ask me any questions you may have.'

And he put a book in my hand and ushered me out of his workroom. Later, I looked at the book. It was called *The Basis of a Happy Marriage*. The basis of a happy marriage? Was this something to do with bicycling expeditions in the country? I opened it. It was full of diagrams of human genitalia. Some were male, some were unfamiliar to me and therefore presumably female. Generally, they were pictured singly, but sometimes they seemed to be deep inside each other.

I closed it, swallowing hard. I had expected some kind of discussion of bicycle design. What I hadn't expected was a no-holds-barred demonstration of sexual techniques, which is what I had got. It was a fearful gear change for a young lad to experience.

I did read the book, of course, and it was actually quite a good book. It was the sort of book that might have been written by a visitor from Mars. It explained all the physiological reactions of

237

our bodies during sex. It explained some things which I had never understood and put me right over other things which I thought I had understood. It also said there was no harm in masturbation, which was a great relief as I could see that that was something I was probably going to be stuck with for a long time, though the book did not give any particular advice or hints on how to masturbate with style, which was a shame.

The main achievement of the book, though, was to devote 200 pages to the act of sex without once making you anxious to try it. Perhaps that was what my father had intended. To put me off the whole idea.

The next time I was in his workroom he asked me, without looking at me, if I had looked at the book. I said I had.

'Good!' he said. 'Then you will now appreciate even more than before the problems of trying to design a unisex bike saddle. Men have external genitalia to accommodate. Women do not. You would think that they would have to have different saddles. But they do not. Our saddles are always the same thin triangle, sometimes so thin that they are hardly a triangle, pretty uncomfortable for both sexes, and I firmly believe that the reason for this design is the reluctance of the first Victorian saddle builders to face up to the differences between the sexes. Poor chaps! What could they do about it? They were probably mechanics in workshops in the Midlands, good at making things and yet totally ignorant of the female form, which in those days was swathed under acres of clothes. The only way a bike mechanic could have done research into the female body was by going to an art gallery, finding a nude female statue and taking measurements, and then getting arrested. I suspect that, rather than take that risk, they decided to just make a common saddle for everyone. If the bike saddle is thin and Spartan for both sexes it seems to have solved the problem. But it has not! It has merely shelved it.'

'Father,' I said, 'when you lent me that book, was that designed to replace our sex talk? Is that the nearest I get to learning about sex from you?'

'And so,' said my father, 'we must think of a revolutionary solution to the saddle problem. We must start again from scratch. We must rethink from the ground up.'

It was useless trying to get my father to discuss something if he wanted to talk about something else. I knew he would return to the subject sooner or later, as soon as he had formulated a reply.

'So, come on!' he said. 'Let's go and pay a visit to Farmer Dutton!'

'Why Farmer Dutton?'

'Because any farmer will do but he is the nearest.'

Mr Dutton did indeed have a farm nearby where he had lots of cows, and a cockerel that made a racket when the wind was right, and a barn full of bales where we children used to climb and play castles when he wasn't looking.

'The one thing that unites all farms, big or small,' said my father as we drove there in our car, 'is that a farmer can never bear to throw anything away. When something goes wrong with a bit of machinery he buys a new one and keeps the old one, intending to mend it, though he never does. When something gets clapped out he keeps it for spare parts. Tools, bags, implements, rolls of piping . . . Somewhere in every farm you will find a graveyard of old things stashed away, unmended and forgotten. A treasure trove. That's why rural museums are overflowing with ancient things. They've got them that very morning fresh from the farm.'

And sure enough, when we got to the farm, my father muttered something to Mr Dutton who nodded and took us round to a yard at the back which not only had all the items mentioned above but also a caravan that nobody used any more, an ancient plough and a rusting sports car. It wasn't any of these that they headed for, however, but an old tractor which Mr Dutton immediately got to work on, unbolting the tractor seat and handing it over to my father.

'If ever you decide to get the tractor going again, you can have the seat back at once,' said my father.

'Not much fear of that,' said Mr Dutton.

'That's what I thought,' said my father.

On the way back I asked him why he wanted a tractor seat.

'Well, it's only an experiment,' he said, 'but I thought we might try the world's first comfortable bicycle seat and see what happens.'

Enlightenment struck. He was going to try screwing a tractor seat on to a bike! After enlightenment there swiftly came feelings of scorn and then embarrassment.

'Father! You can't put a tractor seat on a bike! It would look ridiculous!'

'Only because we are used to the present ridiculous object called a bike saddle.'

'But . . .'

'Don't be blinkered by your prejudices, child,' he said. 'We have already established in principle that, when bicycling, the human body rests on far too narrow a shelf or cliff ledge. In principle, it makes sense to widen that cliff ledge. Or shelf. You have agreed with that principle. Now, when I am turning the principle into fact, you are growing nervous. But you can only find out if something works by trying it! Benjamin Franklin must have looked ridiculous flying a kite in a thunderstorm, but did that deter him from inventing the lightning conductor?'

Well, we did fix the tractor seat to a bicycle and it was indeed incredibly comfortable and suitable for lady or gent alike and nobody laughed at us in the street when we rode past on it, for the simple reason that when you sit on a tractor seat you more or less cover it and very few people realise you are sitting on one. No, on comfort grounds it was fine. Where it failed was on mechanical grounds. In order to absorb the shock of passing over bumps and rocks, a tractor seat is made springy and bendy. When you're riding a bike, you need something absolutely firm to push against so that you can drive the pedals round. If a tractor driver had to pedal his tractor he wouldn't have a soft seat. So the tractor seat turned out to be fine for tractors, not so fine for bicycles. And because your legs were moving up and down they rubbed against the front of the seat, which then had to be cut away . . .

I once rode down to the local shop on our tractor-bike. I locked it up and left it outside. When I came out ten minutes later, there was a crowd of at least a dozen people staring silently at the bicycle-with-a-tractor-seat. I unlocked it and rode away, still surrounded by that unsettling silence.

I am sure you don't want to hear any more about a failed bicycle seat design. I certainly don't. What you want to know more about is my sex education. That's what I would want to know more about if I were you.

Mother Gives a Sex Talk

'Now that we have finished experimenting with bicycle seats,' I asked my father, 'do you want that book back?'

'What book?'

'*The Basis of a Happy Marriage.*'

'That depends. Do you think you know enough about bicycle design now?'

'Yes.'

'Do you think you know enough about sex now?'

'No.'

'Then keep the book and go and ask your mother for some advice.'

'But, Father, you haven't told me anything yet!'

My father looked at me gravely.

'It is a well-known fact that when fathers teach their sons to drive, they become bad drivers. When fathers teach their sons to play golf, they always become bad golfers.'

'That's not true!' I said. 'Most of the best sportsmen started out being encouraged by their fathers!'

'Encouraged, yes,' he said. 'Not taught. Only encouraged. And I am encouraging you to go and talk to your mother. Now go!'

I went and found my mother.

'Father has been trying to give me a talk about sex,' I told her.

'Not before time,' she said. 'I've been asking him to do it for two years. Did he show you that book?'

'Yes.'

'Lord save us. I've looked at that book myself and I didn't understand much of it. Anyway, it's written by a man for men.'

'Yes, but I'm going to be a man,' I said.

'That's true,' she said, 'but you won't be having sex with men. Will you?'

'No.'

'So you've got to understand how women work, sexually.'

'Right,' I said.

I don't think I had ever been so embarrassed in all my life. Talking to my mother about sex! Even worse, her talking to me about it!

'I can't remember much about the book, but I don't think he says much about the way women feel, does he?' she said.

'No,' I said. 'I think he's much more interested in temperature changes and pulses and heartbeats and, um, what happens at the moment of, um . . .'

'That's right!' she said. 'I remember now! He approaches sex as if it were some kind of engine performance, to be monitored, oiled and watered. You can sort of imagine the author appearing beside your bed with an oily rag, looking down at both of you as you get on with it and saying, "Well, that seems to be ticking over nicely. I'll leave you to it. Give me a ring if you overheat." '

Never in all my born days did I expect to hear my mother talking about such things in such a way. I must have gone puce because she smiled and leant over and pinched my cheek.

'This isn't helping you much,' she said. 'Actually, assuming you know what happens when people make love, there are only a few helpful things that I can tell you. One is not to make it like an Olympic event. Men think that in sex the longer they last and the more often they do it, the more successful they are. I am afraid that's not true. And all those myths about how wonderful it would be to have both your climaxes at the same time, not true. It doesn't work like that. The only real secret is to try to give pleasure to the other person. Then you'll get it back.'

I waited, scarlet with embarrassment and interest.

'Yes?' I said.

'That's it,' she said. 'That's all I know. Well, all that's worth knowing. But it's all wrapped up in there.'

'That's all you learnt from my father?'

'Oh, I didn't learn it from him. I got it from the *Reader's Digest*. But it seemed to work pretty well.'

'Oh.'

'But all this sex business is not so very important. It's only a prelude to much better things.'

God, this was better. What things?

'What things?'

'Oh, love, and getting married, and having children, and settling down . . .'

244

She must have seen the expression on my face because she burst into laughter.

'I'm not going to do any of those things,' I said, with dignity. 'I'm just going to . . .'

'Make love to the girls?' she said.

'Yes,' I said, going what I later knew to be poinsettia-red.

'Oh, there's something else about sex I forgot to tell you,' she said. 'The girls know.'

'Know what?'

'That that's what you want.'

'Do they?'

'Oh, yes. Girls know that boys want to go to bed with them.'

'Oh. So . . . do they?'

'No. Not usually.'

'Why don't they?'

'Why should they?'

'Wouldn't they enjoy it?'

'They might, but not with a boy who didn't know how to do it properly.'

'With who then?'

'Someone older.'

'Oh.'

'But probably not at all. If they went to bed with someone, they'd only get the reputation of being the sort of girl who would go to bed with someone.'

'Oh.'

Suddenly it all seemed terribly confusing. I looked at my watch. There was plenty of time to wait before I did anything.

'I think I'll go and play table tennis with Ralph.'

'All right, dear.'

Ralph Gives a Sex Talk

Ralph and I had quite different styles when it came to table tennis. As you might imagine, he had a swashbuckling approach, very flamboyant and erratic. When his shots came off, they were unstoppable. When they didn't, they got lost under the furniture. By contrast, I was quite methodical, better at defence than at attack. I must have seemed quite stolid to Ralph, always careful to return the ball, always careful to keep it low over the net. When I did occasionally cut loose and try an aggressive drive, it always took him by surprise.

'Whoa there!' he would say. 'Steady on, D'Artagnan!'

One of his secret identities was as one of the Three Musketeers, though it was only secret to the extent that he could never remember which one he was. He once came across Oscar Wilde's remark to the effect that the names of the Three Musketeers were Athos, Pathos and Bathos and the memory of this never failed to crack him up, though I have to say I had heard much better jokes on the radio.

'It's your serve!' said Ralph.

Without thinking, I had been throwing the ball back to him after every point and he had been throwing it back to me.

'Your mind wasn't on the game,' he said, after beating me easily. 'What's up?'

'I . . .'

Brothers don't talk to each other a lot about sex. At least, *we* didn't. At least, *I* didn't.

'The thing is that Father started giving me a sex

talk today and then mother did as well and, well, I'm a bit confused about the whole thing.'

'I'm not surprised,' said Ralph. 'Did our father show you that book? *The Basis of a Happy Marriage?'*

'Yes.'

'*Sacré bleu!'* said Ralph. (Some people swear like troopers. Ralph preferred to swear like a Musketeer.) 'No wonder you are looking confused. He showed me that book too and it set back my development by a year.'

'Why?'

'Well, it took me a year to read it and understand what the author was on about and by the time I had realised it was all a waste of time, I had lost a year.'

'Why was it a waste of time? Because it was only aimed at married people?'

'No, no, no, no. Sex is the same in marriage as outside it, except, they say, that if you're married you don't have to get the last bus home afterwards. No, because the guy who wrote it didn't tell you the one vital thing about sex. That it's a trap.'

'A trap!?' I exclaimed.

'Yes. A trap. Oh, a very nice sort of trap. But a trap all the same.'

'How is it a trap?'

'Well, it's something invented by nature to keep the species going. If men and women didn't make love, they wouldn't have babies. If men and women didn't enjoy making love, they wouldn't do it and the species would die out. So nature has ensured that men and women enjoy making love and thus have babies. In recent history mankind has found different ways of avoiding having babies, so now

247

we can enjoy making love without getting people pregnant. We have outwitted nature. Mark you, nature will think of some revenge.'

This was all so dreadfully ahead of me that my head span.

'Unfortunately,' added Ralph, 'if we have managed to outwit nature, we still haven't managed to outwit girls. Girls know that we are just after one thing.'

'That's what mother said!' I said.

'And there is only one way to get it,' continued Ralph.

'She didn't mention this bit,' I said. 'What is the way to get it?'

'Well, from my reading of theatre history and from my theatre experience at school and from other sources I will not specify, I have learnt that girls let their guard down when they think that boys are not interested in them.'

'I thought you said that we were all after just one thing.'

'All of us, except those that are . . . different.'

'Different?'

'Oh, for heaven's sake! Do I have to spell it out to you?'

'Yes.'

'Q-U-E-E-R,' spelt Ralph.

I fell silent. I was out of my depth again.

'Girls do not feel threatened by queers,' said Ralph. 'For obvious reasons. In fact, it is quite the opposite. They love the company of queers. They all have the same interest in clothes, and hair, and décor, and music and things. And men, of course. So girls' defences are down against queer men.'

Nowadays we would say 'gay'. Then it was

always 'queer'. Nowadays, people complain that the proper, traditional use of the word 'gay' has been ruined. Nobody ever said that about the proper traditional use of the word 'queer'. I wonder why not.

'But what's the point of being queer and putting girls at ease if you don't want to take advantage of it?' I asked.

'Ah! But there's such a thing as being a bit queer,' Ralph said. 'People in the theatre are like that most of the time. You don't have to be really queer to be like that. They call it being a bit "camp". It doesn't impress men, but girls love it. That's what I find, anyway. If you're one of the girls and you're actually a boy, you'd be surprised how much you can get away with.'

I thought about this. It made sense. Then a thought occurred to me.

'You're not a . . . I mean, you're not queer are you, Ralph?'

'Only when it suits me,' he said enigmatically.

I thought some more about it. It all seemed so difficult. Then another thought occurred to me.

'How do you think the Three Musketeers did it?'

'Did what?'

'Got the girls.'

'Well,' said Ralph, 'I expect they bought them a drink and said, "Hey, mademoiselle, has it ever occurred to you that although we are called musketeers, we only fight with swords and you never see our muskets?" And the girls said, "Ooh, I never thought of that. Let's have a look at your musket, then." And after that they played it by ear.'

I was still a bit lost. It isn't often you get three sex talks, all on the same day, all from members of your family. Some instinct told me to bide my time. And, although it is outside the scope of this story, it all bore fruit years later when I met an American girl and, with a drink or two inside me, unconsciously followed Ralph's advice and fluttered my eyelids at her as if I were gay. And then further disarmed her by telling her all about my father's attempts to build a new improved bicycle seat, which she found hilarious. By the time we were in bed together, I was in a position to follow Mother's advice and get pleasure by giving it. That worked, too.

Thanks, everyone.

Superstition

'Look at that!' said my father one day, as we were all driving in our car together somewhere. 'Twenty-nine seagulls in a group! That's unlucky!'

He pointed while we all sat tight and said nothing. Experience had taught us it was dangerous to engage his attention in any way while he did not have both hands on the wheel.

There was, in fact, a large group of seagulls following a tractor in a field nearby, but how he knew there were twenty-nine of them baffled me. After his hands had returned to the wheel, Ralph decided to challenge him.

'And if there were only twenty-eight?'

'Still unlucky.'

'And twenty-seven?'

'Still unlucky. *Any* amount of seagulls is unlucky. Seagulls are unlucky per se. They are nasty, vicious creatures. When you see them inland, it means there is bad weather at sea.'

(In those days, seagulls were still sea creatures and not as fond of inland refuse dumps as they are now.)

'Would one seagull be unlucky?'

'Yes,' said my father stoutly. 'Though not as unlucky as twenty-nine,' he conceded.

'I can never understand why you have these little superstitions, Father,' said Ralph. 'Most of the time you are quite rational and logical and systematic—indeed you pride yourself on it—and then you come up with these batty sayings which have nothing to do with science at all.'

'Actually, being rational and logical can be a superstition in its own way,' said my mother. 'If you insist on being it, I mean. Scientists are sometimes very superstitious about rationality. But there are some times when logic is not enough.'

'I know where this is leading,' said my father. 'This is leading us back to Catholicism and the Higher Truth.'

'Well, it is a higher truth,' said my mother, modestly putting it in lower case.

'Nonsense. Religion is just another kind of superstition,' said my father. 'But with religion, instead of saying things like "One for sorrow, two for joy," people say equally superstitious things like "Three in one and one in three."'

'Darkling here we worship thee.' My mother couldn't help completing the hymn couplet.

'Darkling!' said my father. 'There you go, you see! What does darkling *mean*? Why do people in church sing things they don't understand?'

'There are lots of things we don't understand,' said my mother. 'We don't understand what we are doing here and where we are going.'

'Yes,' said my father, narrowly avoiding a cyclist, 'but that doesn't mean we have to increase the number of incomprehensible things by putting them in a hymn and making people sing them. Darkling! Darkling here we worship thee! What does it *mean*? How do you darkle? Or is it, "Charlie is my darkling"? What does it *mean*?'

'I'll look it up,' I said, to help restore peace.

Ours is the only car I have ever come across where there was a dictionary permanently on board to help settle arguments. I have seen pubs where they keep the *Guinness Book of Records* to settle disputes, but the *Guinness Book of Records* would have been of no use to our family. We didn't argue about things that could be settled by statistical records. If *Guinness* had included things like which was the truest religion, or the most useful proverb, or the most ominous number of seagulls in a group, we would have got a copy immediately. As it was, we had a dictionary, and I can't remember a journey when it wasn't used.

'Darkling,' I said. 'A literary word. It means growing dark, or having connotations of darkness.'

'Growing dark,' said my father. 'So the line from the hymn means "Growing dark here, we worship thee." And what does *that* mean?'

Nobody answered. Nobody answered when father was spoiling for a fight over religion. I sometimes hoped, even though I shared his disenchantment with religion, that a loud voice would come out of nowhere and say, 'Never mind

252

what "darkling" means, my son, just keep your eyes on the road!'

'Perhaps, if you were more religious,' said my mother, 'you would be less superstitious. If my religion really is a kind of superstition, then I think it is a superior kind to yours. I believe in God the Father, God the Son and God the Holy Ghost. You believe it is unlucky to look at the new moon through glass. Which do you think is the more sophisticated?'

'I am not superstitious!' expostulated my father. 'Name one way in which I let my life be governed by superstition!'

'Catching leaves,' said my mother. 'You almost had a heart attack the other day.'

Ah, she had him there! That was true. Every autumn, the season which was now upon us, my father delighted in trying to catch old dry leaves as they fell from the trees. He said that you had to catch ten and then you would be safe from bad luck. Well, the other day it had been cold day with a breeze and the leaves had started falling from the old walnut tree in the back garden and he had gone out to stand underneath and try to catch them. He had been out there a long time. It is not easy. I have tried it myself. You cannot predict the flight path of a leaf. Leaves are either very cunning or very stupid. Either way, they easily get past you. On this occasion father had gone red in the face and been forced to give up before he got to ten.

'I'd forgotten about that,' he said. 'Thanks for reminding me. I had only got to nine. One more to get.'

By this time we had almost got back home. I could see exactly what was going to happen next.

253

We would park the car outside the house. Ralph, Mother and I would go indoors to put on the kettle and settle down. Father, however, would go into the back garden and try to catch his tenth leaf.

I was wrong.

Fate must have overheard my prediction and decided to disprove it.

As we slowed down near our house, a gust of wind blew a whole lot of leaves from the tree next door to us, some kind of willow.

They fell across the car in a whirling shower.

Father was driving with the window open.

The leaves flew round the car.

Instinctively, he made a grab for one.

This caused him to twist the steering wheel.

(I can still see all this, in slow motion, in my mind's video playback.)

This caused him to drive very slowly into the car parked in front of us at the kerb, which belonged to the same man as the willow tree belonged to.

'Damn,' said my father.

He slowly uncurled his fist and revealed that he had a crumpled willow leaf in it.

'Still, at least I caught it.'

'It didn't bring you much luck, did it?' said Ralph. 'What price superstition now?'

'Well,' said Father, 'you don't know that it won't bring me luck. Maybe the luck is still to come. Maybe I was lucky in not having a worse accident.'

'You're talking like a Catholic now,' said my mother. 'I recognise the twisted logic. A Catholic can justify anything.'

Looking back, I can't think of many families who, after a traffic accident, would sit there discussing whether it was caused by bad luck or

not. Any other family would have:
   1) Indulged in loud recriminations OR
   2) Got out to inspect the damage OR
   3) Fled immediately.
But no, we had to sit there and discuss it in terms of superstition which explains why, when our neighbour Mr Murphy turned up to see what had happened to his car, having seen the accident out of the window, he was surprised to find us still sitting there, talking away.

He went to the point where the two cars were touching.

He examined both cars thoroughly.

He came to the window which my father had opened.

'Well, there's lucky for you,' he said. 'My car is unscratched. Yours seems to have all the damage.'

He strolled back indoors while my father sat there, open-mouthed.

'Now you'll have to claim for insurance,' said my mother.

My father said nothing.

We all knew why this was.

It was because of the incident with the car insurance.

Car Insurance

Nobody liked to remind Father of the time he had tried to claim damages from himself.

It had come about like this.

There had been a time when we had had to travel a long way to stay with some friends for the weekend. The friends were too difficult to get to by rail, so we decided to drive. Unfortunately, our car was unreliable at the time, so Father decided to do something quite out of character: he hired a car for the weekend.

I am not sure why it strikes me as being so out of character for him. If your car is out of action, it is logical to hire a car. Father was always logical. And he was not especially mean with money. So why does it seem out of character? Perhaps because he was quite a private person and did not like the idea of driving a car in which someone else had also recently sat as the temporary owner. He occasionally had the same feeling about hotel rooms.

'Whenever we stay in a hotel,' he told me once, 'we have to conceal from ourselves the fact that someone else used all these facilities the night before. They sat on the same lavatory seat. They rolled on the same mattress. They put their socks in the same drawer. People say how horrible it is to have had burglars in their house—well, in a hotel it's exactly the same thing! But in a hotel the previous intruders have paid for the privilege of using the territory we are now occupying and someone has cleared up after them so we pretend that it never happened. We have to try to wash it out of our minds. And yet sometimes I wake up in the middle of the night in a hotel and think to myself, "Last night a total stranger lay his head on this pillow!" and I shudder a little.'

'Do you feel the same way about sitting in a seat on a bus which someone else has just got out of?' I asked. 'Or a theatre seat? Do you feel invaded there?'

'No,' he said, 'it never occurs to me. It's a funny thing, that sometimes previous ownership disturbs me and sometimes it doesn't. It's not just me. Everyone feels the same. Nobody feels that an old house is demeaned because other people used to live in it. Rather the opposite. The same with antiquarian books, and paintings, and things like that. Nobody ever calls a painting by Monet a cast-off, second-hand painting. But once you start wearing second-hand clothes, you do feel demeaned. There is nothing antiquarian about cast-off clothes. They are just dead men's clothes.'

Anyway, he reluctantly hired the car, and we drove to our friends' house for the weekend, and we came back again, and as the place that hired out cars was not within walking distance, my mother agreed to drive our accident-prone car behind the hire car back to the depot in order to pick up Father after he had deposited the hire car.

He left the hire car in the road outside our house with the engine still running.

He went into our drive to get out our own car for my mother.

He drove out into the road and, as he exited, he accidentally clipped the wing of the hire car.

Drawn by the noise we all rushed to have a look.

The collision was not nearly as bad as it had sounded. It had not caused a lot of damage. It had, however, definitely caused damage. The sort of damage that hire-car companies love to see because they can furrow their brows and talk about collision damage waiver and personal responsibility and a little box which you failed to initial, all of which means that you are responsible for paying for damage which you thought you were insured against.

'Hmm', said my father, surveying the dents. 'Better go and face the music, I suppose.'

And off he went to the car-hire company, who duly noted the damage and asked him to describe the accident.

'Who was driving the hire-car vehicle at the time?' asked the man in charge, who Father thinks was called Terry, though I am not sure about this because although Terry is now one of the most popular names in Britain, I don't think there was anyone in the country before 1960 who was actually called Terry, just as there was no-one called Tracey, or Wayne, or Sharon, or Kim . . .

But I digress.

'There was nobody actually in the car at the time,' my father said. 'Though the engine was running because I had left it running as I was about to jump back in and use it.'

'Was it on a public highway?' said Terry.

'Yes.'

'Oh, dear,' said Terry.

'Why "Oh, dear"?' asked my father.

'Well, if the engine was running and it was on the road,' said Terry, who had been here before, 'then you were legally in charge of the vehicle. That's not too bad, really, I suppose. I just need to know who was driving the other vehicle. Did you get their details?'

'Yes,' said Father. 'I was driving the other vehicle.'

There was a silence.

'I thought you were driving the hire car?'

'No. I was in charge of the hire car. You just explained that to me.'

'Well, legally, that comes to more or less the same thing. But how did it come about that you were driving the other car?'

Father explained that he was just moving the car out of the drive for Mother and happened to collide with the hire car. That was all. It was as simple as that.

'It's not really as simple as that,' said Terry. 'What we have here is a traffic accident in which both cars have apparently been driven by the same person.'

'Seems pretty simple to me,' said my father. 'Keeps it all in the family. Nobody else involved. Amicable conclusion.'

Terry stared at Father.

'Nothing is ever simple in insurance,' he said. 'I've been in the car-hire business for ten years and the only way that any insurance wrangle can be worked out is by confrontation. They have to fight it out. Challenge and counter-challenge. Both sides say they are innocent and then they slug it out. All right, maybe one side sometimes admits guilt, but at least there are two different sides. I have never in my life known the same party to be on both sides in a traffic accident.'

And nor, it turned out, had the insurance industry. News spread like wildfire that there was a lowly traffic accident in Shropshire somewhere in which the same man had been driving both vehicles and was therefore asking himself to pay costs and damages. There was nothing in the insurance rules which covered this. They had never thought to insure themselves against a case in which the same man was driving two cars. It was always assumed that when two cars collided, they would be driven by different people.

It is a reasonable assumption.

I feel proud, now, that it took my father to shatter it.

At first, apparently, there was shock and horror in the industry, followed by complete hilarity. The two insurance companies involved in the case were so proud of being the two companies involved in the case that they both applied to the *Guinness Book of Records* to have the case recognised as a record—the first case in which plaintiff and defendant were the same person—but sadly they never quite made it, as the *Guinness Book of Records* had also had submitted to it some piffling case in which a burglar had mistakenly raided his own premises and been arrested for it and they thought that was more interesting.

Well, the case was, indeed, amicably settled and my father never had to appear in court and explain how he had been driving a car which had collided with another car which he had also been driving.

But these things linger. Many years later I was present at a grand dinner given by the insurance industry, one of those dinners where the industry congratulates itself so much that you know there is something gravely wrong with it. And there were speakers who spoke seriously about insurance (and people were very bored), and there were comic speakers who had no idea about insurance but had been hired for the night merely to be comic (and people laughed a lot but were very bored), and there was one speaker who did know about insurance and was very funny and he told this story about the traffic accident in which the driver of both cars was one and the same person and

260

everyone roared with laughter . . .

And afterwards I went up to him and said, 'That was a good story. And of course it was true. And I know it was true, because it happened to my father.'

And the speaker told me not to be silly. He told me that it was just a funny story which had been told to him by a lot of old-timers, a hoary old insurance chestnut made up to exemplify something which couldn't possibly happen because the insurance world was too smart to let it happen.

So I didn't insist.

After all, he had never met my father.

Elementary, My Dear Ralph

Whenever I see someone wearing a deerstalker, or smoking a curly pipe, or flourishing a violin or hypodermic syringe I immediately think of . . .

Have you guessed?

Well, you're wrong.

The person I think immediately of is my brother Ralph.

More especially, at the time he was going through his Sherlock Holmes phase.

I suppose we all go through Sherlock Holmes phases.

I went through one myself, after I had read the Conan Doyle story called *The Dancing Men* in which Holmes cracked a fiendishly complicated code. He did this because he knew which letters were most commonly used in English and could therefore identify them with the most common signs in the code.

I spent the next year trying to investigate and create codes using Holmes's knowledge of the frequency of letters. I still remember the popularity order of letters: E was the most common, followed by T, A, O, I, N, S, H, R, D. One Christmas I set out to solve the code of the junior club of my favourite weekly comic. 'Hello, members!' chortled the club leader. 'Here is a special message to everyone, written in the club code so that only members can understand it!' Then followed the message in code. It took me half an hour to crack it using the Holmesian letter table. The message was, somewhat unsensationally, 'The compliments of the season to all our members.'

Ralph had quite a different quest for the Holmesian Grail. If I wanted to think like Holmes, Ralph wanted to *be* like Holmes—to look like him, sound like him, behave like him. He wanted to play the part, in fact.

Where he got the deerstalker from, I don't know. But I know where he got the curly pipe from. It was from Father's smoking cupboard. Father didn't smoke much, but he occasionally liked to load and fire a pipe on festive occasions, so Ralph knew exactly where to go to get a pipe that looked like Sherlock's.

Unfortunately, Father knew exactly where to go to get it back again. Father had always been convinced that one of us was going to start smoking one day. He knew that we would raid his supplies to do it. So he kept a strict eye on how much tobacco was left at any given moment and when he spotted that a pipe was missing, he made a beeline for his elder child.

Ralph admitted having the pipe.

But he denied ever having smoked.

'Why on earth would one take a pipe, if not to smoke it?' demanded Father. 'What else can one do with a pipe?'

'You can be Sherlock Holmes,' said Ralph stoutly.

'Be Sherlock Holmes?!' said my father. 'I've heard of some pretty pathetic excuses in my time . . .'

I suppose it is in a grown-up's nature always to believe the most disreputable explanation for any delinquent behaviour, so Ralph was convicted of being a premature smoker and sentenced to lose his pocket money for three weeks. He felt this was very unfair.

'I'll get my revenge somehow,' he muttered to me. 'Just you wait and see, Father dear. I shall get my own back.'

'You don't sound very much like Sherlock Holmes,' I said. 'You sound much more like all those criminals he caught. Do you remember how, before they were sent to prison, they usually shook their fist at him and said, "You've got the best of me this time, Mister 'Olmes, but just you wait and see who gets the last laugh!"'

'Getting a bit above our station, aren't we, Watson?' remarked Ralph coolly. 'I would advise you not to underestimate my powers.'

'I think it's Father's powers we ought to worry about,' I said. 'I thought he solved the problem of the missing pipe very neatly. Perhaps I should adopt him as my famous detective instead of you.'

Ralph abruptly cut short the conversation at this

point in a very un-Holmeslike manner by launching himself at me and trying to punch my head off which ended, as usual, in fisticuffs and laughter.

But it was I, several days later, who precipitated the final drama.

Ralph had become increasingly restless over this period. When there was nothing to engage his mighty intellectual powers he became easily distracted and resorted to copious use of drugs.

'Not at the peppermints again?' I remarked. 'That's the third packet today.'

'I need some problem to work on,' he said, pulling on the deerstalker and staring out despondently into the rain which had kept us indoors. 'Somewhere out there there must be some poor soul who needs my help.'

'Hello, what's this?' I said.

I had been idly leafing through a book which I had got down from the bookshelves, one of those big books which look so good on the shelves that it usually doesn't occur to anyone to get them down. Bound volumes of the *Illustrated London News*, books on the birds of Africa, histories of the search for the North West Passage—that sort of thing. The volume I had got down was a big picture book on the native mammals of America and I was goggling at a moose when the postcard fell out of the book.

'What's what?' asked Ralph.

'Someone's left a postcard in this book.'

'So what?'

'It's got writing on it.'

'So what?'

'I'd love to know who wrote it.'

'Why?'

'Because it's a love message.'

I think Sherlock Holmes in real life would have shown no interest in a message of love, but it aroused Ralph's attention quickly enough.

'Let's see,' he said.

The postcard that fell out of the chapter on bears in America had a picture of a seaside town on the front and some writing on the back. The writing was lively but not tidy and sprawled right across the back of the postcard. It read as follows:

Dear darling,

What a wonderful trip and I am sorry you had to go back so soon. Belfast was lovely. Give my love to Rootie, but make sure you don't give her yours! See you very soon.

All love, Aggie.

'Very instructive,' said Ralph, and he got up to leave the room.

'Where are you going?' I shouted.

I knew soon enough, when he returned carrying a large magnifying glass.

'If you examine the postcard carefully,' he said, 'there are several interesting features.'

'Are there?' I said.

'Certainly,' he said. 'For one thing, the writer has written across the whole of the back of the postcard.'

'Isn't that normal?'

'Not at all. The normal thing is to write a message on the left-hand side and the name and address of the recipient on the right.'

'You're right,' I said, impressed by this

observation, elementary though it was. 'Why hasn't he done this?'

'"She", I think,' said Ralph. 'The writing is a woman's. The language is a woman's. Men tend not to talk about "wonderful" and "lovely".'

'Right,' I said. 'So why has she not done that? To make more room for the message?'

'I think not,' said Ralph. 'That message could easily have been written in half the space. No, I fancy the reason was because the postcard was being sent in an envelope.'

'Why?'

'Who knows? Possibly because the writer didn't want anyone else to read it. Perhaps because she did not know where the recipient was living . . .'

'I don't understand.'

'If she expected the postcard to be forwarded, she would send it in an envelope. There is never enough room on a postcard to cross out one address and insert another. But there always is on an envelope.'

I could see how Watson felt now. Admiring. And resentful.

'Here is another interesting thing,' said Ralph, turning the card over. 'The scene on the card.'

Underneath the seaside scene was the caption 'Newcastle in Summertime'.

'What do you deduce from that, Watson?' said Ralph.

I tried to ignore the scent of humiliation in the air.

'Um, that after this trip to Belfast had finished, Aggie went to Newcastle, which was probably her home town so she must have been a Geordie . . .'

'Most unlikely,' said Ralph. 'The scene is of

266

Newcastle seafront. But Newcastle is not on the sea. It is on the River Tyne. That is why it is called Newcastle-on-Tyne. It has no sea front.'

'Then where . . . ?'

'There are all sorts of places called Newcastle. Newcastle-under-Lyme, for instance. Why 'under Lyme', you may wonder? It is an interesting story, but not relevant to this case. What is far more relevant is that not far from Belfast, down on the coast of County Down, there is a pleasant seaside resort called Newcastle. I infer it is there that Aggie went after her dear darling had gone back home to England.'

'So they came to Belfast together, but dear darling went back after a while and Aggie went on to Newcastle?'

'It seems so.'

'Who was Rootie?'

'Steady on, Watson,' said Ralph. 'We haven't worked out yet who dear darling was, though all the evidence points overwhelmingly to one person.'

'Evidence? What evidence?'

'The evidence of the postcard being in the book. Normally one keeps letters and postcards in one's desk. One does not keep correspondence in a book on American mammals. Unless, of course, there was some sentimental attachment . . . Let us see . . . Ah yes! As I thought!'

Ralph had turned to the very beginning of *The Native Mammals of the American Continent* and pointed to a handwritten inscription inside the front cover.

'To you and Rootie. Hope you will both be very happy. Love from Aggie. June 1937.'

'There you have it,' said Ralph.

'Have what?' I said.

'The writing in the book is exactly the same as on the postcard. Therefore Aggie has given this book as a present to dear darling and Rootie. We can safely infer that those two were getting married and that this was a wedding present. Now, this is something of a change of roles for Aggie. When she wrote the postcard, she was writing it to her dear darling and warning him not to take any notice of Rootie. Let me see, where was it . . . Here we are! "Give my love to Rootie, but make sure you don't give her yours!" Aggie is warning her darling to keep his hands off Rootie. Yet in June 1937 it is all over. She is giving them a wedding present. Aggie has lost. Rootie has won.'

'Yes, but . . .'

'Mother and Father were married in June 1937, were they not?'

'Yes, but . . .'

'I think it is fairly clear that Father is dear darling. Mother is, equally, Rootie. Who Aggie was remains to be discovered.'

'Nobody has ever called Mother Rootie.'

'Remember that her middle name is Ruth. What more natural nickname for a Ruth to pick up in her youth than Rootie. The very sort of nickname, too, one would be anxious to discard in later life.'

I looked at my brother. Not only was he unconsciously talking more and more like Sherlock Holmes, he was looking like him—keen, thin, pinched, bright-eyed like a hunter on the trail.

'It seems extraordinary to think of Father going off to Northern Ireland with another woman,' I said.

'One never likes to think of one's parents as being like other people,' said Ralph reprovingly. 'But it would be awful if they were not like other people. Would you like it if Mother and Father had never cast eyes on anyone else before they got married?'

'Well,' I said, 'I'd quite like it if they hadn't gone off to Northern Ireland with someone else.'

'Good old Watson,' said Ralph. 'Always the stickler for correct family behaviour.'

'How are we going to find out who Aggie is? Shall we go and ask Mother?'

'I don't think that would be a good idea,' said Ralph. 'I think we might go and pay Father a little call.'

And so, that very evening, we went to see Father in his workroom.

'Hello, boys,' he said cheerily, looking up from his work. 'Like to see a little gadget I'm making which will make it easier to get corks back into wine bottles?'

'No thanks, Father,' said Ralph. 'There's something we have to talk to you about.'

'Dear me, what is it?'

'Oh, it is just a little matter I am anxious to clear up,' said Ralph, sounding more like Holmes than ever. Father looked at him curiously.

'Father, do you remember someone called Aggie?'

'Aggie?' he said, startled.

'Yes, Aggie.'

'I have known one or two girls called Aggie,' he said. 'Which one was this?'

'The one you went to Belfast with in 1936 or 1937,' said Ralph.

'Belfast . . .' said Father. 'Belfast . . . Belfast . . . Belfast . . .'

Sometimes, you get a gut feeling that someone is playing for time.

'Belfast . . . let me see . . .'

'Capital of Northern Ireland,' said Ralph shortly.

'I don't think I have ever been there,' said Father.

'Not with a girl called Aggie?' said Ralph.

'Not with or without a girl called Aggie,' said Father. 'I am sure I would remember if I had been to Belfast. With a girl called Aggie. Anyway, the thing is that corks expand when taken out of wine bottles, so the problem I have to overcome is . . .'

After we had extracted ourselves from his room and his cork problems, I turned on Ralph.

'Well, you got that wrong, didn't you? Brilliant deduction!'

'Got it wrong?' Ralph looked surprised. 'I didn't get it wrong. I was spot on. It was just that Father chose to deny it, that's all.'

'Oh.' I thought this over. 'Well, if he denies it there's nothing you can do about it. After all, he hasn't committed a crime or anything. You can't force him to tell the truth.'

'There's more than one way to get a bull out of a china shop, Watson,' said Ralph, and didn't refer to it again till we were all sitting at supper.

'Mother,' he said suddenly during a lull in the conversation, 'you once had a great friend called Aggie, didn't you?'

'Yes, I did,' said Mother, surprised. 'When I was a girl. And after that, too. We saw a lot of each other. But she faded away from my life after your father and I got married. Never saw much of her again, which was sad, really, as we were great friends.'

'Was she very pretty?' said Ralph, resolutely avoiding Father's eye, which was working overtime.

'Pretty? Yes, she was quite attractive. Wouldn't you say so?'

This to Father, who gulped and said he supposed she was not unattractive.

'I've got a photograph of her somewhere in the family album,' said Mother.

'Gosh, I'd be jolly interested in seeing it,' said Ralph.

'I'll get it,' said Mother.

She left the room and Father leant forward and spoke very fast and urgently.

'I don't know what your game is, but I don't want any of the past raking up and I don't want any reference to Belfast and I don't want me dragged into this. Understand?'

'So my pocket money will be restored, then?' said Ralph, gazing back at him innocently.

Father looked at him.

He looked at Father.

It was a very long moment for me.

Then we heard Mother coming back.

'Yes, you can have your pocket money,' said Father.

After we had looked at the photo of Aggie Satterthwaite (that was her name, and she was indeed quite pretty) and after we had finished supper without further incident, I grabbed hold of Ralph outside.

'That was blackmail,' I said.

'Not at all, Watson,' he said. 'All I ever want to

do is see that justice is done. I think we may say that in this case that has been achieved.'

The Exchange Student

Father suddenly decided one year that we should have more exposure to foreign languages.

'Good!' said Mother. 'Let's go abroad, then!'

But that wasn't in his mind at all.

What he was thinking of was arranging for a French exchange student to come and stay with us.

'That won't expose the boys to foreign languages,' said Mother. 'The French boy will have to speak English while he is here. That's not a foreign language. Not to our boys. It would be much better to go abroad.'

'Ah, but they will be going abroad on the second half of the exchange! Whichever one of ours goes back in exchange will have to speak French over there!' said Father.

'Well, he'll have to learn how to speak it on the boat going over, then,' said Ralph, who distrusted any languages which belonged to other people.

I had my own reasons for not wanting visitors.

'I don't want to have a French exchange student coming over here and playing with my Meccano!' I said.

I had just started the complicated matter of making a historical reconstruction of the scaffold on which Charles I had died and I didn't want anyone to know about it. The history master that term had announced a prize for the best artistic rendering of a scene from seventeenth-century

England and after hesitating over the idea of a painting of Oliver Cromwell's warts ('Paint me, warts and all!' Cromwell had said to his portraitist and I thought it would be quite surrealist to do a painting just of the warts, and very time-saving too) I had decided to do a Meccano reconstruction of the death scene of Charles I.

(I had always been interested in the mechanics of death. When I was about ten, I had once had to be cut loose from a rope after losing consciousness while researching the art of lynching.)

'It's no good,' said Father. 'I have already sent off the application form.'

Shock and horror. It was already ordained. We were going to have a foreign teenager billeted on us, who would then play with my Meccano and muck around with Ralph's model theatre.

Then we forgot all about it for months and months.

And then suddenly one day the child arrived.

His name was Jean-Marie.

Or her name was Jean-Marie.

It was a very bisexual sort of name.

But then he was a very bisexual sort of person.

Or, if it was a she, she was.

'Are you a boy or a girl?' said Ralph, the first time all three of us were alone together.

It was not an unjustified question.

Jean-Marie was either a pretty-looking boy or a boyish-looking girl.

He, or she, dressed very stylishly.

'*Répétez, s'il vous plaît,*' it said.

'*Etes-vous une jeune fille ou un garçon?*' said Ralph.

(All those years of French lessons had paid off

273

at last!)

The creature blinked for a moment and then opened its mouth in protest.

For the first time in my life I was to encounter the way the French mind works.

'Am I a boy or a girl?' it said. 'Why must you always categorise things? Why must you use these labels to sort things into their little drawers? Why is it important if I am a boy or a girl? I am a person! Yes, I am a person and proud of it! I love people! The world is full of people, all different, all with their own interests that make them different from each other, and all you can say is, "Are you a boy or a girl?" Have you no more interesting questions than that?'

I had never seen Ralph looking so flummoxed. I don't think he had ever encountered the French mind before either. For the rest of the week (the child was only with us for a week) neither of us referred to the problem again in Jean-Marie's presence, only behind his or her back.

I must have assumed that Jean-Marie was enough of a girl not to be interested in Meccano because by Thursday I had started work again on Charles I's death scene, building the grandstand and the execution block and even a small axe, which is almost impossible with Meccano.

I was wrong about our guest.

'What is it?' said a voice behind me.

It was Jean-Marie.

I explained.

'How barbaric!' Jean-Marie said.

'Well, I think the French did it too,' I said. 'You chopped off kings' heads as well. Less than two hundred years ago, actually.'

(At last all those history lessons had come in useful!)

'Oh, pouf, I am not bothered about chopping off kings' heads,' said Jean-Marie. 'That is very acceptable. It is the method I am talking about. This axe! How brutal!'

'What other way is there of chopping someone's head off?'

'The guillotine, of course! The French invention! It was invented by a Frenchman especially so as not to be painful!'

'Oh?' I said. 'And what Frenchman was that?'

'Dr Guillotin, of course,' said Jean-Marie, with the hauteur that only the French can manage (which is why hauteur has a French name I suppose). 'He invented it specially so that there would be no suffering like what the axe made. You know sometimes the axe took five or six times to cut the head off? But with the invention of Dr Guillotin, with the diagonal blade and the heavy fall of the blade, zut! *Comme ça! C'est instant!* Look, I will show you . . .'

And Jean-Marie started pulling out bits of Meccano from the box, despite my protests, and fairly soon had started to construct a very passable copy of a guillotine. For the blade he used an old Stanley knife I had been using for cutting cardboard which he rigged to a Meccano framework with a groove in it formed by two pieces of Meccano separated only by a washer and . . . Well, you don't want to know the details, but we got it working. I say 'we' because I got interested in the problem too.

Finally, we got it going up and down. We even borrowed a small basket from the kitchen cupboard for the heads to fall into. But we had no heads. We had nothing to test it on to see if it really cut heads off.

'Ralph might have some figures he doesn't need,' I said.

'You mean his dolls?'

'They're not dolls!' I said. 'You must never call them dolls! They are theatre figures. They are acting in his plays. He is studying the theatre. When he grows up, he wants to be a famous . . .'

'A famous what?'

'I am not sure,' I confessed. 'Director, producer, actor, playwright, one of those things. But he is very serious about his figures.'

'Girls are very serious about dolls,' said Jean-Marie. 'But they are still dolls.'

What a very French thing to say. We went to see Ralph.

'Ralph, got any figure you don't need?'

'Why?'

It must have looked a bit worrying to him, me coming in with the enemy, Jean-Marie, obviously in cahoots with him.

'We want to cut his head off,' said Jean-Marie.

'You *what*?' said Ralph.

I explained about Charles I and my model. I explained about the guillotine. I explained about Jean-Marie and Meccano and the Stanley knife.

'So we just wondered if you had got any figure you didn't need, so we could see if the guillotine worked?'

Ralph got up and went over to his box of figures and rummaged for a bit.

'You could have this,' he said finally.

He held up a small, rumpled figure wearing

276

boots and rough country clothes, about six inches high.

'Is it a farmer?' I said.

'Sort of,' said Ralph. 'A gamekeeper, really.'

'Why don't you need him? Wasn't he a very good actor? Have you fired him?'

These were the kinds of thing that Ralph sometimes said about his figures. I remember once hearing him roar with anger and coming out in time to see him throw a little figure wearing a crown downstairs, shouting, 'You're hamming it all up on purpose! You're making a mess of everything! Just because you did Polonius all right, you think you can do anything! Get out and never come to me for another part!' After which he had paused dramatically then gone downstairs to retrieve the figure, whispering to me, 'You've got to show them who is boss.'

'It wasn't his fault,' said Ralph, holding the gamekeeper, 'but I was trying to devise a stage version of *Lady Chatterley* and it just didn't work. So he had to go.'

'What's *Lady Chatterley*?' I asked.

'Book about gamekeeping,' he said shortly. 'Now, where's this guillotine?'

According to legend, the revolutionary crowds round the guillotine got very excited, a bit drunk and very noisy. We were the exact opposite. As the gamekeeper was inserted into the correct place, with his head over the basket, and the blade was wound up slowly on one of those little Meccano handles, we fell very silent. He may only have been a six-inch long gamekeeper due for execution, but there was something a bit macabre about the performance.

'Maybe he will be reprieved at the last moment,' I said.

'By whom?' said Jean-Marie.

I said nothing.

By now he had wound the blade up to the top and the little catch had clicked. He had rigged up another string to release the catch.

'Lord,' said Ralph, 'we commend the soul of thy servant . . .'

Too late. Jean-Marie had pulled the string. The blade flashed down the descent, hit the gamekeeper's neck and bounced up and down on it several times. The gamekeeper was unhurt.

'Do you think that counts as divine intervention?' said Ralph.

'No, I don't,' said Jean-Marie. 'The blade is not heavy enough, that's all.'

We spent the next five minutes getting the heaviest little metal weights we could find and taping them to the top of the blade. We had one or two dry runs and almost cut off my finger in the process. It was looking good. Then it was time to put the poor little gamekeeper through the ordeal again.

Jean-Marie started winding the blade up again.

Abandoning his previous role as a solicitous priest, Ralph suddenly shouted, 'So perish all enemies of the people!'

I had a sudden impulse to snatch the little gamekeeper up and rescue him.

Too late.

The catch clicked, the blade whizzed down and, heavy enough now, sliced off the gamekeeper's head.

It fell into the basket.

278

We all cheered.

'*Vive la France!*' shouted Jean-Marie.

'*Vive la Revolution!*' cried Ralph.

'Good shot!' I said.

'Good shot?' said Ralph. 'God, how English. Look, I could go and see if I have got any more characters in the box I don't really need.'

'Yes, go on!' said Jean-Marie.

It must have been like that in the French Revolution too. Blood lust. The crowd baying for more victims. One head after another. It was the same here. Ralph and Jean-Marie went and got a Shakespearean foot soldier and beheaded him, then an old man with a white beard who was probably Biblical in origin.

'You've got to stop now!' I said. 'We know it works properly! What's the point of cutting off any more heads?'

But what is one wishy-washy liberal against two revolutionaries?

The Old Christmas Crib

Christmas was always a problem, at least when it came to choosing which service to go to. Because my mother was a Catholic and my father was an ex-Protestant with strong agnostic leanings, and even stronger atheist tendencies, the solution was always going to be something of a compromise. The final arrangement was that we would alternate the two religions, going to Mass one Christmas and the local C of E service the next, and so on alternately.

'Excellent system,' said my father. 'Catholic church for believers. Protestant church for non-believers. Excellent.'

Yes, it was a good system in its own way, but it had one flaw, which was that very often, when Christmas came around, nobody could remember exactly what we had done the year before.

'I am sure we had the Protestant service last year,' said my mother one Christmas. 'I can remember all the tins of baked beans and the cauliflowers.'

'You're thinking of the Harvest Festival,' said my father, who could tell what my mother was thinking even when she couldn't. 'They don't decorate churches at Christmas.'

'Which is odd,' said my mother. 'Christmas is the time when everyone gives presents, so you would think churches would also be festooned with presents which could be given to the poor later.'

'Yes, but present-giving is secular,' said my father. 'It's not a God-based custom. It's not mentioned in the Bible and it's not sanctioned by the Pope or the Archbishop of Canterbury. Whereas Harvest Festival . . .'

'I wonder if the Pope gets any Christmas presents,' said my mother. 'He hasn't got any family. Who makes things Christmassy for him?'

'The Cardinals,' said my father. 'They all creep into his bedroom in the middle of the night and leave a stocking for him full of handsome new Papal headgear, and low-sugar communion wafers, and vintage Communion wine, and photographic books of places he has visited in the year, and in the morning the Pope wakes up and finds what Father Christmas has left.'

'You're not suggesting that the Pope believes in Father Christmas, I hope,' said my mother.

'Why not? He believes in more unlikely things than that. He has to, being Pope.'

We used to have countless conversations like this in my house, conversations which started with something quite random but always got back on to religious wrangling eventually. My father once noticed me getting a bit upset about it and said to me, 'Don't worry about these little head-to-head battles that your mother and I have! After all, they would be much worse if they were about something serious. But they're only about religion. What was it that Lord Melbourne said about religion? Something about it being all very well in its own way, but it shouldn't be allowed to invade one's private life . . .'

(I suppose, looking back, that the *laisser-faire* way they argued meant they really loved each other. You can tell when a married couple is arguing to wound, or even kill. There's something in the air, something acrid and poisonous. Conversely, when a good married couple has an argument their hearts are never really in it— they're always looking for something better to do. Here's the test: if you ask a married couple what they were arguing about the night before, it's a good sign if they can't remember. It's a bad sign if one or other side can remember every line of dialogue. It's very bad if both sides can.)

That year it was obviously the year after a Catholic Christmas because we didn't go to Mass. I can also remember that it must have been 1953 because when the family traipsed off to the big local church for the morning service on the Sunday before Christmas Day, some of the decorations in the church were left over from the Coronation. As usual, the church, which had probably been nearly empty the previous Sunday, was now full of the normal absentees. A Christmas tree had been installed. And someone had gone to the trouble of doing a Christmas crib, over which many of the congregation were bending to have a look before taking their seats. There seemed to be an air of excitement among them which you don't ordinarily associate with a Nativity scene. We went to have a look as well.

'Oh, my heavens!' said my mother. 'Whatever have they done here?'

I looked in at the crib. It contained the expected figures. Joseph, Mary, the baby, donkeys, oxen, a couple of wise men . . . but what was that? It was a scale model English bobby standing by the door in full police uniform! And what was that behind him? A Turkish belly dancer? Yes, it certainly looked like the figure of a Turkish belly dancer. And there was a British soldier standing over the baby Jesus with a rifle at the ready . . .

'What on earth is the vicar playing at?' said a voice behind me.

'Perhaps it's meant to mean something,' said someone else doubtfully.

'It's in shocking bad taste,' said the voices. 'Someone ought to do something . . . Perhaps it's sabotage . . . There weren't any belly dancers in the Bible, were there?'

I thought it was rather exciting, but I didn't say anything. None of us said anything. We just went to a pew and sat down. Because we knew. We knew who had done it. It must have been Ralph. My

282

dear older brother. The theatrical impresario.

As you already know, Ralph was passionate about the theatre. In the way that other children accumulated sea shells, or conkers, or bits of broken machinery (or I accumulated train-spotting manuals, or gadgets that had once worked and which could therefore now be dismantled), Ralph collected stuff about the theatre. Books, texts, programmes, then bits of scenery, costumes and props. I didn't know what he was talking about most of the time, especially when he said 'props'. I thought he meant some mysterious things that stopped the theatre falling down.

'It's short for properties,' said Ralph scornfully. 'You can't be in the theatre if you don't know that!'

'But I don't want to be in the theatre!'

'Good,' said Ralph. 'You'd only walk into the flats the whole time.'

'Flats?'

'Oh, for heaven's sake . . .'

And he would flounce off and resume work on his doll's house.

Mother and Father were taken aback the first time he said he wanted a doll's house.

'Boys don't play with doll's houses!' said Father. 'I'm not having any son of mine hanging curtains or dressing dollies in a doll's house!'

'It is a little unusual,' said Mother, more mildly.

'I don't want to *play* with it,' Ralph said stoutly. 'I want to use it as a theatre.'

And when he finally got the gift of a big, second-hand, slightly battered doll's house that was too dingy for any sensitive girl to use, that was exactly how he used it.

'The outside is worn and needs painting,' he

told me. 'Which is exactly right for all those Chekhov plays set in a dilapidated country house!'

'Chekhov?'

'Oh, for heaven's sake!'

I had quite early on discovered what delicious turns of temper I could induce in Ralph by feigning ignorance of matters theatrical so I never lost an opportunity to do so, even when I knew full well what he was talking about.

'And the interiors are ideal for all those drawing-room comedies, for Oscar Wilde's plays, for instance. And Bernard Shaw's. It's amazing how many of Shaw's plays are set in posh surroundings considering how left wing he was meant to be.'

For hours he would fiddle around with figures to his heart's content, staging scenes, working out entrances, getting people up and down stage. I once pointed out to him that what he was actually doing was playing films, not theatre, that the doll's house was much more like a movie set than a stage setting. That stopped him in his tracks for a moment. Then he bounced back.

'Ah, but even if only one room represents the stage, I like to keep track of what the other characters, the ones off-stage, are doing at any one moment. You've heard of Method acting? This is Method directing!'

The figures became very real to him. Not just as characters in his plays, but as actors in their own right. He gave them names. I remember there was one little red-haired lady called Yvonne who got most of the best female parts in Wilde, Chekhov and Sheridan. One of his lead male actors was called Gilbert. Another one was called Arthur.

He tended to treat these figures as real people and even invented little stories for them regarding their private lives as actors.

'I am afraid Arthur has been drinking again,' I overheard him say once. 'I shall not be sending him on as Duncan tonight.'

'Who's Duncan?' I said.

'Have you never read the Scottish play?' he said.

'What Scottish play?' I said.

Ralph ground his teeth and retreated into a superior silence. On another occasion, I seem to remember, I found him ticking Yvonne off. She was married to Gilbert, but was having an affair with the little figure called Alex, opposite whom she was playing currently in some play by Noel Coward.

'You can do what you like in other plays,' he was saying strictly, 'but when you are in a play of mine you behave yourself, young lady.'

So after we had seen the Christmas crib in the church that Christmas Sunday and I then found myself sitting on the end of the family row beside my brother, I had no doubt that I was sitting next to the guilty party. (I had actually recognised the British soldier as one of his faithful figures.) During the service I leant against him and asked in a whisper if he had done that to the crib.

'Yes, I did!' he said. 'And a good job too! About time someone gingered it up. Every year that damned crib has looked so boring, like . . . like . . . well, a bit like a scene out of Queen Victoria's private life!'

'Queen Victoria?'

'Well, the Virgin Mary is always number one like the Queen. Joseph always hangs back like Prince

Albert. The three wise men shuffle in like Disraeli, Gladstone and . . .'

A fierce look from Father stopped him in his tracks. We got through the service in silence after that, apart from a bit of singing of course, and left the church afterwards, pushing our way through the crowd gawping at the crib. As soon as we got outside, into the cold dark evening, my father rounded on Ralph.

'I am extremely cross with you, Ralph. I take it that that was your work, the disgraceful additions to the Nativity scene?'

Before Ralph could say anything, the vicar appeared. He hurried over to us.

'Father, I am so very sorry about what happened,' began my father. The vicar ignored him. He turned to Ralph.

'Ralph, I think you know what I am going to say, don't you?'

'Yes,' said Ralph. 'It didn't quite work, did it?'

'No, I am afraid not,' said the vicar. 'Well, it did in a way because it was a big talking point and everyone paused for ages at the crib, which they never have before, so it did sort of work, but I think the figures you chose were just a little advanced for the audience. I think we need some more everyday characters. A gardener, perhaps? An AA man? A lollipop lady?'

'An AA man would be nice,' said Ralph. 'I think I have one at home somewhere.'

'Just a moment,' said my father. 'You knew about this, Father?'

'Knew about it?' said the vicar. 'Well, of course! Ralph and I planned it together. It was his idea, actually. He came to me and suggested that we

286

might give the traditional Nativity scene a bit of a rethink. Shakespeare can be done in modern dress, so why not Christmas? Briliant idea! And then he thought that a mixture of ancient and modern . . . But didn't he tell you about all this?'

'No,' said Father. He turned to Ralph.

'I am extremely cross with you, Ralph. I do think you might have let us in on the secret.'

'Yes, Father,' said Ralph.

'He's a clever boy,' said the vicar.

'Yes, Father,' said Father.

'Bring the AA man round tomorrow morning, and anyone else ordinary you can find,' said the vicar and bustled off into the dark.

We walked back home in silence.

Supper was quite quiet, too.

The subject was not referred to again by either side.

Christmas rolled on in its usual merry way. We wrapped presents, sang carols, cooked things, opened cards and, finally, on Christmas morning, did our stockings.

Then came Christmas lunch.

'You can all come in now!' sang out Mother.

We all trooped in and gasped at the sight of the turkey.

It stood in the middle of the table, huge, sloping upwards, a crisp skin reaching a peak.

The slopes were pristine, unbroken.

But on the peak there was planted a small Union Jack.

On either side of the flag there was a small figure in climbing-gear clothing with snow goggles and an ice axe.

Clearly, it was Hillary and Tensing, conquering

the turkey.

We gave Ralph a round of applause, he bowed and then we all sat down to Christmas lunch.

Liquorice Allsorts 1

What do they mean by "Liquorice Allsorts"?' said my father crossly one day.

We had been having evening supper round the kitchen table. One moment he had been staring into space at the shelves. Next moment he had exploded with wrath and asked, as just noted, what they meant by Liquorice Allsorts.

'What do you mean, what do they mean?' said Ralph.

'Look at the box up there on the shelf. See what it says. "Liquorice Allsorts". But how do we know when we buy a box of Liquorice Allsorts that we are getting *all* sorts? How many sorts are there in all? How do we know that they haven't missed some out? How do we know that some boxes do not have more sorts than other boxes?'

'Which question do you want answered first?' said Ralph.

Father ignored him. He still had more questions to ask.

'How do we know that they are not keeping back the best sorts for their best customers? Or for members of the Bassett family?'

'Who on earth are the Bassetts, dear?' said my mother. 'Do we know them?'

'They are the people who make Liquorice Allsorts!' cried my father. 'It says so on the box!

288

Look! Bassett's Liquorice Allsorts! Well, what's to stop these Bassetts from keeping the best Allsorts back and eating them themselves?'

'If they did, they'd be very fat by now, dear.'

'Or perhaps,' said my father, 'perhaps they only put a selection in each one and we never get the full range.'

'That's unlikely,' said Ralph. 'Why would they do that? It's much more likely that it's all done by machine. I bet there's a machine dealing them out, like a croupier distributing cards, the same ones every time. One Allsort with pips on, one sandwich Allsort, one with the coconut paste . . .'

'Yes, yes,' said Father. 'We all know the regular ones. It's the missing ones I'm interested in!'

'There aren't any missing ones!' said Ralph.

'How do you know?' said Father.

'Because . . . because . . . because it's always the same selection every time!' said Ralph. 'Have you ever come across an Allsort in one selection which wasn't in the next one you had?'

The trouble with arguments is that after a while people run out of facts with which to hit each other over the head and fall back on opinions. Then it gets even worse. They run out of opinions and fall back on speculation. When an argument becomes mere speculation, it's time to call a halt. I felt it was incumbent on me to step in and call that very thing.

'Look!' I said. 'Ralph, Father, this is really silly! You both sound as if you are great experts on Liquorice Allsorts, but I bet you couldn't even name the usual ones.'

'Yes I could,' said Ralph. 'There's the three-layered one . . .'

289

'Stop!' I cried. 'Let's do this scientifically. I'll open that box of Liquorice Allsorts and you two take it in turns to name a different kind until we've been through the lot. OK?'

They said that it was OK and I got down the box and opened it and put up the lid so they couldn't see and said, 'Right, Ralph, name one.'

'Well, I don't know their names, but there's the three-layered one. Liquorice in the middle, sort of sweet paste top and bottom.'

'What colour paste?'

'Brown.'

'Father?'

'Five-layered one. Two layers of liqorice, three of paste.'

'Ralph.'

'Um, the ones with fluffy coconut stuff round a liquorice centre. Different colours.'

'What colours?'

'Um, pink and yellow.'

'Father?'

'The ones with tiny bobbles on. Blue. And pink.'

'Ralph?'

'I think that's it, isn't it? No, hold on, there's the little cylinder one, like a log, with a thin wrapping of black round a white core.'

The only one they couldn't remember, funnily enough, was the black spiral twist. I say 'funnily enough' because that is the only Allsort which is all liquorice and nothing else. (I discovered years later that the one with little bobbles on is the only Allsort which has no liquorice at all—the inside is a kind of hard aniseed jelly.)

'Well, apart from the black twist,' I said, 'you've got them all. That's all the Allsorts there are. And

290

it's not really very many. Leaving aside the colour variations, I reckon there are only six different kinds of Liquorice Allsort.'

'Which makes it all the more likely that there's another sort we don't know about,' said Father.

'Less likely,' said Ralph. 'If they had another Allsort, they'd be desperate to use it. Bassetts *must* be desperate to ring the changes. After all, they're already varying the colour on some of the shapes just to make it seem as if there are more Allsorts than there really are. If you had another Allsort up your sleeve, you'd chuck it in the box!'

At this point Mother re-entered the fray.

'Why don't you write to the Bassetts and ask them? I am sure they'd tell you.'

'Who are the Bassetts?' said my father.

Liquorice Allsorts 2
(Historical Interlude)

'No son of mine will ever be an artist!' thundered Josiah Bassett. 'Never, d'you hear! Our family have been in the liquorice business for three generations! That's what we do! We make and sell liquorice! We are the kings of liquorice! Not damned artists!'

It was breakfast time in the Bassett household. The year was 1900. The queen was Victoria. The weather was rainy. That was because it was Yorkshire. The atmosphere was frosty. That was because it was breakfast time in the Bassett household and Josiah Bassett, head of the Bassett family, had come down to find his second son,

291

Arthur, talking excitedly to his mother, Hannah, about the latest art news from Paris. Josiah Bassett wasn't interested in Paris. The French showed little interest in importing Bassett's liquorice, so Josiah didn't see why he should show any interest in anything French.

'His name is Camille Pissarro,' Arthur had been telling his mother enthusiastically, 'and by using hundreds of little coloured dots, he builds up an entire picture...'

'I must forbid you to talk about art at breakfast,' said Josiah, entering the room. 'If you can't talk about something sensible, don't talk about anything at all.'

'And when do you think the best time to talk about art would be, Father?' said Arthur. 'If I left it to you, we would never talk about it at all.'

'And a good thing too,' said his father. 'When I was a lad, we never talked about art. There was no need to. If my father ever bought a painting, it was to cover up a damp patch on the wall. There were ten paintings in the dining room, all on the same wall. Visitors used to wonder why. "Because it's the north-facing wall," he used to tell them, "and that's where the rain comes through."'

'And did your father ever look at the paintings?' said Arthur icily. 'I don't suppose he ever once bothered to examine the work of the artists he had patronised!'

'Oh yes, he did!' said Josiah. 'Only once, but he did. I distinctly remember him looking up at a big painting of some boats in a river which hung over the sideboard and saying, "Bloody hell! Now the damp's coming through *Sunset Over the Severn*! We'll have to get a new picture and all!"'

'What a philistine,' muttered Arthur.

'What did you say?' roared Josiah.

'I said, "What a philistine!"' Arthur roared back.

'Please, not at breakfast!' pleaded Hannah. 'You know how the servants listen when we argue. Then they have arguments in the kitchen themselves in imitation of their betters!'

'Morning, Mother, morning, Father,' said Hugo Bassett, the eldest son, strolling into the breakfast room, yawning languidly. 'Am I in time for the first family argument of the day? Nothing like a good ding-dong to get the circulation going. Who's winning this time?'

'It's not a question of winning or losing, dear,' said his mother diplomatically. 'It's just that Arthur is very keen to go to the art academy to learn how to paint and Father says that . . .'

'Father says that he should go down the liquorice mines like everyone else in the family!' stormed Josiah. 'Even you went down, Hugo!'

'That's because I couldn't think what else to do,' said Hugo. 'No talent for anything, you see. But old Arthur here . . .'

'Are you taking your brother's side?' stormed Father.

'Am I? Good Lord, I believe I am. That will never do. Let me change sides immediately and even things up dramatically. Take it from me, Arthur,' he continued, turning to his brother, 'your place is here with the Bassctts. You must help us develop our Allsorts and marry and have children, and they too will go into the family firm and smell of liquorice from dawn to dusk.'

For you must remember, dear reader, that in

those days they had no television and no soap operas and all the drama they had was provided by their very own family sagas. You often hear people saying that in the old days they had to provide their own entertainment. What they don't tell you is that that entertainment often involved fistfights, illegitimate children, murder, incest and endless family feuds.

'Arthur marry?' grumbled Josiah. 'Chance would be a fine thing. I don't see our Arthur marrying. He's not so much an Allsort, more of an Othersort.'

'And what does that mean?' asked Arthur indignantly.

'This painter friend of yours in Paris, what's his name? The one who paints little dots?'

'Camille Pissarro?' said Arthur, amazed that his father would show even this little interest in painting.

'Camille Pissarro!' jeered his father. 'What sort of a nancy boy name is that? Camille is a girl's name! Is that what you want to do—run off to Paris, and change your name to a girl's name, and wear a smock, and paint little dots like a girl? Pah!'

Arthur went pink. Then he went pale. Then he went red. Then he turned puce. From a distance, in fact, he looked very much like an Impressionist painting being worked on, or perhaps more like a Fauvist canvas, which was surprising as the Fauvist movement had not yet even started.

Then he walked over to his father and grasped him firmly by both lapels.

'Listen to me once and for all, Father. An artist is not a nancy boy. He has to be tough. He has to be strong. He has to have belief in himself. You are

294

not like that. All you had to do to be a liquorice millionaire was be born. You grew up in the lap of luxury and you took over when your father got rheumatism from his damp paintings and died. You have never done anything strong or tough in your life. Leave that to the artists.'

Josiah sat open-mouthed. Not for years had anyone talked to him like that. With an effort, he recovered himself.

'All I ask, Arthur, my boy, is that you reconsider your decision. Look at Hugo. He is big and strong. He made liquorice his life. Could you not do the same?'

They all looked at Hugo. He was, in fact, not big and strong. He was slim and slightly effete. If anyone was big and strong it was Arthur. Arthur might have been a painter, but he must have wielded mighty heavy brushes, for his forearms were bulging with muscles.

Hannah, his mother, voiced what they were all thinking.

'My dear ones, I think we should start this all over again. I cannot help feeling that we have all been totally miscast. Perhaps we will get a chance later in the book to come back as we were really meant to be.'

They all nodded in relief. It had all been a terrible aberration. If only they could get a chance to do it all over again, but very differently. In real life this never happens, but in an epic family saga—who knows? Could they not be recast?

Author's Note: we'll let you know.

Liquorice Allsorts 3

'Who are the Bassetts?' said my father.

'They are the people who make the Liquorice Allsorts,' said my mother. 'At least, that's what you told me. Don't you remember?'

'Yes, of course,' he said.

'Then write to them and ask about the missing Allsort.'

Mother, of course, had no interest in whether there was a missing Allsort or not. All she wanted to do was put an end to this pointless all-male wrangling. She didn't want to hear her lovely family spend the rest of their lives arguing about Liquorice Allsorts, so she had issued a challenge to Father much in the same way that Austria had issued an ultimatum to Serbia in the fateful summer of 1914. Both of them must have thought they were in a win/win situation. Austria knew that Serbia would be humiliated or invaded; Mother knew that Father would either have to do something about his theory or shut up.

(As it turned out, Austria miscalculated badly, not only causing the First World War but losing its empire into the bargain. Mother, on this showing, would have made a better job of handling the 1914 European crisis.)

It was at this point that the interesting differences between Father, Ralph and me emerged.

Father said he would certainly write to the Bassetts and establish the truth, as truth was what he was after. Of course, he did nothing of the kind.

I said I thought it was a waste of time writing to the Bassetts, as big companies never write back to little boys, but I did write anyway.

Ralph said nothing, but started looking very thoughtful, as if he was composing the letter in his head, which indeed he was.

In other words, Ralph saw it as an artistic challenge, a chance to write a part for a character (himself), while Father saw it as a hypothetical situation which needed no action.

I saw it as a business opportunity.

I based this theory on a letter I had once written to the makers of Marmite. When I was about thirteen I was teased by boys at school because I always pronounced it as 'Marmeet', which I did because I knew that that was how the French pronounced the word originally. The other boys all pronounced it as 'Marmight' because that was how everyone in Britain pronounced it except me, and to prove their point they would then hit me. So I avoided saying the word at all, which I managed to do by switching to eating Bovril instead of Marmite, but at the same time I wrote a letter to the makers of Marmite asking them to back me up in my pronunciation.

And I got an answer!

A man from the marketing side of things wrote back to say that customers could pronounce the product any damned way they wanted to, as long as they bought the stuff (I am paraphrasing). He then complimented me on my loyalty to Marmite and enclosed a large jar of the stuff.

What a surprise!

Especially as I had meanwhile developed a taste for Bovril.

And now had to reacclimatise myself to Marmite.

Which suddenly tasted very salty.

Still, I had learnt the lesson that if you write appreciatively to a manufacturer, you are almost certain to receive free samples by return. Before I even started to shave I already had three tubes of shaving cream waiting for me to use them. One was Erasmic, one was Palmolive and one was Ingrams. I can't remember on what pretext I had written to each one, but it had worked wonders— and they were all pretty good, too, despite the names. Erasmic? Why? Why would a shaving cream name itself after a Dutch philosopher?

But I digress. Immediately after we had had our far-reaching, long-ranging family discussion about Liquorice Allsorts and whether there was a missing Allsort, I wrote a letter to the makers of Bassetts Liquorice Allsorts.

Dear Mr Bassett,

My family and I have long been enthusiastic eaters of your Liquorice Allsorts. Recently, however, we had an argument about whether the selection of Allsorts is the same in every box, and in order to settle this argument I am writing to you for a decision. Do you in fact supply the same selection to every box, or does it vary from time to time?

The reply was not long in coming. I received a package through the post with a note as follows:

Dear Sir,
  Thank you very much for your kind letter. I take the liberty of enclosing a complimentary box of Liquorice Allsorts.
  Yours sincerely,
  Complaints Department.

This was very much along the lines I had expected. I knew from previous experience with Marmite, Bovril, Palmolive, Erasmic, etc., that complaints departments were so relieved when you didn't actually have a complaint that they would mail out free samples to reward you. They never answered your letter directly. They simply sent you a free sample. Nowadays, of course, complaints departments are no longer called complaints departments. They do not admit the possibility of complaints any more. They call themselves customer relations units or consumer smarminess departments and they exude oily charm. What they don't do much any more is send free samples.

My father never wrote a letter to the liquorice people, although he said he would. But Ralph did, much to my surprise. He had one simple inquiry. He wanted to know where all the different shapes of Liquorice Allsorts had their origins, from the layered ones to the ones with little coloured bits on the outside.

He got a letter back.

It said that they did not know for sure.

But there was a myth in the company that the Liquorice Allsort with little coloured bits on the outside had been inspired by a member of the original Bassett family.

The story went that one of the late Victorian Bassetts had refused to go into the liquorice business and had become a painter. He had gone to Paris to study art, where had encountered Camille Pissarro. Pissarro had believed in building up pictures from small dots of paint. Back home in Yorkshire, he had persuaded the Bassett family to apply this technique to liquorice.

The Liqorice Allsort with the little coloured bits was, if you like, the world's first *pointilliste* sweet.

'What a load of rubbish,' said Ralph.

I don't know.

It's not the sort of story a PR department would make up.

So I fancied there might be a bit of truth in it.

The Book Disposal Problem

'It doesn't make sense,' my father used to say. 'It just doesn't make sense. There's no sense in it. I can't see why people do it. Why on earth . . .'

This sort of statement always acted as a warning that he had spotted a hitherto unidentified problem floating in the heavens and was about to start work on a solution. The problems varied wildly. Once he became obsessed with the need to teach semaphore to deaf-and-dumb people. Another time, he tried to devise a use for birds' nesting boxes in the winter. Often it was to do with waste. It might be to do with the way bath water was wasted. Or the way wind energy was wasted. (How he would have loved wind farms! In fact, I think they may actually have been invented before he died. Yes, I am sure they were, because I remember him saying to me one day, 'If you ran a wind farm, would you call yourself a wind farmer? It makes sense. But it doesn't sound right, does it? I mean, people who ran windmills didn't call themselves "windmillers", did they?')

But it was the problem of book disposal that had suddenly struck him on this particular day. People bought books. Then they read them. Then they kept them.

'What's the point of keeping books once you've read them?' he would say, usually as he gazed at our extensive bookshelves. 'How many of them ever get read again? How often do you read the same book twice? I mean, look at this one. Gerald Durrell. *My Family and Other Animals*. I remember reading this when it first came out, and very good it was too, a lot better than his brother Lawrence's twaddle, but when you've read it once . . .'

His voice trailed away as he opened the book and started reading it again for the first time in goodness know how many years. Fairly soon he was chuckling, and then he was ensconced in an armchair, and soon after that he had reread the whole of *My Family and Other Animals* and thoroughly enjoyed it. What he hadn't done was notice that he had just undermined his whole theory, or indeed that every time he brought his theory up, he ended by rereading another book on our shelves.

But he had a good point nonetheless. There are a lot of books which never get reread. So what is the point of keeping them?

'They sit on our shelves, taking up a lot of space and not paying their keep. They're like hotel rooms which are never occupied, or cars which are driven once a year, or . . .'

'Or windows which are kept shut all the time,' offered Ralph helpfully.

'Yes,' said Father.

'No!' said Father, spotting that Ralph had tricked him yet again. 'Even when a window is closed, it can still be used for looking through.'

'But most of the time our windows are not being looked through,' said Ralph. 'In fact, it's very rarely that a window is actually being looked through. So, is a window useless most of the time?'

'No,' I said. 'It's keeping the cold and wind and rain out most of the time.'

'Thank you, my boy,' said my father.

'Actually,' I said, 'there are times when windows are kept working non-stop round the clock. Think about the windows in a greenhouse. They're not really for seeing through so much as keeping the heat in and making things grow. So that's a case of windows being useful *all* the time.'

'That's not true,' said Ralph. 'Half the year there's nothing growing in greenhouses at all. That's not exactly being useful. And the rest of the time people grow lots of things that people don't really want to eat. Like tomatoes.'

It's an odd thing, but although most people do like tomatoes, a few people genuinely can't stand them and Ralph had always been one of them.

'Just because *you* don't like them, doesn't mean they're useless,' I said. 'Everyone else likes them. Why can't you?'

'Maybe I am genetically predisposed not to like them,' he said.

'Genetically predisposed?!' I said. 'Not to like

tomatoes? That's impossible!'

'Not at all,' he said. 'Remember that less than 400 years ago nobody in Europe had ever tasted a tomato. They only brought them over from America because people were getting tired of potatoes and tobacco and chocolate. But for thousands of years before that people had never eaten tomatoes in Europe and nobody, not even Jesus, knew what they tasted like. Then suddenly for 400 years you get people eating tomatoes all the time. So it stands to reason that some people will have retained an inherited inability to deal with tomatoes. I am proud to be among that number, reflecting the tastes of our forebears!'

'Good job you're not an Italian, then,' said my father.

'Why?'

'Well, Italian cooking is based more on the use of the tomato than anything else, more so than any other cuisine in the world. All the Americans could do with it was make ketchup, but the Italians built a whole culture on it. Imagine what it would be like to be an Italian who didn't like tomatoes!'

We thought about it. At least, the other two did. I was busy trying to see a chink in Ralph's logic. I thought I saw one.

'How can you say that people over 400 years ago had no taste for tomatoes? They never had the chance to find out. Nobody had ever offered them one. People in the Middle Ages didn't have a distaste for tomatoes. They just didn't have tomatoes, that's all. You might just as well say that some people in the Middle Ages had a fear of flying. They couldn't have! There *was* no flying.'

'Yes, but you can have an allergy to something

303

you have never seen,' said Ralph. 'You hear occasionally of people having bad reactions to peanuts. But there were thousands of years when we never saw a peanut. So how could we get an allergy to one?'

My father banged the table till things started falling off it.

'Stop it!' he shouted. 'Stop running away with the argument! Stop stealing my anger! What about the books?'

It was quite true. Ralph and I had such a tendency to argue—more like a need, really, being brothers close in age—that we tended to cut out third parties in arguments. Father would start a debate with Ralph, I would take Father's side (because he was against Ralph) and pretty soon I would be arguing directly with Ralph, Father forgotten.

'What books?' said Ralph, genuinely puzzled.

'The books we read once and will never read again.'

'Ah, yes. Them.'

We all looked at the bookshelves.

I don't know which unread books the other two decided to focus on, but in my case I ended up staring at *Lord Nelson's Selected Letters*.

I got the point immediately.

I had never read Nelson's letters and even if I had I couldn't visualise wanting to reread them. If I wanted to know what it was like to be Nelson, I would read a Hornblower book. I couldn't visualise *anyone* wanting to reread Nelson's letters, not even Lady Nelson—and perhaps her least of all, if what I had heard about their relationship was true.

I ran my eye along the shelf.

I came back to Nelson's letters.

They seemed the best of the bunch. And I had already given them the thumbs down.

'I agree,' I said.

'So do I,' said Ralph.

He told me later that the book that had decided it for him was *The Complete Ostrich Farmer*.

'Well,' said Father, 'it might very well be that some of these books which we would like to get rid of are actually quite valuable and worth selling. It's possible, but I severely doubt it. I have on several occasions in my life helped to man a book-stall at jumble sales and the one thing I have learnt from that experience is that a few books are valuable, a lot of books are worth very little and most books are worth nothing at all. An experienced book-jumble man once told me that even at a penny each, most books are impossible to shift and that charity collectors regularly reject up to 50 per cent of the stuff they are offered. At the end of the day, most books remain unsold even at a penny each. That means they are impossible to give away.'

'And that means, if I am not mistaken,' said Ralph, 'that if you can't sell them and can't give them away, it leaves only one course of action. We will have to throw them away.'

'You can't do that,' I said. 'There's something wrong about throwing books away. It's a bit like killing them.'

'It's very like killing them,' said Father.

'I agree,' said Ralph. 'But is there any other choice?'

'Yes,' said father. 'There is.'

We looked at him expectantly, as if he were a

305

magician who had suddenly thought of another place where the rabbit might be.

'Second-hand bookshops,' he said.

'But you have already said we can't sell them!' said Ralph.

'Who said anything about selling?' said Father. 'There is more than one way of getting a book into a second-hand bookshop.'

We looked at him as if he were a bit batty. How could there be any other way of getting a book into a bookshop?

'What you do is, you go into the second-hand bookshop with a small stock of unwanted books in a bag or a basket and, as you slowly go round the shop, you gradually put your books back on to the shelves. Your travel books go back in Travel, biographies in Biography and so on. You are enriching the bookseller's stock. You are finding a safe home for unwanted books. You are giving these books a chance to find a new owner. It is like the principle behind the Battersea Dog's Home, except that it's done with books. It is the very opposite of shoplifting! It is quite legal, and it helps everyone.'

We thought about it. It made a lot of sense. It also made a lot of nonsense. There was a silence.

'Which one of you would like to start?' said Father.

The same silence continued on our part. We also avoided his eye and found a sudden interest in our watches.

'All right,' said Father, 'I'll go and do it. It's my job as the inventor of the process to test it. Though I can't see any flaw in it.'

'To be on the safe side, hadn't you better start

small?' said Ralph. 'Rather than take in an armful of books, and perhaps get arrested for shoplifting, why not just take one? Just for a test run? Pop it on the shelves and get out quick?'

'Yes,' said Father. 'Good idea.'

We set about selecting a book for him to take, a book which under no circumstances anybody would ever want to consult again and finally settled on a Portuguese-Italian dictionary. God knows where it had come from.

Next Saturday morning, Father looked up at our bookshelves, said he was proud to play his part in initiating an era of gradually decreasing books, put the Portuguese-Italian dictionary in a shopping bag and set off.

He returned an hour later. He was still carrying the bag. And there still seemed to be a book inside it.

'Father . . .'

He held up his hand.

'Just a moment. Listen. Say nothing. What happened was this. I went into the bookshop. I browsed around for a while until I found the dictionary section. I then put the Portuguese-Italian dictionary on the shelf. But I thought it would look very odd to the bookseller if I went straight out again, so I browsed for a while in the biographies and the memoirs. Thought I would do that for about ten minutes. Unfortunately, before I had finished my ten-minute stint, I started reading a book and got very interested in it. The long and the short of it was, I bought it.'

He avoided our eye.

'I achieved the main object of our mission,' he said. 'I established that it was possible to do the

307

opposite of shoplifting. I established that it was possible to give books to bookshops without them knowing it.'

'What we have got to do now,' said Ralph firmly, 'is learn how to put books into shops without taking other books out and paying for them!'

'Never mind, Father,' I said, trying to act as peacemaker. 'You did your best. What book did you buy?'

'A fascinating book by a man you never think of as a writer,' he said, and he showed me his proudly purchased copy of *Lord Nelson's Selected Letters*.

'Father . . .' I said. But I hadn't the heart to go on.

Although he had established the principle that you could surreptitiously get rid of unwanted books in second-hand bookshops, we never quite got the system going. Indeed, it received a further setback a couple of weeks later when Mother was trying to establish the meaning of some Portuguese word she had picked up.

'We haven't got a Portuguese dictionary, alas,' said Father.

'No, but we've got the old Portuguese-Italian dictionary somewhere, haven't we? If we looked the word up there the Italian should give us a clue. Find it for me, dear, would you?'

Father said nothing. Shortly afterwards he put his coat on to go out. Ralph and I followed him out into the garden.

'Father!' said Ralph. 'You can't do it! You can't just march into a shop and take the dictionary back! It's not ours any more!'

'Leave me alone!'

'Father,' I joined in, 'you'll get in a fight with the bookseller and be arrested when he sees you taking a book out!'

'Look,' said Father, 'I'm only going to go in there and look the word up! All right? I am not going to take our book back. It's not our book any more, in any case.'

'In that case,' said Ralph, 'it's not really worth going there to look the word up. It's only a Portuguese-Italian dictionary. Why not consult a proper Portuguese-English dictionary?'

'Maybe they haven't got one there.'

'Why not go to a proper bookshop and look it up? Why not go to the library and look it up?'

Father thought for a long time and then he came back in and took his coat off.

'I'll do it tomorrow,' he said.

I don't know if he ever did it tomorrow, but I do know that that is how we came to have two copies of Lord Nelson's letters and no Portuguese-Italian dictionary.

Final Chapter

A fortnight before I went to university, my father asked me to come in and sit down as he wanted to have a talk with me, so I went into the room he used as an office, or rather the room he used as a dump but which he also worked in, and I obediently sat down on the one chair which did not have newspapers and books on it.

That meant that he had to stand.

I stood up and offered him my seat.

He took it.

That meant that I had to stand.

He then produced a sheet of paper from the desk and handed it to me.

'In a couple of weeks you will be at university and your childhood will be over,' he said. 'So this is the bill.'

'The bill for what?' I said.

'Your childhood,' he said.

I looked at it.

It was, indeed, the bill for my childhood.

Eighteen years' worth of expenses, which he had neatly tabulated.

It came to nearly £2,000.

I asked him if I could sit down for a moment.

He looked round for a free chair, but could not see one.

I made as if to sit in his lap.

He stood up immediately.

I sat in his chair and tried to gather my thoughts.

'This is a huge amount for a poor student to pay,' I said.

'You are not a poor student yet,' he said. 'That starts next week. In any case, I have only charged the little extras. I am a reasonable man. It is not as if I have charged you for your education. Nor for your clothes, or your health, or our family holidays.'

For what, then?

I looked at one item at random.

It said, 'To buying pumpkin for Hallowe'en celebrations, October 1956—£1/5/6.'

I was thunderstruck.

I was not, however, dumbstruck.

'Father, it is not customary to charge children for the expenses of their childhood, especially the little pleasures.'

'No,' said my father, 'it is not. But it should be. Raising children is a ridiculously expensive business. Christmas alone is enough to bankrupt most people. It is only fair that the load should be spread between parent and child, thus giving the child a feeling of involvement and shared responsibility . . .'

'Yes, but charging me for a pumpkin for Hallowe'en in 1956!'

'What is unfair about that? I never wanted to celebrate Hallowe'en. It is a horrible American idea. I was opposed to it all along. If I finally bought a pumpkin, it was only because I was overridden by you and Ralph and Mother. It is only fair that I ask you to share the expense, now that you can afford to do so.'

'Yes, but hold on a moment,' I said. 'As I remember, the pumpkin was hollowed out and used as a candle-holder to put in the window. The contents were converted into soup and into pumpkin pie. I distinctly remember you eating your fair share of soup and pie. You benefited from the pumpkin personally! And yet you wish me to foot the entire bill!'

My father's expression changed gear. He thought for a moment and then picked up a pen.

'I am not an unreasonable man. You are right. I too was a beneficiary from the pumpkin purchase. I shall not charge you for the pumpkin. The pumpkin is on me.'

He crossed it out and handed the bill back to me.

'Is there anything else you wish to query?'

The next item that caught my eye was one that said, 'To purchase and posting of picture postcard in Perigord, 1955—9d.'

'Why on earth have you charged me for a holiday postcard?' I said. 'We must have sent loads of postcards. Why just one?'

'Because that was the only one you sent personally,' said my father. 'Do you remember? You sent it to the headmaster of your school.'

'I did *what*?'

'We were on holiday in France that year and we were sending postcards to family members one day and someone said it was such a shame that we only sent cards to family, who already knew perfectly well where we were on holiday, and not to people who didn't know. And someone else said that if we sent cards to our teachers at school, we would be one up on everyone else, because nobody ever sent cards to their teachers. *And* it would make teachers feel wanted. And so Ralph persuaded you to send a card to your head teacher.'

It was true. It all came back to me now. Ralph had gone on at me, saying that teachers probably never got any signs of affection at all from their pupils and that if they got just one card, the sender of that card would shoot up high in their estimation. I said I didn't want to shoot up high in the headmaster's affection. Ralph said, 'Not affection, estimation.' I said that either way, I didn't see the point. Ralph said it was an investment for the future. I said, 'That is the only kind of investment there is, an investment for the future, there is no such thing as investment for the past.' Ralph said not to be so bleeding clever-clever and to write a postcard to the headmaster. We had a brief fight and I lost and then I wrote a postcard to the headmaster, saying that I was having a good holiday and had been practising my French.

When I got back to school, the headmaster took me to one side and thanked me for my postcard and said he had been very touched by it. In twenty years of teaching, no pupil had ever sent him a holiday postcard before.

'But don't worry,' he said. 'I won't tell anyone you sent it to me. That would only make trouble for you.'

For the first time I realised that teachers are human. I even asked him if he had had a nice holiday.

'I had to take my mother to Dorset,' he said. 'It was very pleasant. *Mais il pleuvait tout le temps.*'

'What?' I said.

'That's French for 'it rained all the time'. I thought you had been practising your French?'

Ha ha, very funny.

What I had forgotten was that father had paid for the postcard in the first place.

'I don't see how you can charge me for the postcard to a teacher,' I said. 'That was a duty, not a pleasure.'

Father thought about it for a moment.

'I am not totally unfeeling,' he said. 'I am prepared to forgo the postcard. And the stamp, as well.'

My father had always taught me, among other things, to check every item on every bill, as there were always a few things which crept in which shouldn't be there at all, and to dispute as much as possible. Check and haggle, haggle and check, that was his motto.

So although the next fortnight was occupied with buying clothes and scholar's kit for the future, it was just as much taken up with going over my past in minute detail.

'"To the purchase of one hundred bookmarks, red—£2/10/0." I don't remember buying any bookmarks. What on earth is that all about?'

'You and Ralph were avid book readers, for which I am very grateful,' said my father. 'It civilised you and it gave your mother and me a lot of peace and quiet. But you had a dreadful habit of leaving books around which were half-read, lying face down at the place you had got to. Very often these books got tidied up and your place was lost. I can remember you getting very upset on several occasions. So when I spotted a bookshop selling bookmarks cheap in bulk I bought a hundred. After that, whenever I spotted a book which you were halfway through reading, I stuck a bookmark in the place and closed it. Do you not remember finding bookmarks in your books?'

'Yes,' I said. 'But I thought it was Ralph up to his games, putting the bookmark in the wrong place in my book.'

'No, no,' said my father. 'I always put it in the right place.'

'Then perhaps Ralph came along afterwards and moved the bookmark from the right place to the wrong place. Because it always seemed to be in the wrong place.'

My father frowned.

'Well,' he said, 'I will give you the benefit of the doubt. Let us call the bookmarks a present from me which misfired.'

And he crossed out the bookmarks from the list.

Most of what I remember of my last fortnight before going to university was spent like this. I would find an item on the bill which I disputed. He would dispute my disputation. I would fight back. He would then give in. After a week of jockeying for position I had got the bill down to under £1,000, but that still seemed a massive amount of money to me. I was about to become a student. Weren't students always poverty-stricken by definition? How could I possibly pay my father £1,000?

'"To purchase of raffle tickets at village fete, summer 1957: twelve tickets at a shilling = 12 shillings." What on earth is that for?'

'Well, you buy a certain quantity of tickets, all of which have different numbers, and if you get the winning number . . .'

'Yes, Father dear, I know what a raffle is! What I want to know is why I should be implicated in the purchase of raffle tickets so long ago! Did any of the tickets win anything?'

'We have not been notified yet,' said Father, carefully drawing out a small packet of tickets from a small drawer in the desk, 'but one never knows.'

'This raffle was two years ago! They would have got in touch by now!'

'I fear you are right. But it is always worth keeping raffle tickets. Even if the number does not win this time, it may win on another occasion.'

'Hold on,' I said, thinking this one through. 'Does this mean that you take along all the raffle tickets you have ever bought each time you go to a place where there is another raffle?'

'Something like that,' he said. 'It works, too.'

'I don't believe you!'

'Well, it worked once.'

'I still don't believe you.'

'Your mother will back me up on this one,' he said. 'She was there when it happened.'

We could hear her moving around in the kitchen so we summoned her to Father's room. Father didn't get up. I went to get a chair for her. She sat down.

'Your son does not believe that I once won a raffle prize with a ticket purchased at a quite different event. Tell him about it.'

'You mean, at Ashby de la Zouch?'

'Ashby de la Zouch? No, it was at Ragley Hall.'

'Ragley Hall?'

This wasn't a very good start. Eventually, they both agreed that it had been at a castle somewhere in East Anglia where they had gone on the day of a big summer fair, or what they now call a fayre. Ralph had been there, but not me for some reason, which helps to explain why I didn't remember it.

'Anyway, your father bought a few raffle tickets which he stored away with his other left-over tickets which he had brought along as usual and when they announced the prizes, he found to his delight that he had won a picnic basket.'

'That's not quite true,' said my father. 'The most you could say was that one of my old tickets appeared to have won a picnic basket. They shouted out "Pink 133!" and there among my collected pink tickets was 133. I couldn't claim immediately, of course, in case there was a genuine authentic winner. But whoever it was didn't seem

316

to be coming forward, so I took the plunge and stood up to claim it, waving my little pink ticket.'

'And then . . .' said my mother.

'And then,' said my father, determined to finish the story, 'and then someone else stepped forward, also waving a pink ticket. You'll never guess who it was.'

'The genuine winner?'

'No.'

'The police?'

'No.'

'Sir Anthony Eden?'

'No.'

'Ali Baba and the Forty Thieves?'

'No, no, no, no!' said Father exasperatedly. 'It was Ralph! Your wretched brother had the winning ticket!'

'But . . . how could he have got it? Had he *bought* it?'

'No,' said my father.

'Had he brought an old one along?'

'No,' said my mother.

'Then . . .'

'It was quite simple,' said my father. 'Ralph was standing near the back, listening to the prize announcements, not wishing to be near me when I was arrested for fraud. Just when the prize for the picnic basket was announced and I stepped forward with "Pink 133" a woman just behind him gasped and said that she also had that ticket. Seeing me going up for the prize, Ralph saw which way the land lay and he said to the woman, "You must let me handle this" and took her ticket from her and marched up to the stand to confront me.'

'And did you confront him back?'

317

'Your father couldn't really,' said my mother. 'He would have lost in a showdown. So he pretended he had misread his ticket number.'

'Did I say 133?' he had said. 'Sorry! It was 313! My mistake!'

He turned over the memory miserably in his mind.

'Very good thing too,' said my mother. 'He gave up cheating at raffles after that. He always pretended it had been something to do with testing the laws of chance, or the law of averages, or something scientific, but of course it wasn't—it was cheating pure and simple.'

'In which case,' I said, 'I certainly don't see why I should have to pay for your old raffle tickets!'

'Fair enough,' said my father, and crossed it off the list.

'Oh, this isn't the "bill for your childhood" performance, is it?' said Mother crossly. 'You're not going through that dreadful routine again? It was bad enough with Ralph.'

'Don't worry,' said my father. 'We're almost there now. We've got it down to about £500.'

'£500?' I said. 'I thought it was about £1,000?'

'Well, I've been crossing off a few items when you weren't looking,' said Father. 'I am a reasonable man, after all.'

I had a look at the bill.

He had crossed off 'Hire of elephants for birthday'. And 'Cleaning up bill after Coronation party'. And 'Out-of-court settlement with Icelandic newspaper'. And 'To purchase of false noses'. And 'To procuring of outsize paper clips'. And 'To hire of donkeys'. And 'To course of jam-making classes' . . .

318

'What is all this?' I said. 'Jam-making? Icelandic Newspapers? Giant size paper clips? Will someone please explain . . . ?

'It's all crossed off,' said my father.

'Hire of elephants?' I said.

'The elephants never turned up, anyway,' said my father. 'Oh, for heaven's sake, if you're going to start querying items which I have already crossed off, we're never going to get anywhere! First you say you shouldn't pay it, then you say you can't understand why you're not paying it!'

'Look, dear,' said my mother, mollifying as always, 'I think it's very nice that you and your father have spent this afternoon before you go away to university revisiting your youth together. Seeing where you both are together. Seeing how you got here. Seeing where you go from here. This really isn't about money. It's about saying goodbye to each other.'

'Saying goodbye?' I said, startled.

'Saying goodbye?' he said, startled.

'Of course it is,' said Mother. 'Most people never find a good way of saying goodbye and good luck at university. I think this is admirable.'

'How did Ralph take the bill for his childhood?' I said.

'Ralph was very different from you,' said Father. 'He refused to go through the bill and look at all the itemised payments. He accepted everything.'

'So he paid it?'

'Paid it? Lord, no. Not at all. He offered to toss me for it, double or quits.'

'Good God. And did you?'

'Yes,' said Father. 'And I lost. So we were quits.'

'Good God,' I said again. 'So Ralph and you

319

settled the whole thing in seconds. And you and I have spent nearly a fortnight haggling over it.'

'You and Ralph are very different creatures,' said Father.

'Everyone's different,' said Mother. 'I am quite different from your father.'

'What if Ralph had lost the toss?' I said.

'He wouldn't have paid,' said Father. 'He would have thought of some grand and wonderful gesture instead. And I would have looked forward to it. But he would never have paid up.'

'And I am quite different from Ralph,' said Mother. 'To put it another way, none of us is like Jesus. But we are all different from Jesus in different ways.'

My father and I looked at each other.

'Tell you what,' said Father. 'I'll let you off the whole bill except for the last item. Is that fair?'

He drew a sharp pencil line through every item on the bill, from top to bottom, leaving only a single one at the end.

This final entry said, 'To producing your childhood bill, including materials and labour: the sum of three guineas (£3/3/-).'

I said, 'Hold on! You're expecting me to foot the bill for a bill which has been withdrawn?'

He said, 'Yes, I am.'

I said, 'I have to pay the expenses for something which doesn't exist?'

He said, 'Yes, I think you have to.'

My mother said, 'You should, you know. Your father worked extremely hard to produce that bill. It cost him a lot to withdraw it. If you pay something towards it too, you will be a free man.'

I suddenly saw what this was all about. It really

was about the end of my childhood. And very few people ever get the chance to do it as neatly as this.

'Will you take a cheque, Father?' I said.

'No,' he said. 'It's not that I don't trust you. It's just that you haven't got a bank account yet.'

I looked in my pockets. I hadn't got the cash on me. So from Father's desk I drew a piece of paper towards me and wrote on it.

'What are you doing?' he said. 'That doesn't look like any form of known currency to me.'

'No, Father,' I said. 'You see, I am trying to be symmetrical. You drew up a bill for my childhood. I am now going to start a bill for your old age. On this I shall put everything you owe me, so that in due course you can settle your bill and pay me back.'

I showed him what I had written at the top of the paper.

FATHER AND MOTHER
OLD AGE ACCOUNT
In credit: £3/3/-, owed from printing of bill
for son's childhood account.

'You mean,' said Father, 'you are celebrating freedom from your parents by getting into debt to them?'

'Of course,' I said.

'I shall be interested to see how your life progresses hereafter,' he said.

'So shall I,' I said.